HOCKEY GOALTENDING

Brian Daccord

Editor

Human Kinetics

Library of Congress Cataloging-in-Publication Data

Hockey goaltending / Brian Daccord, editor.
    p. cm.
  Includes index.
  Prev. ed. cataloged under author Brian Daccord.
  ISBN-13: 978-0-7360-7427-8 (soft cover)
  ISBN-10: 0-7360-7427-9 (soft cover)
  1. Hockey--Goalkeeping. 2. Hockey goalkeepers--Training of. 3.
Roller hockey. I. Daccord, Brian, 1964-
  GV848.76.D33 2009
  796.962'27--dc22

2008032109

ISBN-10: 0-7360-7427-9
ISBN-13: 978-0-7360-7427-8

Acquisitions Editor: Justin Klug; **Developmental Editor:** Kevin Matz; **Assistant Editors:** Laura Koritz, Elizabeth Watson; **Copyeditor:** Patricia MacDonald; **Proofreader:** Anne Meyer Byler; **Indexer:** Betty Frizzéll; **Graphic Designer:** Robert Reuther; **Graphic Artist:** Tara Welsch; **Cover Designer:** Keith Blomberg; **Photographer (cover):** Dave Sandford/ Getty Images; **Photographer (interior):** Neil Bernstein, unless otherwise noted; **Photo Asset Manager:** Laura Fitch; **Visual Production Assistant:** Joyce Brumfield; **Photo Office Assistant:** Jason Allen; **Art Manager:** Kelly Hendren; **Associate Art Manager:** Alan L. Wilborn; **Illustrator:** Keri Evans; **Printer:** United Graphics

Human Kinetics books are available at special discounts for bulk purchase. Special editions or book excerpts can also be created to specification. For details, contact the Special Sales Manager at Human Kinetics.

Printed in the United States of America   10 9 8 7 6 5 4 3

The paper in this book is certified under a sustainable forestry program.

Human Kinetics
Web site: www.HumanKinetics.com

United States: Human Kinetics
P.O. Box 5076
Champaign, IL 61825-5076
800-747-4457
e-mail: humank@hkusa.com

Canada: Human Kinetics
475 Devonshire Road, Unit 100
Windsor, ON N8Y 2L5
800-465-7301 (in Canada only)
e-mail: info@hkcanada.com

Europe: Human Kinetics
107 Bradford Road
Stanningley
Leeds LS28 6AT, United Kingdom
+44 (0)113 255 5665
e-mail: hk@hkeurope.com

Australia: Human Kinetics
57A Price Avenue
Lower Mitcham, South Australia 5062
08 8372 0999
e-mail: info@hkaustralia.com

New Zealand: Human Kinetics
P.O. Box 80
Torrens Park, South Australia 5062
0800 222 062
e-mail: info@hknewzealand.com

ACKNOWLEDGMENTS

I am very grateful to have the opportunity to work with motivated goalies. I sincerely appreciate the opportunity to be a mentor and thank the goalies and parents who entrust me with this responsibility. To be associated with the tremendous goaltending coaches of the Goaltending Consultant Group is an honor, and I thank them for their contributions to this book. The support that I receive from my parents, and their interest in my endeavors, encourages me to take on ambitious projects such as this one. Most of all, I am very fortunate to have a loving wife and children who support me in pursuing my passion of coaching goaltending.

Thank you to all of the colleagues that have played a role in putting this book together.

- John Carratu and Chris Dooley of Stop It Goaltending
- Dave Flint of Northeastern University
- Bill Troy, Rob Gagnon, and Tony Gould of the Cushing Academy facilities
- Erik Kaloyanides of the Athletic Evolution facility
- Justin Klug, Jason M. Muzinic, Kevin Matz, Gregg Henness, and Neil Bernstein of Human Kinetics
- Todd Brown and Mike Sheehey of Nike Bauer
- Adam Naylor of Telos
- The goalies and players who participated in the book's photo and DVD shoots

CONTENTS

DVD CONTENTS

Strength Training Exercises

Plyometric Exercises
   Lower-Body Sumo Squat
      Jumps
   Lower-Body Stride Jumps
   Lower-Body Split Jumps
   Upper-Body Power Drops
   Upper-Body Kneeling One-Arm
      Put
   Upper-Body Kneeling Side
      Throws

Dynamic Flexibility Exercises
   Lunge Walk
   Lateral Lunge Walk
   Shuffle
   Russian March
   Spiderman
   High Knee Exercise
   Butt Kicks
   Carioca

Improving Quickness and Agility

Drop Drills
   Underhand Catch Drill
   Goalie Explosiveness Drill
   Wall Drills
   Stability Ball Drills

Ladder Drills
   Forward One In
   Forward Two In
   Close the Five Hole
   Three-Point Shuffle
   Scissors
   Carioca

Save Techniques

Upright Stance and Butterfly Stance
Butterfly Steer Save
Low Shot In Tight
Long Shot Up High
Butterfly Smother Save
Butterfly Pad Save Leg Extension
Half Butterfly Save
Butterfly Paddle Down
Butterfly Stand-Up Smother Save

Glove Save
Blocker Save
The Long Body
Dive to Glove Side
Dive to Blocker Side
Butterfly Slide Save
Butterfly Slide Block
Butterfly Slide Smothers
Butterfly Push From a Down
   Position

Crease Management Skating Techniques

T-Glide
Drop Step
Shuffle Step
Step-Outs
Step-Out to the Side

Butterfly Slides and Pushes
The Butterfly Push
Momentum Changes and
   Continuation
Reverse Rotations

Postsave Recovery

Behind the Net Coverage

Battling Traffic: Puck Retention and Moving the Puck

Skating Drills

Total Running Time 70 Minutes

FOREWORD

Goaltender is arguably the most important position in all of sports, and certainly he or she is the most important player on the ice. A good goalie can make or break a team! Have you ever considered what it would be like to be Marc-Andre Fluery or Chris Osgood under the intense scrutiny and pressure of the Stanley Cup Finals! Well it doesn't have to be the Finals for all goalies alike to feel the need to get better under pressure. Playing goal is a unique position and it demands fundamentally sound principals to get you through the most difficult times that the game can offer. *Hockey Goaltending*, by Brain Daccord, has brought these principals to life for all skill levels!

With the new rules in hockey that range from shrinking the goaltending equipment to limiting the tactics that a defensive player can use to control an offensive player, the goalie's job is harder than ever. Flexibility, strength, agility and, most importantly, flawless technique are necessary to succeed as a goaltender in the modern game. *Hockey Goaltending* has everything you need to develop these facets of your game. There are exercises and drills in this book for developing strength, flexibility, agility, and reaction time, as well as explanations of the critical techniques, old and new, to win in today's game. *Hockey Goaltending* also tells you how to pick equipment, keeping in mind the new sizing specifications that are a result of the recent rule changes, and has great advice on becoming, and staying, mentally tough in a position that demands a strong mental approach.

But perhaps the most valuable and unique element to the book is the inclusion of a DVD which allows you to see the techniques in a dynamic and fluid way. You can follow the butterfly slide through the whole slide or see how to track a puck behind the net through its entire movement. Goaltender is a dynamic and fluid position and it's extremely useful to see the techniques illustrated this way alongside the in-depth explanations the book provides.

There are many elements that make a great goaltender—athletic ability, tireless work ethic, self-discipline—but *Hockey Goaltending* is a great manual to help you succeed as a goalie. It shows you the different techniques you'll need to help you develop into a versatile save maker!

John Vanbiesbrouck
All-time winningest American-born goalkeeper and United States Hockey Hall of Fame inductee

PREFACE

In a recent interview, I was asked why Patrick Roy is one of the greatest goal-tenders in NHL history. A number of reasons immediately came to mind . . . athleticism, competitiveness, the ability to read the play, and the skill of main-taining composure in pressure-packed games. But the true test of greatness is performing at the highest level over a prolonged period of time, and Patrick Roy was able to do this because he continually evolved his game throughout his career.

Recently, the hockey authorities have been on a mission to create more offense in the game. The new rule changes range from shrinking the goaltend-ing equipment to limiting the tactics a defensive player can use to control an offensive player. Goalies can object all they want, but it is not going to stem the tide of rule and regulation changes favoring putting more pucks in the net. Goalies need to continue to refine their skills and implement systems that give them the best chance of stopping the puck and having success. The changes in the game have led to a number of improvements in goaltending techniques as well as tactical developments, and this book will bring today's motivated goaltenders up to speed and offer a number of ways to improve their game.

In this second edition of *Hockey Goaltending,* I have asked some of the top goalie coaches in North America to contribute their expertise, from equipment to techniques and tactics, to help today's modern goalies dominate the game. The new hockey climate has put the goaltender position in the spotlight as goalies have an even greater impact on the game than in years past. These contributing coaches are all members of the Goaltending Consultant Group and collectively train some of the top goalies in the NHL, the minor leagues, college hockey, and major junior hockey. Whether you are a beginner or a seasoned veteran, male or female, this book will help you improve your game on and off the ice and help take you to the next level.

Several factors contribute to a goalie's success. *Hockey Goaltending* takes you through these factors, offering information to make you better in every facet of the position. The first chapter addresses equipment and making sure goaltenders are properly geared up for success, a process that can seem over-whelming at times because of all the choices and the expense. Getting stronger and increasing flexibility are goals that can be achieved off the ice, and *Hockey Goaltending* offers drills and exercises to increase strength, flexibility, speed, quickness, and agility in chapters 2-4. A full explanation of save techniques will be detailed in chapter 5. Chapter 6, on crease management, includes a breakdown of skating techniques and positioning and their importance in goaltending. Chapter 7 instructs goalies on what to do after the initial save and covers tracking the puck as well as blocking and reacting strategies.

Chapter 8, on offensive attacks, will teach goaltenders how to play all the key situations with confidence including killing penalties. One of the most dangerous situations for a goalie is when the attack comes from down low and chapter 9, on behind-the-net coverage, teaches goalies how to handle wraparounds, passouts and walkouts. Chapter 10, "Battling Traffic and Playing the Puck," concludes tactical and technical instruction with a focus on scrambles, tips, screens, and ultimately playing the puck with your stick. Chapter 11, "Goalie Sense," includes 13 points on how to maximize your potential as a goalie and chapter 12, "Developing a Shutout Mind-Set," opens the door for goaltenders into the world of mental-edge training and its importance to a goalie's success. Finally, *Hockey Goaltending* offers forms that goalies can use not only to track goals against but also to set goals and follow dreams. For coaches, there is even information on how to deal with your goalies as well as how coaches can best utilize a goalie coach within the team setting.

Each topic covered in *Hockey Goaltending* includes pictures to illustrate technique and positioning. Many of these pictures are in frame-by-frame sequence, which allows readers to see the movement of the goaltender in a step-by-step manner, making it easier to break down and replicate the moves. Along with the pictures, each chapter highlights a current NHL goaltender and uses his particular skill set to reinforce what is being described in the book. Throughout the pages you will find coaches' tips to help you understand and implement techniques and concepts. *Hockey Goaltending* also includes a companion DVD which will put all the instruction from the book into motion. Throughout the book look for the DVD Icons for material included on the DVD.

Being a goalie is a great opportunity to have fun and compete, but it also carries responsibilities, as your teammates will depend on you. Work hard at practice and in games, and take advantage of every opportunity you have to get better. *Hockey Goaltending* will be a powerful resource for you, so keep it handy and refer to this book when you have a specific question or need a refresher. Most important, go out and show your passion for the most dynamic position in the greatest game on earth, and have a great time doing it.

chapter 1

GEARING UP TO STOP PUCKS

John Carratu

Before you participate in any activity, it is important to have the right equipment. This is no different for goaltending, as equipment plays a major role in protection and performance. For you to play at the top of your game, you must be able to play without fear. This means wearing equipment that allows you to concentrate on stopping the puck without worrying about getting hurt. Along with offering safety, your equipment must also be mobile— mobility is essential in order for you to execute proper mechanics. Finding the right combination of protection and performance at a reasonable price is the key to successful choices in equipment. With all the choices out there, it can be a difficult and overwhelming task to find the gear that is best suited for you and your style, and this chapter will assist you in making great decisions.

It is important to note that the equipment specifications have changed recently at the higher levels. Within two years all equipment that goalies wear will have to meet the specifications. The NHL began implementing the specifications for smaller goaltender equipment in order to increase the number of goals scored, and these regulations are now being introduced at all levels. At first goalies were disappointed by the changes, believing—like everyone else at the time—that they would make tending goal more difficult. What in fact has happened is that the smaller equipment allows for increased mobility and quickness, and goalies can execute proper mechanics better than with the larger gear. The change in goaltender equipment specifications has prompted a flurry of sales activity, and this chapter will walk you through each piece of equipment and include suggestions and helpful tips.

THREE PS: PROTECTION, PERFORMANCE, AND PRICE

In choosing equipment, it is essential to consider the combination of protection, performance, and price. Believing that you won't get hurt stopping a puck is necessary for a goaltender to play without fear. With that said, a goalie must also be able to move without feeling encumbered by his equipment. The hat trick is scored when you can meet the previous two criteria at a reasonable price. It is important to note that although a particular make and model will be a great fit for one goalie, it may not be right for another. This is why it is important to try different equipment to see what suits your needs best. This section offers advice on all three Ps.

Protection

Finding gear that offers the proper protection will help you develop the confidence you need to man the pipes. Being a goaltender requires you to stand in front of a solid vulcanized piece of rubber that can travel at speeds in excess of 100 miles per hour (160 kilometers per hour). Protection is a major concern for both the player and the parent. Unfortunately, there will be bumps and bruises along the way because that is a part of the game, but proper protection of a goalie should be a major priority.

A few main areas need to be addressed when outfitting a goalie, including the head, upper torso, midsection, and legs. It is important to make sure that all the major joint areas are properly protected. Arm and chest pads should have proper clavicle and sternum protection, and the elbows need to be properly protected as well. Make sure there is hard plastic or heavy-duty, high-density foam in these areas. Pants should fit properly to protect the thigh, hip, and groin area; goalie pants have more protection than do player pants in order to absorb shots and protect from injury when going down to make a save. Leg pads should have proper protection to protect the front and inside of the knee. A well-protected goalie can perform his job with a high degree of confidence! What you really want to look for are any gaps in protection that a puck would be able to penetrate. This is why it is important to try gear on and move around while mimicking saves. While doing this you can see how the equipment responds to certain actions and if the protection remains consistent without restricting movement.

Performance

As a goalie you demand maximum performance from yourself, and your equipment must meet those demands too. Your equipment has to perform at a high level over a long period of time. Actively seek out the makes and models that are best suited for your style of play. Equipment can vary to satisfy the needs of goalies who rely more on blocking techniques versus goalies who prefer to rely more on reflexes. This may even come in the form of a single or double break in the same model pad. In general, a blocker likes equipment more rigid than a reactor. Equipment quality usually will be reflected in the pricing of the gear. It is a pretty safe bet that if the equipment costs more, the stitch count is higher and a better-density foam has been used, as well as lighter and stronger materials. Keep yourself educated about new trends in the equipment you will be wearing. With the new size specifications for goalie equipment now in place at the pro, college, and junior levels, and shortly coming to youth hockey, older equipment will soon be illegal. The smaller equipment allows a goalie to move better, but some blocking coverage and protection have been lost. Remember, you want to be able to be confident so you can perform at your optimal level!

Price

The final consideration when selecting equipment should be the price. Many parents shy away from the thought of their young player becoming a goalie. The stress, the strain, and the agony are all cited as reasons, and we are just talking about the cost of the goalie equipment on the family budget! It is true that you are playing not only the most important position in hockey but also the most expensive. And few of us are lucky enough to have a team purchase our equipment, so it is important to maximize every dollar spent.

This section will help you save big dollars while allowing you to feel fully protected when making big saves. Remember that the most expensive equipment may not necessarily be the best, depending on your age and playing style.

Stick It to Them   One expense that can add up throughout a season is the cost of sticks. If you prefer the traditional wood stick over the newer composite models, this is one way to save. Buy your sticks in bulk, which is smart for many reasons. First, if you buy your sticks in quantities of 3, 6, or 12, you may get a much better rate from your local pro shop. Second, you will be using the same stick throughout the season, letting you have the same consistent feel while you play. Finally, you will never be stuck trying to find a make or model. Of course it is essential that you be comfortable with the stick before buying in bulk.

Find an Older Goalie Buddy   Develop a friendship with a goalie who is a year or two older. As your friend outgrows equipment, you can purchase the used gear at considerable savings. Another advantage is that you can talk with this goalie and learn about the equipment: what he liked and what might need improvement. This is a great idea for players 12 and under, and the savings can be tremendous.

Develop a Lasting Relationship With an Established Pro Shop or Dealer   Become a regular customer at a pro shop that specializes in goalie equipment. You'll get great services, find out about the latest in equipment innovations, and be able to negotiate better deals if you're buying full sets of equipment. Shops will be happy to give some type of discount if they are guaranteed to sell multiple pieces of equipment.

Find Small Independent Companies That Custom-Make Goalie Equipment   A number of smaller companies are making excellent equipment at reasonable prices. They offer great personal services and are often able to customize your equipment in a way that store-bought gear cannot. Seek these companies out, and you will be wonderfully surprised by the service, price, and performance level of the equipment you purchase.

Search the Net   If you know what you want and are comfortable purchasing through the Internet, there are some great deals online. The challenge with this method is not having the opportunity to try the gear on before you buy it. If you are well educated about goalie equipment, you can save considerable money this way.

Adjust Your Equipment and Adjust Your Savings at the Same Time   Before you spend money on new gear, check to see if your present equipment can be adjusted. Many arm and chest pad sets are laced together in the shoulder area, and a slight adjustment can add that needed inch or two in the arms. Many models of leg pads now offer adjustable knee cradles that can help get an extra season out of the pads. Gloves have Velcro straps around the wrists that can be loosened if needed. Knowing this might be a way to get an extra few months of usage out of your comfortable equipment.

Closeout Models Offer Great Savings   Every year or so, equipment companies come out with new models, offering newer innovations, materials, and styles over last year's model. Eventually a company will close out a model or stop producing that style. If you are currently using a specific model and enjoy the performance but find that it is being closed out, don't be saddened—look for the opportunity to save. Many stores or Web sites will offer considerable savings to sell off their inventory as the newer models are arriving. You will get a great price and avoid that "adjustment" time of getting used to new equipment because you will be wearing the same gear you are already comfortable with.

Returns Offer a Unique Way to Save on Equipment   Goalies at the highest levels are fanatical about their equipment. Their gear is custom made, and a lot of time is spent producing it. If the equipment does not meet the specifications of the goalie, it is returned to the manufacturer. The manufacturer will often pass the gear along to pro shops. Ask the dealer at some of the bigger goalie equipment stores, and you'll be surprised at what might be out there. The quality is superior, as are the savings, and you might end up wearing the same equipment as your favorite goalie!

The most common mistake that goaltenders make is buying the brand and model that a particular NHL goalie is wearing or the one that has the best graphics. This equipment may look the same as the gear in the stores but may have several unique features. Don't get caught up in the graphics. Use the three Ps to make well-educated decisions on equipment.

COACHES' TIP

GOALTENDING EQUIPMENT

When choosing equipment, it is important to select each individual piece on its own merits (see figure 1.1). Many manufacturers promote the fact that their pieces are designed to integrate well with each other, and this should be a consideration. This being said, there are many goalies who mix equipment makes and models. Experience is the key here, and the more equipment you have tried, the better you will understand what you need. If you do not have experience you must rely on others, such as sales clerks and other goalies. Try to find people with experience who can steer you in the right direction. Ask questions regarding fit, weight, durability, and cost differences. Try to learn as much as possible, and relate that information with style of play.

  Once you have purchased your equipment, maintenance will play a role in performance and comfort. Make sure to air out your equipment after each use because equipment will stiffen up and smell if it is kept in a bag. Check your gear frequently to make sure the toe ties, straps, and strings are all in good shape. You may also want to check out the pockets that hold protective foam as well as the buckles and straps of your mask. This section gives you valuable insight into choosing each piece of equipment.

Figure 1.1 As a goalie, you'll need a lot of equipment. Select each piece on its own merits, keeping in mind the three P's.

Underwear and Socks

Most goalies today choose to wear performance clothing under their equipment. Performance gear is traditionally lightweight, fits tightly to the body, breathes well, and pulls moisture away from the body. This is a great choice because the form fit helps the muscles warm up faster and helps you stay dry throughout the game. Many goaltenders wear underwear that covers the whole leg and arm, while others choose the T-shirt and shorts option. The performance material is comfortable to wear, and there is a choice between a number of manufacturers. Under Armour is a popular selection in performance wear, but most manufacturers are producing their own performance wear. If you play in a colder climate, perhaps a mock-neck style is a good option.

One recent innovation is the performance top, which consists of a Kevlar-reinforced turtleneck that protects against lacerations. This option allows a goaltender to move more freely than does the traditional throat guard. Another popular new product with goalies is compression shorts that are intended to help prevent groin pulls, which are common among goaltenders. Elastic straps are strategically placed within the shorts to help prevent injury.

It is important to wear what feels comfortable and to keep your clothing clean for hygienic reasons. Your body is very sensitive to uncomfortable underwear, so if your underwear rubs the wrong way or is in any way annoying, it can be a distraction. With the fear of Staph infection, it is also important to wash your underwear after each use.

Most goalies now opt to wear the team socks that go with their uniforms, when in the past goalies sometimes wore a one-piece sweatpant. Socks attach to either a garter belt or to hockey shorts that have Velcro strips to grip the socks.

Cup

A goalie-specific cup is now a necessity with the number of shots being absorbed by the body. The goalie cup allows the impact to be absorbed through the midsection and prevents painful injuries. The female version of the jockstrap is called the jill strap. When selecting a goalie cup, bring your pants to make sure the equipment interacts comfortably. You should not feel inhibited when squatting into your stance or performing a butterfly.

Recently, older goalies have found that placing a smaller cup inside a larger cup (double cupping) provides the best protection. Hockey equipment manufacturers are now producing a model that consists of a cup within a cup for goalies who face harder shots and require the extra protection. Double cupping is not a requirement for younger goalies and is a consideration beginning at the bantam level.

Skates and Sharpening

When purchasing a new pair of skates, go to an experienced dealer and find the proper brand and model to fit your foot. Choosing a skate is similar to choosing a shoe, and skate sizing is traditionally one shoe size smaller for comfort and impact reasons. Your heel must not rise when skating, and the skate must be wide enough for your foot. A hockey shop can also punch out areas of the skate if the fit needs adjusting. If your skates are not comfortable, your play will suffer dramatically. When purchasing skates, bring your leg pads with you so you can find where the straps fit best in order to help interlock the two pieces of equipment. Frequently check to make sure the plastic is not cracked, the eyelets are functional, and no rust buildup is present.

Break skates in before tryouts or major tournaments. Skates are usually very stiff at first and can hinder movement. Also they can feel and skate differently from what you have been wearing. Don't lose your competitive edge trying to adjust to your new skates. The newer materials incorporated into today's skates dramatically reduce break-in time. Wear the skates at practice while continuing to use your old skates in games until you feel comfortable enough to use them in a game.

You must also take into consideration the amount of blade that rests on the ice and the sharpness of your blade. Goalie skate blades are mostly flat, with very little or no rocker for balance. Some goalies are opting for slightly more rocker to assist in skating, and the give and take is in the balance.

Today's goalies are keeping their blades sharper then ever. With all the down-low movements, it's easy to see why. The inside edge of the skate must grip the ice firmly to allow a goalie to execute butterfly pushes and perform momentum changes with power. Get skates sharpened between one-half and three-quarters of an inch (1.3 and 1.9 centimeters) based on preference, and sharpen after 7 to 10 hours of use. Older, more experienced goaltenders sharpen their skates from a three-eights cut to a half inch (0.9 to 1.3 centimeters). The sharper cut provides more grip, precision, and crispness to skating. Adequate strength is required to use a deeper hollow, so a goaltender with too deep a cut who finds his edges dig into the ice too deep and therefore gets his feet stuck is better off with a duller blade (less hollow).

Some goalie skates allow you to replace the blade and not the whole plastic cowling. Purchase an extra set, and keep them readily available. If you crack a blade or lose an edge, they could come in handy.

Pants

A good investment once a player hits his peewee years is the goalie-specific pant. Goalie pants offer increased protection for the thighs and hips. This equates to more padding covering a greater amount of surface. It will eliminate the sting from shots and improve puck absorption. Do not buy pants that are too bulky, or you will lose mobility. You should also bring leg pads and arm and chest protectors to ensure proper equipment interaction when purchasing your pants. Most goalies wear their chest pads over their pants. By moving up and down, you can tell if the chest pad shifts smoothly or if the pants inhibit the movement of the chest pad or vice versa. The chest pad and the pants should not be fighting each other.

Leg Pads

The leg pad has become the trickiest piece of equipment to properly fit. Many companies make models to suit butterfly- and hybrid-style goalies (see figure 1.2). The butterfly goaltender usually prefers a stiffer pad with maximum blocking area coverage, while the hybrid goaltender focuses on mobility. For the younger goaltender, a stiff pad may be cumbersome and can make movement more difficult. Here are the characteristics that differ between a butterfly pad and a hybrid pad.

Butterfly Pads

■ Generally stiffer in knee and thigh for sealing and five-hole coverage (no funneling effect in five hole)

Figure 1.2 Hybrid pads (left) and butterfly pads (middle and right).

- High-density foam construction to provide stiffness but longer rebounds (less absorption)
- Stiffer from top to toe to enhance seal along ice
- Shallower leg and boot channel to enhance natural rotation of the goal pad

Hybrid Pads

- More flexible in knee and thigh
- Softer materials used in the shin for impact absorption (rebound control)
- More flexible in boot, particularly in scoop area for a deeper crouch in tight
- Deeper leg and boot channel, providing for a more traditional secure fit

Goal pads have three varying degrees of flexibility depending on the location of the breaking point(s):

1. Break at bottom of the knee (where shin and knee meet). Extremely stiff and upright pad.
2. Break at bottom and top of knee (nothing in middle). Provides some flexibility at top section.
3. Break at bottom, middle, and top. Provides flexibility throughout knee and thigh area. This is enhanced by incorporating flex darts in the outside roll to further increase the overall flexibility of the pad.

MARTIN BIRON

In goaltending there are a few popular catchphrases. "Playing big," "filling up the net," and "moving efficiently" are ways to describe positive characteristics found in top goaltenders and fit Martin Biron to a T. Biron is 6 feet 3 inches (190 cm) and 170 pounds (77 kilograms), and through a big but compact stance he covers a lot of the net. With recent rule changes in equipment, Biron was forced to downsize his equipment and has adapted well to smaller gear and his mobility has improved. Previously regarded as a blocker, he now demonstrates his athleticism and combines progressive blocking technique with patience and the ability to react to shots. His butterfly style eliminates holes, and there is not a lot of excess movement when he plays. His ability to adapt to the new equipment helped Biron lead the Flyers to the 2008 NHL conference finals.

When watching Martin Biron play, you will see how he maximizes his size and is an intimidating goalie to shoot against, as his opponent is usually left with very little net to shoot at. The former QMJHL star has played parts of nine NHL seasons with Buffalo (1995-1996 and 1998-1999 through 2006-2007) and most recently is manning the pipes for the Philadelphia Flyers. He compiled a 134-115-25 record, 2.53 GAA, .909 save percentage, and 18 shutouts in 300 career regular-season games with the Sabres. Biron is second on Buffalo's all-time list in shutouts (18) and third in games played (300) and wins (134). Originally he was drafted by the Sabres in the first round (16th overall) of the 1995 NHL entry draft.

A number of alterations can be made to a goal pad, so here are a few tips.

Toe and Foot Area

Sliding toe bridges, toe ties, and so on are available to secure the pad to the skate; find what works best for you by trying the various options. Make sure the inside of the pad is flat, allowing movement from the butterfly position. Certain pads will also be cut and angled in this area based on your stance. The concept behind this is to tightly close the five hole when in the butterfly. Make sure the skate is secured in the ankle channel and can move as needed. When you are butterflying, the skate will actually shift slightly in the pad, but when you are upright it must fit in the channel.

Inside Leg Protection

Make sure the calf, ankle, and knee have proper protection. A shot should not be able to find a seam and cause injury. This area can also help trap pucks that might sneak under the pad. Look for high-density foam to ensure overall protection. Inside leg protection also keeps the knee from dropping below the lower portion of the leg when down in the butterfly. In this situation, the inside padding is in contact with the ice and therefore props the knee up, reducing the strain on the joint. Less material on the inside of the knee can increase stress on the knee joint when down.

Knee Cradle

The area where the knee rests when in a butterfly is now a major component of the leg pad. Make sure there is proper protection and your knee is aligned properly. The knee should not be lower or higher in the cradle, and the cradle should be sized properly. Many pads have adjustable knee cradles to ensure proper fit. If the knee cradle is too high or low, your knee will not be in the proper position when going down and therefore not properly supported.

Thigh Rise

The thigh rise is the area above the knee rolls. Many goalies are opting to increase the pad size here because it does cover more net and allows the butterfly to close quicker. Be careful not to lose mobility by purchasing pads that are too big in this area.

One problem that goalies have is with thigh board and pant integration, and therefore it is important to wear your skates and pants when trying on the pads. A thigh board that gets caught in the pant when going up and down will constantly need to be shifted. Look for no catching of the thigh board when performing recovery moves for the butterfly.

COACHES' TIP Take the time to select your leg pads properly. Leg pads are often your most expensive gear. Buy the pad that is best suited for your style of play. Bring skates and pants when buying pads to ensure proper equipment interaction.

Arm and Chest Protectors

Once an overlooked piece of equipment by manufacturers, the evolution of the arm and chest protector has improved greatly over the years. Special attention is provided to the shoulder, elbow, and collarbone area. Many models now have built-in neck guards for additional protection. This has helped reduce the risk of upper-body injuries tremendously.

When purchasing an arm and chest protector, take mobility into consideration. You don't want to be so bulked up you can't move. Find the proper balance between protection and mobility. You must be able to perform without feeling inhibited while at the same time being protected. Also, learn how to adjust all the straps and laces to ensure proper fit and comfort level. You want your upper-body equipment to be fastened tightly enough that it does not shift while you play while at the same time not be so tight that it restricts your movements. Many models now have the arms laced in so you can adjust the length of the arm within the unit.

Bring your mask, pants, and gloves when purchasing your arm and chest set. Make sure the pants interact properly and you don't feel constricted in the midsection. It is imperative that the chest pad and pants move independently and are not encumbered by one another. If they do not integrate well, you will feel this right away and will not be comfortable in your movements. Make sure the gloves and elbow floaters are even so there are no spaces left for a shot to sneak in. Also, make sure the shoulders don't rise so high that it interferes with your mask and head movement.

Blocker

Traditionally, all blockers look very similar. Most blockers have some curvature at the top in order to cover more area of the net from a shot originating from ice level. Differences in blockers come from the placement of the palm, the number and placement of straps, and thumb and pinkie protection (see figure 1.3).

Make sure the blocker feels comfortable and there is a snug fit in the palm and proper weight distribution through the whole hand. Now that most goalies have adopted the butterfly, it is essential that there be proper protection for the inside of the wrist area. This protection allows you to maintain a blocking position with your blocker without the fear of a puck sneaking through. It is important that the protection not inhibit your range of motion in the wrist. Also, check to see that proper protection is offered for all the fingers.

Figure 1.3 There are many variations of blockers and catching gloves so select the ones that best suit your playing style.

Most blockers are angled at the top to help control rebounds. The angle varies from model to model, and the amount of curvature at the top of the blocker is a personal preference for a goaltender. A butterfly goalie will choose a greater angle at the top of the blocker because this will block more of the angle of flight from a butterfly position. Find a blocker that suits your playing style.

The palm placement has changed in many models. Some are placed higher at the wrist to maximize coverage in the length area. Some are off-centered toward the wrist to offer extra area in the width. A higher palm placement may not suit a goaltender who paddles down a lot because it can make it difficult to get the stick flush. A butterfly goalie who likes to pull the blocker in tight may prefer a palm placement that is closer to the inside in order to improve blocking area coverage to the perimeter.

Blockers now come with a thin or thick board feature. A thin board lets you feel the puck better, but it makes rebound control a bit more difficult. The opposite holds for the thicker board. Again, experiment to find what works best for you.

Catching Glove

Most goalies agree the catching glove is the most important piece of gear they own. From catching the puck to handling the stick, the glove has to do it all, and you need to feel good while doing it. Take extra time when purchasing a glove—it is that important to your game.

Find a glove that closes and retains the puck and feels comfortable on your hand. The break, or fold, of the glove varies from model to model. Some gloves have a single break, while others have a double break. A double break allows you to close the glove easily with just the fingers. The single break requires the use of your thumb as well. A blocker like J.-S. Giguere would likely prefer a single break as he likes to maximize coverage and allow the puck to enter the glove, while Ryan Miller would probably opt for a double break because he prefers to catch the puck cleanly.

The angle of the break is also very important and reflects how you hold your glove. Goalies now place their gloves anywhere from a 3:00 o'clock position to a 12:00 o'clock position. The angle of the break should allow you to catch the puck cleanly with respect to the angle of how you position your glove. If you use the wrong angle, you may find that pucks you think should be going in your pocket are hitting closer to your thumb or palm and popping out.

The pocket of the glove now offers a variety of options. The depth of the pocket is essential. If you like to play the puck, opt for a shallower pocket as Martin Brodeur does. Using a large pocket makes it more difficult for a puck to bounce out, but it takes longer to get the puck out of your glove in order to play it with your stick. The design of the pocket ranges from the traditional T-trap to an inverted T-trap style. Find the style that gives you the proper feel for the puck at all times.

Make sure there is adequate protection for the back of the hand. There should be no areas where a skate blade can cut your hand, but the protection should not keep you from flexing your hand back. This protection must also be enough to withstand a slash with a stick. Slashes and skate cuts can be painful and scary injuries. The glove must also offer proper weight distribution so that you are dictating the glove position rather than the glove determining how it is being held. Familiarize yourself with all the features of your glove so you can maximize your performance. Resist the urge to buy a glove that is too big, as it will hinder a variety of aspects of your game.

Mask

The most personalized piece of equipment for a goalie is the goalie mask. The evolution of the mask since the days of Jacques Plante is nothing short of remarkable. The sight line, protection, and performance help a goalie play with a level of confidence that once was not there. Only two types of masks should be considered. Whichever you choose, make sure it is certified for the league and level you are playing in. The first choice is the traditional helmet and cage (see figure 1.4) worn by players. This is a fine selection for young goalies and offers proper protection for their age. There is no need to purchase a new mask for a mite- or squirt-age goalie, although it may add enjoyment to the position.

The other style is the popular goalie mask. The benefit of a mask over a helmet and cage is that the mask deflects the puck to reduce the pressure of its impact. This reduces the chance of pressure cuts or any trauma to the head. Since younger players do not generate enough power in their shots for this to be a concern, the mask is not necessary until the peewee level but is still preferred. Simply put, the lightweight and functional mask offers the best protection for a goalie.

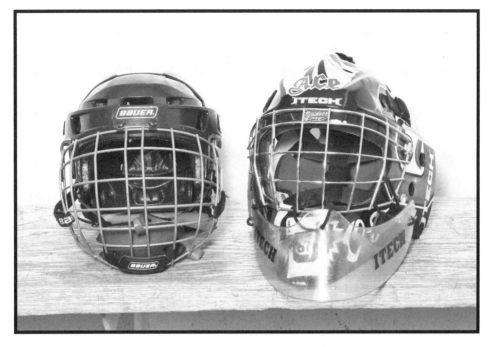

Figure 1.4 The traditional helmet and cage (left) and the popular mask over a helmet and cage (right).

When making your mask purchase, look for a Kevlar or fiberglass weave to ensure the best protection and proper sight lines. These sight lines will vary from model to model, and it is important that you look through the correct bars in the mask for proper puck tracking. The mask should feel comfortable and not put additional strain on the neck. Make sure the backplate covers the whole back of the head, with no exposure, and the mask straps are properly secured. The chin cup should offer additional comfort and ensure that the mask stays on during scrambles or collisions.

Most mask manufacturers suggest that a mask be replaced every two seasons. The reason is that a mask takes constant abuse while in your hockey bag. The bag is thrown in the back of the SUV, on the locker room floor, and so on. Therefore, purchase a mask bag or put your mask in the thigh of your pants to prolong its usage. Finally, do go to an experienced, authorized dealer. Fit and protection are essential, and an experienced hockey shop will help immensely. This is not an area where you want to compromise safety.

Most goalies wear a plastic throat protector to protect the neck area against shots. The throat protector is attached to the mask with string and should not be fastened too tightly so it does not restrict head movement. Many goalies also opt for a throat guard that protects against possible lacerations from a skate. Throat guards are recommended even for very young goaltenders, especially if the kids like to pig-pile the goalie at the end of the game.

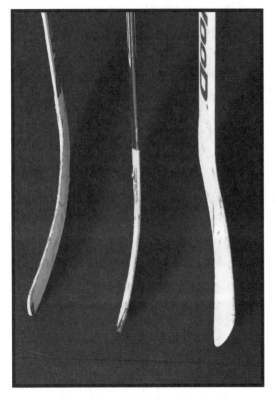

Figure 1.5 Stick curves come in many patterns, each with its own benefit.

Stick

Your stick has many important features that affect much of your style (see figure 1.5), so it is essential to pick a proper one. A younger goalie's performance will be dramatically affected if the stick paddle is either too big or too small. The following breakdown will help you make smart decisions.

Material

Goal sticks are either wood, foam (wood handle with polyurethane foam core paddle and blade), or composite. Many companies are making composite goalie sticks that come with a hefty price tag. The composite will last longer and maintain flexibility and consistency, while a traditional stick allows for a better feel for the puck and therefore better puck control. A composite stick is the lightest option and the easiest for younger goalies to control. Older, stronger goalies generally are able to clear the puck with more velocity with a composite stick.

Although composite sticks are popular, some goalies are returning to the traditional wood–fiber laminate sticks. With the price difference, you can order several wood–fiber laminate sticks for the price of a single composite. As technology rapidly advances, the composite stick should soon have the same give or feel of the traditional stick.

Lie

The lie is the area between where the paddle and blade meet in a stick. The lie will affect your hand positioning and how the blade stays on the ice. When steering pucks, the blade of the stick must be flat and therefore can be affected by the lie. The lie will also come into play when a goalie plays the puck with his stick. Try different lies in order to find the one that works best. Goaltenders who hold the blocker in tight to the body will prefer a higher lie. The lie of a stick may differ from one manufacturer to another. When purchasing a stick, bring to the store an old stick so you can match it up with the new one.

Paddle Height

The paddle height will affect a goalie's stance and movement. The most common mistake when purchasing a stick is buying one with a paddle that is too big. The longer the paddle, the more difficult the stick will be to control. The length of the shaft will also reflect the length of the paddle, so a small goalie with a high paddle will also have a long stick. This is a concern because goalie sticks are balanced and should not be cut down like player sticks. Difficulty controlling the stick is more prevalent the younger the goalie is. A paddle that is too short may cause a goalie to hunch over too much, affecting balance.

Goalie preference comes into play when selecting paddle height. The perfect height makes the stick easy to maneuver, allows the goaltender to feel comfortable in his stance, and allows for proper blocker height when down in a butterfly. Make sure a qualified salesperson helps you with this, and keep track of your paddle height.

Curve

For young goalies, it is important to find a stick with as little curve as possible so they can learn how to properly control a stick. An advanced goalie should decide how much of a toe or heel curve is needed. Learning how to pass and shoot a puck is essential as you develop as a goalie. You must be able to make a flat pass as well as shoot the puck high and hard off the glass. A curved stick allows you to control the puck when moving it with your stick blade as well as for passes, clears, and rims (pucks played around the boards).

Rocker

The degree of rocker plays a role in getting height on the puck. The more rocker, the better the chance of getting height. It is difficult to lift the puck with a flat rocker, although a flat blade allows for better balance. The goal is to find a rocker that allows you to get the puck airborne without affecting your sense of balance.

Pro, Intermediate, and Junior Models

Pick the size stick that is recommended for your height and weight. Too often young goalies are using the wrong size stick, and it has a dramatic effect on their performance. Don't buy a stick thinking you will grow into it or with the intention of cutting it down; your hands will be too small for the shaft region of the stick and cutting the shaft will cause an imbalance with the stick.

Stick Taping

Stick taping is another issue that is decided by goalie preference. Traditionally, sticks are taped heel to toe. This helps prevent snow buildup and friction on the stick. Keep a knob on the butt end of the stick, too. This will keep the shaft from sliding out of your hands during a poke check and make it easier to pick up the stick when dropped. Many goalies tape the area where the shaft and paddle meet. It helps dampen vibrations and reduces the wear to the palm of your blocker. Stick with white tape, as it is easier to see the puck off the stick and follow rebounds.

COACHES' TIP   Once you find a stick you like, take it with you when buying new sticks. Make sure new sticks match up, and check the lie, curve, rocker, and paddle height.

CLOSING THOUGHTS ON EQUIPMENT SELECTION

Buy for comfort and protection. Buy what feels right, not what is the newest gadget on the market. If you can't find exactly what you want, special-order direct from the manufacturer. It may take longer, but the value is well worth the wait. If you need additional work done, alter your gear as needed to meet your style.

It is always a good idea to be prepared to fix your equipment. Keep an extra bag with your gear filled with the following items:

- Laces of all sizes
- Mask accessories
- Emery board for stick and nails
- Bandages
- Sweet Stick or skate stone
- Tape
- Multipurpose tool set
- Straps or clips for pads

chapter 2

GETTING STRONGER

Dave Flint

A well-designed strength program is critical if you want to be an elite athlete. It can help prepare your body for the rigors of a long season and ultimately help you stay healthy throughout the course of the year. Many uneducated goalies believe that if they lift weights they will get too big and slow and will lose flexibility. Nothing could be further from the truth—increasing lean muscle mass can make you stronger, quicker, and more agile, all important components of being a good goalie. The days of not lifting weights and using training camp as your time to get in shape are a thing of the past. To be the best goaltender, strength training needs to be a year-round part of your training program.

STRENGTH TRAINING AND AGE

Age is an important factor when designing a training program. Younger (preadolescent) athletes' bodies are not developed yet, so younger athletes don't have the muscles to lift heavy weights. They are also still growing, so it is important to help them develop a good strength base and balance so they can train with weights when they are older. The older athletes (16 and older) will train with weights more to develop their strength and power.

Preadolescent Goalies

Training programs for preadolescent goalies need to focus on flexibility, core strength, balance, quickness, and agility. Heavy weight training can be detrimental rather than beneficial with this age group. Their bodies are still developing and cannot handle heavy loads. It is a good time to work on coordination and learning the movements of the lifts for when their bodies mature. Most exercises are done with body weight, medicine balls, stability balls, and very light weights, so proper form and technique are taught without the chance of injury.

High School, College, and Professional Goalies

Young high school athletes are still growing at a rapid rate and should not handle heavy weights, as this can affect the athletes' growth plates. As these athletes get stronger and familiar with the lifts, they can start to lift heavier weights. The focus for this group is on building strength, power, flexibility, core strength, quickness, and agility through the use of free weights, stability balls, medicine balls, and other training modalities. Working these areas helps you become a fit, well-rounded athlete, which is essential for becoming the best goalie you can be.

COACHES' TIP Strength training will play a major factor in shooting the puck and holding the crease in traffic. It will be very difficult for an older goaltender to maximize talent without a well-designed program.

TRAINING GUIDELINES

The off-season conditioning program is designed more for developing strength, power, quickness, agility, and flexibility so that you are in the best condition entering your season. The in-season program is more designed as a maintenance program so that you don't lose too much of your strength, power, quickness, agility, and flexibility during the season. If you tried to train as hard in-season as you do in the off-season along with practices and games, you would get burned out sooner or later, and it would have detrimental effects, such as chronic fatigue, loss of muscle mass, or sickness from being run down. Giving your body time to recover is just as critical as training it.

Guidelines for Weight Training

1. Take the proper time to warm up before lifting weights. Perform at least 10 minutes of a general warm-up (e.g., stationary bike or running on a treadmill). This raises the body temperature to prepare the muscles for lifting weights.

2. When lifting heavy weights, always use a spotter to help avoid injury.

3. When trying a new lift, use very light weight or no weight until you are comfortable with the movement. This lets your body become familiar with the movement.

4. Move the weight through a full range of motion in a controlled manner. If you do not move the weight through the full range of motion, you will not get the full benefit of the lift. Your muscles will not get worked as hard as they should. Also, jerking the weights or swinging them through the range of motion could lead to an injury.

5. Breathe correctly. Your muscles need oxygen to perform, so make sure that you breathe. Holding your breath can unnecessarily raise your blood pressure.

6. Don't overtrain—more isn't always better. Overtraining occurs when your body doesn't get adequate rest to allow your muscles to recover. This can lead to injury or decreased performance on the ice and in the gym. If you are starting to feel run down, your joints ache, you are not recovering from workouts as quickly, and you have a lack of interest in training, these are symptoms that you might be overtraining.

7. Consult with your physician before starting a weight training program. Make sure you are fit and in good health to safely begin a training program.

In-Season Training

In-season training should be done to maintain strength and flexibility and to counter the effects a long season has on your body. A good in-season program can be very beneficial down the stretch during playoff time. It can also make the transition into the off-season program a lot easier. In-season programs should be somewhat quick but productive. Workouts should not last more than 45 minutes. With practices or games almost every day, more than 45 minutes in the gym might be too much for your body to handle; your body still needs energy for practices and games. So when you go to the gym, make sure the time you spend there is quality time. If you work hard and can get your workout done in 30 minutes, then that is great. If it takes you longer, that is fine too. Everyone's bodies are different, so find out what routine works best for you.

Off-Season Training

Goalies should not train like forwards and defensemen. The position is unique, and therefore the training is different. Goalies need to be physically strong while maintaining flexibility, agility, and quickness. In game situations, goalies work in short, powerful bursts. Very rarely do they need to work hard for more than 10 to 20 seconds at a time. That is why it is important to build up anaerobic threshold, power, and core strength.

In game situations, goaltenders are called on to explode into their saves and move their bodies into strange positions very quickly and then be able to recover within a second—this is where power and core strength prove beneficial. This program focuses on making you a better athlete. It is broken down into three phases: strength, maximal strength, and power.

Periodization

Periodization is a term used to describe the different phases of a training program. They usually last for three to six weeks depending on the program. The first phase of a typical off-season program starts with lighter weights and higher repetitions. As the training program moves along, the weight increases and the repetitions decrease, moving more toward developing maximal strength and then eventually into power development. The phases progress this way because it is important to develop a good strength base before getting into the more complex movements and heavier weights. At the end of the off-season and entering the preseason, you want to be at your strongest because of the demands that will be placed on your body during the season ahead.

A good option when training goalies in the off-season is to use three phases lasting four to six weeks, depending on how long the off-season is. This allows enough time for the body to adapt, and it also keeps the program from becoming boring.

Phase 1, the strength-building phase, focuses on basic movements and light to moderate weights. The exercises are usually in the 8- to 15-repetition range and in sets of three. A repetition is the movement of the weight through a complete range of motion for that exercise; a group of repetitions is considered a set. The movement should be slow and controlled. This type of lifting builds a strong base of strength to prepare the muscles for the fast, explosive movements that will be performed later on in the off-season.

Phase 2 is called the maximal-strength phase, again lasting four to six weeks depending on the duration of the off-season. The weights will increase in this

RICK DIPIETRO

Rick DiPietro is the star goaltender for the New York Islanders. At 6 feet 1 inch (185 centimeters) and 210 pounds (95 kg), he is solid and strong and ready for the rigors of an NHL season. Being physically strong is important for a goaltender. You need to be able to maintain your depth and command your crease because the latest inter-pretations of the rules have given greater leniency to attacking forwards. Being strong will help prevent injuries and help you hold your post as well as improve your ability to shoot the puck. DiPietro is one of the top puckhandling goalies in the NHL and as a youth would shoot up to 200 pucks a day as part of his off-ice training. DiPietro's commitment to training off the ice is a big part of his success between the pipes.

A former number one draft pick, Rick DiPietro recorded a career-best home shutout streak of 191:04 minutes in 2006-2007. He became the first Islanders goaltender to record two 30-win seasons and started a career-high 18 consecutive games. A prod-uct of the U.S. National Team Development Program, he tied the Islanders franchise single-season record of 32 victories, shared by Billy Smith (1981-1982) and Chris Osgood (2001-2002). DiPietro competed for the United States at the 2006 Olympics and two World Junior Championships.

© Bruce Bennett/Getty Images Sport

phase, and the repetitions will decrease. More difficult lifts are added to challenge the athlete. The repetitions are in the six to eight range, and three or four sets are performed depending on the exercise. After this phase, taking a week off from weight training is recommended to give the muscles and joints some rest before phase 3 begins.

Phase 3 is the power-development phase. Developing power is critical for a goalie's game. A goalie who lacks explosive power will struggle to be successful. This phase includes Olympic lifts, medicine ball exercises, and plyometrics as well as some basic lifts to create a balance between power and strength development. The repetition range is three to eight depending on the exercise, and sets are three or four. A week of rest is recommended after this phase before the season starts. If you worked hard enough, you deserve it.

Free Weights Versus Machines

Free weights usually incorporate a greater range of motion and bring several muscle groups into play to stabilize the weight. They are more beneficial to athletes than are machines, which usually focus on one muscle group and are not sport specific. Machines do have their place for people who have not lifted weights and are trying to build a strength base and also in a rehabilitation setting. Sports are usually played with one or two feet in contact with the ground, which is why the free weights are more beneficial. When performing an exercise on a machine, your body weight is usually supported, and sometimes your feet aren't even in contact with the ground.

With free weights you can do multijoint and multiplane exercises geared toward your specific sport by incorporating the movements used in that sport. You can also vary the speed at which you lift the weight. You can perform a quick, explosive movement, such as a power clean, or lift a heavier weight more slowly through a full range of motion, such as a deadlift. Some valuable goalie-specific lifts are Sumo squats (groin, quadriceps, and hamstrings), lateral lunges (groin, hip flexors, quadriceps, and hamstrings), and diagonal lunges (groin, hip flexors, quadriceps, and hamstrings).

Rest Between Sets

Lifting weights is an anaerobic activity that will cause lactic acid to build up in the muscles. The optimal amount of time needed to remove lactic acid from the muscles is about three minutes. As you get into lifting heavier loads, it is beneficial to allow your muscles enough time to recover. As a goalie, you usually don't have that much time to recover during a game, so try cutting down your rest intervals as your body adapts. Maybe start out at two minutes and then work your way down. By doing this, you can build up your body's tolerance to lactic acid.

Breathing

An important part of lifting that is often overlooked is breathing correctly. Have you ever seen a person lifting in the gym whose face is bright red, and his head looks as if it's going to pop off his shoulders? This person is performing a Valsalva maneuver, which when done often over a long period can lead to heart problems (right ventricular hypertrophy). In the short term it could lead to your getting dizzy or passing out. It is important to remember to exhale during the difficult part of the lift and inhale on the easy part of the lift. For example, when doing a bench press you want to inhale as you lower the weight and exhale as you push the weight up.

If you are going to train, it is important that you train consistently. Training hard and then stopping, only to pick it back up sporadically, will yield minimal results. For the best results, work out consistently and with intensity.

COACHES' TIP

STRENGTH-TRAINING EXERCISES

There are many strength-training exercises to choose from. The following upper- and lower-body exercises are particularly effective for goaltenders.

Upper-Body Exercises

Upper-body strength is important for goalies in situations when there is traffic in front of them so they are able to push off players and hold their ground. It is also important in recovery when they need to push themselves up from the supine or prone position.

BENCH PRESS

Muscles Worked: Chest, Triceps, Shoulders

Procedure:

1. Lie flat on the bench, and grab the bar with a wide overhand grip.
2. Slowly lower the bar to the midchest, pause, and push the weight back up, exhaling on the push. Make sure to keep your back flat on the bench, and don't bounce the weight off your chest.

SEATED SHOULDER PRESS

Muscles Worked: Shoulders, Triceps, Upper Chest

Procedure:

1. Seated upright with your back flat against the bench, push the weight straight up over your head.
2. Lower the weight in the front to your upper chest, pause, and push the weight back up, fully extending the arms. Note that shoulder presses done behind the head put unnecessary stress on the shoulder.

UPRIGHT ROWS

Muscles Worked: Shoulders

Procedure:

1. Start standing upright, with the knees slightly bent and feet shoulder-width apart.
2. Grab the bar with an overhand grip with your hands about 4 inches (10 centimeters) apart.
3. Pull the weight up just below the chin, keeping the bar close to the body (see photo).
4. Pause at the top, and lower the weight slowly.

DIPS

Muscles Worked: Triceps, Chest, Shoulders

Procedure:

1. Start by grabbing the dip bars, supporting your body weight with arms fully extended.
2. Lower your body until your arms are flexed and your chest is about even with the bars (see photo).
3. Push yourself back up to the starting position where your arms are fully extended.

BARBELL CURL

Muscles Worked: Biceps

Procedure:

1. Start with your feet about shoulder-width apart and your knees slightly flexed.
2. Grab the bar with an underhand grip, your hands about shoulder-width apart (you can vary width of grip).
3. Pull the bar up toward the chest by flexing the elbows. Slowly lower the weight to the starting position.
4. Do not rock forward or back to get the weight up.

Lower-Body Exercises

Lower-body strength may be even more important for a goalie's success than upper-body strength. They are both important, but so much movement in goaltending is derived from the lower body. Lower-body strength allows a goalie to quickly get from point A to point B and also helps him recover faster after a save. Following are some effective lower-body exercises for goalies.

SUMO SQUATS

Muscles Worked: Groin, Quadriceps, Gluteals, Hamstrings

Procedure:
1. Start standing upright, with the bar on your upper back and your hands grabbing the bar with a wide overhand grip (see photo *a*). Legs are wider than a normal squat, and the toes are pointed out.
2. Flex the knees and drop the hips while maintaining a flat back. Lower yourself until your knees are flexed at 90 degrees (see photo *b*).
3. Keep the feet flat on the floor and the chin up, and return to the starting position by extending the knees and the hips.

LATERAL LUNGES

Muscles Worked: Groin, Quadriceps, Gluteals, Hamstrings

Procedure:
1. Start standing upright, with the bar balanced on your back and a wide overhand grip.
2. Step directly to your left with your left leg, keeping your foot facing forward and flexing your knee to 90 degrees (see photo).
3. Push back by extending the leg and returning to the starting point.
4. Repeat with the right leg.

CALF RAISES

Muscles Worked: Calves

Procedure:
1. Start by standing with the balls of your feet on the edge of a 6- to 8-inch (15 to 20 centimeter) platform.
2. Hold dumbbells in your hands, or balance a bar on your back with a wide overhand grip.
3. Lower your heels down toward the floor until you feel a stretch in your calves.
4. Raise your heels up by pushing with the balls of your feet against the platform.
5. Once your heels are as high as you can get them, lower them to the starting position.

STEP-UPS

Muscles Worked: Hamstrings, Quadriceps, Gluteals, Groin, Calves

Procedure:

1. Get a box or bench 18 to 24 inches (45 to 60 centimeters) high.
2. Use either dumbbells or a bar balanced on the back.
3. Facing the box, step up with the right leg, and drive the left knee toward the chest (see photos *a-b*).
4. Step off the box and return to the starting position.
5. Step up with the left leg, and drive the right knee up toward the chest.

Core Exercises

Core strength is essential for goalies because of the physical demands that are placed on their bodies. Good core strength will help with quickness, agility, save recovery, strength on skates, and prevention of injuries by allowing you to maintain good form and body position throughout the save. It also keeps your technique and form from getting sloppy when you become fatigued. Here are a few core exercises for goalies.

RUSSIAN TWISTS

Muscles Worked: Low Back, Abdominals

Procedure:

1. Start in a seated position on the floor, with your legs crossed and slightly bent and feet off the floor.
2. Lean back slightly so that you are balancing on your buttocks.
3. Holding a medicine ball, rotate your torso to your left while moving the ball to your left side (see photo), then rotate to your right while moving the ball to your right.

STABILITY BALL V-UPS

Muscles Worked: Low Back, Abdominals

Procedure:

1. Start lying on the floor with your hands extended above your head, holding a stability ball.
2. Raise your hands and feet off the floor toward each other, forming a V with your body.
3. Place the ball between your feet (see photo) and then return to the starting position.
4. Continue by flexing your body back into the V position and passing the ball back to your hands.

MEDICINE BALL SIT-UP AND THROW

Muscles Worked: Abdominals

Procedure:

1. Start in a seated position on the floor, with your knees bent and feet flat on the floor.
2. Have a partner stand about 5 feet (1.5 meters) away.
3. Lie back with the ball extended over your head (see photo *a*).
4. As you sit up, throw the ball to your partner (see photo *b*).
5. Your partner then throws the ball back, and you repeat the exercise.

MEDICINE BALL SIT-UP, STAND-UP, AND SLAM

Muscles Worked: Abdominals

Procedure:

1. Start in the same position as for the medicine ball sit-up and throw, minus the partner (see photo *a*).
2. Sit up with the medicine ball overhead, and then once you are upright, move right into the standing position (see photo *b*).
3. As soon as you are standing, slam the ball down onto the ground in front of you (see photo *c*).
4. Retrieve the ball, sit back down, and repeat.

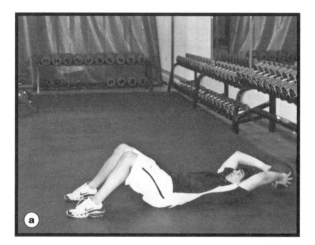

**COACHES' TIP** To create efficiency within your goaltending technique, it is important to have a strong core. It is the core that will stabilize the extremities and allow you to keep a compact stance.

PLYOMETRICS

Goaltending is a position that requires quick, explosive movements. A great way to improve your explosiveness is through the use of plyometrics. Plyometrics are characterized by an eccentric contraction of the muscles followed by a rapid concentric contraction. This allows the muscles to generate more power.

Lower-body plyometrics are done through various jumping, leaping, and bounding movements. A goalie benefits from these types of movements when she has to quickly move from point A to point B to make a save (e.g., on a pass across the crease), when exploding into a shot to make a save, or in a recovery situation. Plyometrics can also be performed for the upper body, which can be important for glove saves and recoveries. Medicine balls are used mostly for upper-body plyometrics but can also be used for lower-body exercises. There are many different exercises that use medicine balls, boxes, or nothing but your body weight.

Guidelines for Plyometric Training

1. As for any training program, consult your doctor before you start. You want to make sure you do not have any underlying conditions or preexisting injuries.

2. Learn proper technique before performing the exercise. Each exercise can have a different technique, so it is best to be shown how to do a particular exercise by a trainer or coach. Improper technique can lead to injury.

3. Make sure you have a good strength base before performing plyometrics. Strength is usually built in the early phases of a training program. Plyometrics usually aren't added to a program until the middle or end phase. A good strength base is important because plyometrics require explosive movements that put a lot of stress on the joints and muscles, and not having a strength base could lead to injuries.

4. In an off-season program, plyometrics should start in the middle of the training plan and go to the end, right before the preseason. This allows you to develop maximal strength and power so you are at your strongest going into the season.

5. Plyometrics can be done minimally in-season as part of a program to maintain power. If you do too much, you might end up overtraining the muscles.

6. When first starting, limit the number of foot contacts (number of times your foot comes in contact with a surface). As you get stronger and closer to the end of your off-season program, you can increase the number. Too many foot contacts early can lead to injury and extreme muscle soreness.

7. When using medicine balls, choose a ball that is the appropriate weight (i.e., one that allows you to perform the desired number of repetitions with some difficulty). It may take a few times to determine the correct weight. If you cannot perform the number of repetitions required, the ball is too heavy. If you can perform the number of repetitions without much difficulty, then it is too light.

8. Perform exercises at maximal effort. Only you know if you are working as hard as you can.

9. Remember, the larger the athlete, the more pressure put on the joints during plyometrics. This may require you to adjust the number of floor contacts to decrease wear and tear on the joints and avoid injury.

10. If you experience any pain during the exercises, stop and consult a physician.

This is just a brief overview of plyometrics. They can be a useful tool and should be part of your training program. It is important to do the exercises correctly to get the maximum benefit and to avoid injury. Following are three lower-body and three upper-body exercises for goalies.

Lower-Body Exercises

Lower-body power is very important for goaltenders. Most movements in the net are explosive, whether you are moving into position to make a save or making the actual save. These exercises are sport specific to the position of goaltending.

SUMO SQUAT JUMPS

Muscles Worked: Groin, Hip Flexors, Quadriceps, Hamstrings, Gluteals, Calves

Purpose: To develop strength and power, primarily in the groin and hip flexors, to help when performing butterfly slides and pushes.

Procedure:

1. Start with your feet wider than shoulder-width apart and your toes pointing outward.

2. Put your hands on either side of your head.

3. Squat down until your thighs are parallel to the ground (see photo *a*), and then explode up as quickly as you can (see photo *b*).

4. As you come down, try to land softly, then repeat.

5. Make sure to keep your head and chest up and use only your legs; don't use your arms for momentum.

STRIDE JUMPS

Muscles Worked: Groin, Gluteals, Quadriceps, Hamstrings, Calves

Purpose: To develop power in the groin muscles and gluteals, which are used so much when skating and when making the lateral movements so commonly used by goalies.

Procedure:

1. Start standing in an athletic position, with your feet about shoulder-width apart and your knees slightly flexed.

2. Push off with your left leg and jump as far laterally to your right as you can, landing on your right leg and touching the ground with your left hand (see photo). Pause for a second and then drive off your right foot as far to your left as possible, landing on your left foot and touching the ground with your right hand.

3. Repeat this process.

SPLIT JUMPS

Muscles Worked: Hip Flexors, Quadriceps, Hamstrings, Groin, Gluteals, Calves

Purpose: To develop power in the lower body to allow for more powerful movement when driving out to challenge a shooter.

Procedure:

1. Start by putting one foot out in front and the other foot behind. The front leg should be bent 90 degrees at the hip and 90 degrees at the knee. The other leg is slightly flexed at the knee and extended at the hip (see photo *a*).
2. Next, jump as high as you can using both your legs and arms.
3. While in the air, switch the leg positions (see photo *b*) and land with the leg that was behind in front and the leg that was in front behind.

Recovery techniques for goaltenders have improved dramatically over the last 10 years. Being able to get up and down quickly gives you the chance to make second and third saves. These flurry saves can make the difference between being a good or a great goalie.

COACHES' TIP

Upper-Body Exercises

These goalie-specific upper-body exercises work on developing upper-body power through the use of medicine balls. Two of the exercises are done on the knees because with the butterfly being used so much today, many movements through the course of a game come when a goalie is on his knees.

POWER DROPS

Muscles Worked: Chest, Shoulders

Purpose: To develop power in the chest and shoulders to hold off players who are trying to screen or to move players out from in front.

Procedure:

1. Start by lying on your back, with your arms extended out in front of you.
2. Have a partner standing on a chair or bench right by your head. Your partner will drop a medicine ball down toward your chest (see photo).
3. Catch the ball, bring it down to your chest, and throw it back up to your partner all in one motion. Do not bounce the ball off your chest or try to catch the ball with your arms fully extended. This is an explosive movement, so it should be done quickly.

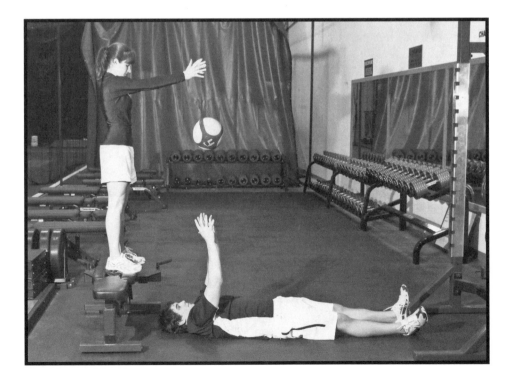

KNEELING ONE-ARM PUT

Muscles Worked: Chest, Shoulders, Abdominals

Purpose: To help you hold your position in front of the net when it gets physical.

Procedure:

1. Start in a kneeling position, with a medicine ball in one hand. Hold the medicine ball at shoulder level with the arm flexed.
2. Twist to that side and then uncoil as you extend the arm and rotate the body, pushing the medicine ball as far away from your body as you can (see photo).
3. If you have a partner, he can catch the ball and throw it back, or you can use a wall.
4. Make sure to train both sides.

KNEELING SIDE THROWS

Muscles Worked: Shoulders, Abdominals, Chest

Purpose: To develop power in the shoulders, chest, and core. Core strength can help with recovery from the butterfly position as well as help you hold your ground when things get physical around the net.

Procedure:

1. Start in a kneeling position, with a partner or wall about 8 feet (2.5 meters) away (to your side).
2. Hold a medicine ball at hip level away from your partner.
3. Twist your torso and your arms, and throw the ball to your partner (see photo).
4. After you perform the desired number of repetitions on one side, switch and work the other side.

OFF-SEASON AND IN-SEASON TRAINING PROGRAMS

Here are some in-season and off-season training programs geared toward goalies of different ages. The off-season program is broken down into three phases and focuses first on building a strength base, then at the end is based more on developing power. The in-season plan is designed to help goalies maintain their strength and flexibility to combat the wear and tear of a long season. Some of the exercises found in these programs are explained in chapters 2, 3, and 4. Due to the scope of this book, we are unable to provide descriptions of all the exercises included in the following tables. It is still important to list them so we can show a detailed program that goalies typically follow. There is also a suggested pregame warm-up workout that can be applied to both younger and older players.

TABLE 2.1

In-Season Conditioning for Ages 16 and Older

Sunday-Wednesday		Tuesday-Thursday	
General and dynamic warm-up			
Ball touches	3 × 20	**Reaction drills**	
Split jumps	3 × 20	Drop drills	5 min
Stride jumps	3 × 20	Turn and catch	5 min
Back squats	Warm-up	Wall ball	5 min
	6-8 reps	Cardio: 40 min (bike, stair stepper, treadmill, elliptical)	
	6-8 reps	**Core**	
	6-8 reps	Stability ball sit-ups	3 × 20
Incline bench press	Warm-up	Hanging leg raises	3 ×15
	6-8 reps	Medicine ball sit-ups	3 × 15
	6-8 reps	Russian twists	3 × 20
	6-8 reps		
Clock lunges	6/leg reps		
	6/leg reps		
	6/leg reps		
Low rows	6-8 reps		
	6-8 reps		
	6-8 reps		
Romanian deadlifts	6 reps		
	6 reps		
	6 reps		
Cool-down and stretching: 20 min			

TABLE 2.2

Off-Season Conditioning for Ages 16 and Older

Phase 1: 4 weeks

Monday-Thursday	Week 1		Week 2		Week 3		Week 4	
Exercises	Reps × wt	Reps × wt	Reps × wt	Reps × wt	Reps × wt	Reps × wt	Reps × wt	Reps × wt
Bench press	10 ×	10 ×	10 ×	10 ×	10 ×	10 ×	10 ×	10 ×
Front lateral pull-downs	10 ×	10 ×	10 ×	10 ×	10 ×	10 ×	10 ×	10 ×
Incline dumbbell bench press	10 ×	10 ×	10 ×	10 ×	10 ×	10 ×	10 ×	10 ×
Seated low rows	10 ×	10 ×	10 ×	10 ×	10 ×	10 ×	10 ×	10 ×
Dips	Fatigue	Fatigue	Fatigue	Fatigue	Fatigue	Fatigue	Fatigue	Fatigue
Back extensions	15 ×	15 ×	15 ×	15 ×	15 ×	15 ×	15 ×	15 ×

Conditioning: 1 mile run — Time

Cool-down and stretching: 20 min

Tuesday-Friday	Week 1		Week 2		Week 3		Week 4	
Exercises	Reps × wt	Reps × wt	Reps × wt	Reps × wt	Reps × wt	Reps × wt	Reps × wt	Reps × wt
Back squats	10 ×	10 ×	10 ×	10 ×	10 ×	10 ×	10 ×	10 ×
Upright rows	10 ×	10 ×	10 ×	10 ×	10 ×	10 ×	10 ×	10 ×
Lateral lunges	8/leg ×	8/leg ×	8/leg ×	8/leg ×	8/leg ×	8/leg ×	8/leg ×	8/leg ×
Seated shoulder press	10 ×	10 ×	10 ×	10 ×	10 ×	10 ×	10 ×	10 ×
Step-ups	8/leg ×	8/leg ×	8/leg ×	8/leg ×	8/leg ×	8/leg ×	8/leg ×	8/leg ×
Shrugs	12 ×	12 ×	12 ×	12 ×	12 ×	12 ×	12 ×	12 ×
Medicine ball sit-ups	15 × 8 kg	15 × 8 kg	15 × 8 kg	15 × 8 kg	15 × 8 kg	15 × 8 kg	15 × 8 kg	15 × 8 kg
Reverse crunches	15 × bwt	15 × bwt	15 × bwt	15 × bwt	15 × bwt	15 × bwt	15 × bwt	15 × bwt
Seated Russian twists	20 × 8 kg	20 × 8 kg	20 × 8 kg	20 × 8 kg	20 × 8 kg	20 × 8 kg	20 × 8 kg	20 × 8 kg

General and dynamic warm-up

Reaction drills: 20 min

Cool-down and stretching: 20 min

The weight (wt) has been left blank as it varies from person to person but should be enough so that the muscles feel fatigued after the number of reps provided. BWT stands for bodyweight.

Wednesday

	Phase 1: 4 weeks			
	Week 1	Week 2	Week 3	Week 4
Agility footwork and drills	General and dynamic warm-up			
	Ladder drills: 15 min			
Pro conditioner	Time – 1 min rest between	Time – 1 min rest between	Time – 45 sec rest between	Time – 30 sec rest between
T-test	Time – 1 min rest between	Time – 1 min rest between	Time – 45 sec rest between	Time – 30 sec rest between
Four-corner drill	3 × each direction	4 × each direction	5 × each direction	6 × each direction
300 yd (275 m) shuttle	Time – 3 min rest	Time – 3 min rest	Time – 2:30 min rest	Time – 2 min rest
Cool-down and stretching: 20 min				

Monday-Thursday

	Phase 2: 4 weeks							
	General and dynamic warm-up							
	Week 1		Week 2		Week 3		Week 4	
Exercises	Reps ×	wt	Reps ×	wt	Reps ×	wt	Reps ×	wt
Bench press	8 ×		8 ×		8 ×		8 ×	
Wide-grip pull-ups	Fatigue		Fatigue		Fatigue		Fatigue	
Stability ball push-ups	10 × bwt		10 × bwt		10 × bwt		10 × bwt	
Dumbbell rows	8 ×		8 ×		8 ×		8 ×	
Incline dumbbell flys	8 ×		8 ×		8 ×		8 ×	
Back extensions	12 ×		12 ×		12 ×		12 ×	
Cardiovascular exercise: 40 min								
Cool-down and stretching: 20 min								

(continued)

TABLE 2.2 *(continued)*

Tuesday-Friday

	General and dynamic warm-up									
Exercises	**Reps × wt**	**Reps × wt**	**Reps × wt**	**Reps × wt**	**Reps × wt**	**Reps × wt**	**Reps × wt**	**Reps × wt**	**Reps × wt**	**Reps × wt**
Front squats	8 ×	8 ×	8 ×	8 ×	8 ×	8 ×	8 ×	8 ×	8 ×	8 ×
One-arm dumbbell snatch	6/arm	6/arm	6/arm	6/arm	6/arm	6/arm	6/arm	6/arm	6/arm	6/arm
Clock lunges	6/leg	6/leg	6/leg	6/leg	6/leg	6/leg	6/leg	6/leg	6/leg	6/leg
Standing shoulder press	8 ×	8 ×	8 ×	8 ×	8 ×	8 ×	8 ×	8 ×	8 ×	8 ×
Lateral step-ups	8/leg ×	8/leg ×	8/leg ×	8/leg ×	8/leg ×	8/leg ×	8/leg ×	8/leg ×	8/leg ×	8/leg ×
Lateral raises	8 ×	8 ×	8 ×	8 ×	8 ×	8 ×	8 ×	8 ×	8 ×	8 ×
Core	Reps × wt	Reps × wt	Reps × wt	Reps × wt	Reps × wt	Reps × wt	Reps × wt	Reps × wt	Reps × wt	Reps × wt
Medicine ball sit-up and throw	15 × 6 kg	15 × 6 kg	15 × 8 kg	15 × 8 kg	15 × 8 kg	15 × 10 kg	15 × 10 kg	15 × 10 kg	15 × 10 kg	15 × 10 kg
Incline sit-ups	15 × bwt	15 × bwt	15 × 8 kg	15 × 8 kg	15 × 10 kg	15 × 10 kg	15 × 10 kg	15 × 12 kg	15 × 12 kg	15 × 12 kg
Rope crunches	12 ×	12 ×	12 ×	12 ×	12 ×	12 ×	12 ×	12 ×	12 ×	12 ×

Reaction drills: 20 min

Cool-down and stretching: 20 min

Wednesday

General and dynamic warm-up

Ladder drills: 15 min

Phase 2: 4 weeks

Agility and footwork drills	Time – 1 min rest between		Time – 1 min rest between		Time – 45 sec rest between		Time – 30 sec rest between			
Pro conditioner × 4										

44

	Day 1	Day 2	Day 3	Day 4
T-test × 4	Time – 1 min rest between	Time – 1 min rest between	Time – 45 sec rest between	Time – 30 sec rest between
Four-corner drill	3 × each direction	4 × each direction	5 × each direction	6 × each direction
300 yd (275 m) shuttle	Time – 3 min rest	Time – 3 min rest	Time – 2:30 min rest	Time – 2 min rest
Plyometrics	**Reps**	**Reps**	**Reps**	**Reps**
Squat jumps	8 × bwt	10 × bwt	10 × bwt	12 × bwt
	8 × bwt	10 × bwt	10 × bwt	12 × bwt
	8 × bwt	10 × bwt	10 × bwt	12 × bwt
	8 × bwt	10 × bwt	10 × bwt	12 × bwt
Split jumps	8/leg × bwt	8/leg × bwt	10/leg × bwt	10/leg × bwt
	8/leg × bwt	8/leg × bwt	10/leg × bwt	10/leg × bwt
	8/leg × bwt	8/leg × bwt	10/leg × bwt	10/leg × bwt
	8/leg × bwt	8/leg × bwt	10/leg × bwt	10/leg × bwt
Ball touches	20 × bwt	20 × bwt	25 × bwt	30 × bwt
	20 × bwt	20 × bwt	25 × bwt	30 × bwt
	20 × bwt	20 × bwt	25 × bwt	30 × bwt
	20 × bwt	20 × bwt	25 × bwt	30 × bwt

Cool-down and stretching: 20 min

Week 9: off

(continued)

TABLE 2.2 (continued)

Phase 3: 4 weeks

Monday – Thursday

General and dynamic warm-up

Exercises	Reps × wt	Reps × wt	Reps × wt	Reps × wt	Reps × wt	Reps × wt	Reps × wt	Reps × wt	Reps × wt	Reps × wt	Reps × wt
Dumbbell bench press	8 ×	8 ×	8 ×	8 ×	8 ×	8 ×	8 ×	8 ×	8 ×	8 ×	8 ×
Weighted pull-ups	6 ×	6 ×	6 ×	6 ×	6 ×	6 ×	6 ×	6 ×	6 ×	6 ×	6 ×
Close-grip bench press	6 ×	6 ×	6 ×	6 ×	6 ×	6 ×	6 ×	6 ×	6 ×	6 ×	6 ×
Low rows	6 ×	6 ×	6 ×	6 ×	6 ×	6 ×	6 ×	6 ×	6 ×	6 ×	6 ×
Medicine ball push-ups	8 ×	8 ×	8 ×	8 ×	8 ×	8 ×	8 ×	8 ×	8 ×	8 ×	8 ×
Back extensions	10 ×	10 ×	10 ×	10 ×	10 ×	10 ×	10 ×	10 ×	10 ×	10 ×	10 ×

1-mile time

Cardio: 45 min

Cool-down and stretching: 20 min

Tuesday-Friday

General and dynamic warm-up

Exercises	Reps × wt	Reps × wt	Reps × wt	Reps × wt	Reps × wt	Reps × wt	Reps × wt	Reps × wt	Reps × wt	Reps × wt	Reps × wt
Sumo squats	8 ×	8 ×	8 ×	8 ×	8 ×	8 ×	8 ×	8 ×	8 ×	8 ×	8 ×
Hang cleans	4-6 ×	4-6 ×	4-6 ×	4-6 ×	4-6 ×	4-6 ×	4-6 ×	4-6 ×	4-6 ×	4-6 ×	4-6 ×
Lateral lunge and pull	6/leg	6/leg	6/leg	6/leg	6/leg	6/leg	6/leg	6/leg	6/leg	6/leg	6/leg
Dumbbell step up and press	8/leg × bwt	8/leg ×	8/leg ×	8/leg ×	8/leg ×	8/leg ×	8/leg ×	8/leg ×	8/leg ×	8/leg ×	8/leg ×
Core	Reps × wt	Reps × wt	Reps × wt	Reps × wt	Reps × wt	Reps × wt	Reps × wt	Reps × wt	Reps × wt	Reps × wt	Reps × wt
Stability ball thrusts	15 ×	15 ×	15 ×	15 ×	15 ×	15 ×	15 ×	15 ×	15 ×	15 ×	15 ×
Stability ball knee tucks	15 ×	15 ×	15 ×	15 ×	15 ×	15 ×	15 ×	15 ×	15 ×	15 ×	15 ×

Medicine ball reverse crunches	20 ×	20 ×	20 ×	20 ×	20 ×	20 ×	20 ×	20 ×
Seated Russian twists	20 ×	20 ×	20 ×	20 ×	20 ×	20 ×	20 ×	20 ×
Reaction drills: 25 min								
Cool-down and stretching: 20 min								

Wednesday

Ladder drills: 20 min

Agility and footwork drills	Time – 30 sec rest between		Time – 30 sec rest between		Time – 30 sec rest between	
Lateral cone hops × 5						
T-test × 4	Time – 1 min rest between		Time – 45 sec rest between		Time – 30 sec rest between	
Four-corner drill	4 × each direction		5 × each direction		6 × each direction	
300 yd (275 m) shuttle	Time – 2 min rest		Time – 1:30 min rest		Time – 1 min rest	

Plyometrics	Reps		Reps		Reps	
Tuck jumps	8 × bwt		10 × bwt		12 × bwt	
	8 × bwt		10 × bwt		12 × bwt	
	8 × bwt		10 × bwt		12 × bwt	
	8 × bwt		10 × bwt		12 × bwt	
Stride jumps	8/leg × bwt		10/leg × bwt		12/leg × bwt	
	8/leg × bwt		10/leg × bwt		12/leg × bwt	
	8/leg × bwt		10/leg × bwt		12/leg × bwt	

General and dynamic warm-up

(continued)

TABLE 2.2 (continued)

Wednesday	General and dynamic warm-up			
	8/leg × bwt	8/leg × bwt	10/leg × bwt	12/leg × bwt
Ski jumps	20 × bwt	20 × bwt	25 × bwt	30 × bwt
	20 × bwt	20 × bwt	25 × bwt	30 × bwt
	20 × bwt	20 × bwt	25 × bwt	30 × bwt
	20 × bwt	20 × bwt	25 × bwt	30 × bwt
Dot drill	15 × bwt	15 × bwt	20 × bwt	20 × bwt
	15 × bwt	15 × bwt	20 × bwt	20 × bwt
	15 × bwt	15 × bwt	20 × bwt	20 × bwt
	15 × bwt	15 × bwt	20 × bwt	20 × bwt
Cool-down and stretching: 20 min				

TABLE 2.3

In-Season Conditioning for Ages 12 to 15

Monday-Wednesday					
General and dynamic warm-up					
Exercises	**Reps**	**Reps**	**Reps**	**Core exercises**	**Reps**	**Reps**
Push-ups on ball	10 × bwt	10 × bwt	10 × bwt	Medicine ball sit-ups	15 × bwt	15 × bwt
BOSU squats	10 × bwt	10 × bwt	10 × bwt	Russian twists	20 × bwt	20 × bwt
Pull-ups on ball	10 × bwt	10 × bwt	10 × bwt	Back extensions	12 × bwt	12 × bwt
Medicine ball step-outs	8/leg × bwt	8/leg × bwt	8/leg × bwt	Reverse crunches	10 × bwt	10 × bwt
Lateral lunges	8/leg × bwt	8/leg × bwt	8/leg × bwt	Supermans on ball	10 × bwt	10 × bwt
	Cool-down and stretching: 20 min					
	Tuesday-Thursday					
Reaction drills	General and dynamic warm-up					
Turn and catch	5 min					
Drop drills	5 min					
Slide board	30 sec × 6					
Juggling	5 min					
	Cardiovascular exercise: 20 min					
	Cool-down and stretching: 20 min					

BWT stands for bodyweight.

TABLE 2.4

Off-Season Conditioning for Ages 12 to 15

Phase 1: 4 weeks

Monday	Week 1 Reps × wt	Week 1 Reps	Week 2 Reps × wt	Week 2 Reps	Week 3 Reps × wt	Week 3 Reps	Week 4 Reps × wt	Week 4 Reps
Warm-up	General and dynamic warm-up							
	Medicine ball circuit × 3; 3 min rest between each circuit, 20 sec rest between exercises							
Chest passes	15 ×		15 ×		15 ×		15 ×	
Russian twists	20 ×		20 ×		20 ×		20 ×	
Lunge and twist	8/leg ×		8/leg ×		8/leg ×		8/leg ×	
Overhead slams	20 ×		20 ×		20 ×		20 ×	
Good mornings	12 ×		12 ×		12 ×		12 ×	
Overhead squats	15 ×		15 ×		15 ×		15 ×	
Push-ups on ball	10 ×		10 ×		10 ×		10 ×	
Sit-ups	15 ×		15 ×		15 ×		15 ×	
Lateral lunges	8/leg ×		8/leg ×		8/leg ×		8/leg ×	
	Cool-down and stretching: 20 min							
Thursday								
	General and dynamic warm-up							
	Stability ball circuit × 3; 3 min rest between circuits, 30 sec rest between exercises							
Push-ups on ball	10 × bwt		10 × bwt		10 × bwt		10 × bwt	
Crunches on ball	20 × bwt		20 × bwt		20 × bwt		20 × bwt	
BOSU squats	12 × bwt		12 × bwt		12 × bwt		12 × bwt	
Dips on ball	15 × bwt		15 × bwt		15 × bwt		15 × bwt	
Supine rotators	20 × bwt		20 × bwt		20 × bwt		20 × bwt	
Lunges on ball	10/leg × bwt		10/leg × bwt		10/leg × bwt		10/leg × bwt	
Pull-overs on ball	12 × wt		12 × wt		12 × wt		12 × wt	
Kneeling on ball	30 sec		30 sec		30 sec		30 sec	
Sissel squats	10 × bwt		10 × bwt		10 × bwt		10 × bwt	
	Cool-down and stretching: 20 min							

The weight (wt) has been left blank as it varies from person to person but should be enough so that the muscles feel fatigued after the number of reps provided. BWT stands for bodyweight.

Phase 2: 4 weeks

Monday				
Warm-up	General and dynamic warm-up			
	Medicine ball circuit × 3; 3 min rest between each circuit, 20 sec rest between exercises			
One-arm put	10/arm ×	10/arm ×	10/arm ×	10/arm ×
Seated Russian twists	20 ×	20 ×	20 ×	20 ×
Hamstring quick kicks	15 ×	15 ×	15 ×	15 ×
Overhead throws	15 ×	15 ×	15 ×	15 ×
Sit up and throw	12 ×	12 ×	12 ×	12 ×
Kick-ups	15 ×	15 ×	15 ×	15 ×
Kneeling lateral toss	10/side ×	10/side ×	10/side ×	10/side ×
Reverse crunches	15 ×	15 ×	15 ×	15 ×
Sumo squats	15 ×	15 ×	15 ×	15 ×
	Cool-down and stretching: 20 min			

Thursday				
	General and dynamic warm-up			
	Stability ball circuit × 3; 3 min rest between circuits, 30 sec rest between exercises			
Push-ups on ball	10 × bwt	10 × bwt	10 × bwt	10 × bwt
Knee tucks	15 × bwt	15 × bwt	15 × bwt	15 × bwt
Reverse BOSU squats	12 × bwt	12 × bwt	12 × bwt	12 × bwt
Pull-ups on ball	10 × bwt	10 × bwt	10 × bwt	10 × bwt
V-ups with ball	12 ×	12 ×	12 ×	12 ×
One-leg squats with ball	8/leg × bwt	8/leg × bwt	8/leg × bwt	8/leg × bwt
Lateral raises on ball	12 × 5 lb (2 kg)	12 × 5 lb (2 kg)	12 × 5 lb (2 kg)	12 × 5 lb (2 kg)
Supermans	12 × bwt	12 × bwt	12 × bwt	12 × bwt
Triple threats	15 × bwt	15 × bwt	15 × bwt	15 × bwt
	Cool-down and stretching: 20 min			
	Week 9: off			

(continued)

TABLE 2.4 *(continued)*

Monday	Phase 3: 4 weeks		
Warm-up	General and dynamic warm-up		
	Medicine ball circuit × 3; 3 min rest between each circuit, 20 sec rest between exercises		
Power drops	15 ×	15 ×	15 ×
Medicine ball sit-ups	20 ×	20 ×	20 ×
Diagonal lunges	8/leg ×	8/leg ×	8/leg ×
Seated two-arm put	10/side ×	10/side ×	10/side ×
Kneeling rocky twists	10/side ×	10/side ×	10/side ×
Medicine ball step-ups	8/leg ×	8/leg ×	8/leg ×
Kneeling chest passes	15 ×	15 ×	15 ×
Wood choppers	15 ×	15 ×	15 ×
Overhead lateral lunges	8/leg ×	8/leg ×	8/leg ×
	Cool-down and stretching: 20 min		

Thursday	General and dynamic warm-up		
	Stability ball circuit × 3; 3 min rest between circuits, 30 sec rest between exercises		
Push-ups on ball	12 × bwt	12 × bwt	12 × bwt
Crunches on ball	20 × bwt	20 × bwt	20 × bwt
Diagonal lunges	8/leg × bwt	8/leg × bwt	8/leg × bwt
Dips on ball	15 × bwt	15 × bwt	15 × bwt
Reverse crunches	15 × bwt	15 × bwt	15 × bwt
Sissel squats	15 ×	15 ×	15 ×
Front raises on ball	12 × 5 lb (2 kg)	12 × 5 lb (2 kg)	12 × 5 lb (2 kg)
Bridging on ball	12 × bwt	12 × bwt	12 × bwt
One-leg triple threats	8/leg × bwt	8/leg × bwt	8/leg × bwt
	Cool-down and stretching: 20 min		

TABLE 2.5

Pregame Warm-Up

Lunge walks	× 2	20 yd (18 m)	Drop drills: underhand catch, overhand catch	10 × 2
Lateral lunge walks	× 2	20 yd (18 m)	Turn and catch	10 × 2
Russian march	× 2	20 yd (18 m)	Wall ball	10 × 2
Shuffles	× 2	20 yd (18 m)	Card toss	15 × 2
Knee to chest	× 2	20 yd (18 m)	Scramble	5 mins × 2
High knees	× 2	20 yd (18 m)	Juggling	2 min
Butt kicks	× 2	20 yd (18 m)	Static stretching: 10-15 min	
Inchworm	× 2	20 yd (18 m)		
Carioca	× 2	20 yd (18 m)		
Forward jog	× 2	20 yd (18 m)		
Backward jog	× 2	20 yd (18 m)		

chapter 3

INCREASING FLEXIBILITY

Dave Flint

Flexibility is the absolute range of motion around a joint or a series of joints. It is unique to each person and to each joint. Just because you may have a flexible lower body does not mean you will have a flexible upper body.

Flexibility is a very important component of any goalie's training program. Goaltending demands that you put your body into awkward positions at a high rate of speed. If you have poor flexibility, your muscles will need to work harder to achieve certain movements. Good flexibility may also help prevent injuries. Today's goalies rely on good flexibility in the hip, groin, hamstrings, and low back. Not to say that other parts of the body are less important, but these areas of a goalie's body are stressed most frequently. Goaltenders use their groin muscles and hip flexors when they perform butterfly slides and pushes and when recovering from a save.

Because of the increased speed of the game over the years, goalies are forced to overextend themselves to make saves now more than ever. Goalies are required to make more acrobatic saves over the course of a game and the season. These are reasons why it is critical to become as flexible as you can. Improving flexibility not only is important to help prevent injuries but also is a critical part of your training program to help you become the best goalie you can be. A goalie who does not commit to his flexibility may not reach his full potential.

DYNAMIC VERSUS STATIC-PASSIVE FLEXIBILITY

Dynamic flexibility is the ability to perform dynamic movements through a full range of motion in a controlled fashion. Dynamic warm-ups have become increasingly popular because the movements are sport specific and they do a better job of preparing your body for activity. This is especially important before games and practices because of the amount of quick, explosive movements that goalies make throughout the course of each game or practice.

Static-passive flexibility is the ability to hold an extended position for a period of time (15 to 30 seconds) by using your body weight or an object to support your limb. This type of flexibility training is recommended after workouts as part of your cool-down to help increase your range of motion. Dedicate at least 15 minutes per day to postworkout flexibility training. Static-passive stretching enables goaltenders to put their bodies in unusual positions to make spectacular saves. It is very tough for a goalie to reach his full potential if he lacks flexibility.

TYPES OF STRETCHING

There are seven different types of stretching, all or some of which have been introduced to you over your years of playing: ballistic, dynamic, active, passive, static, isometric, and PNF.

- Ballistic: Ballistic stretching involves using your body's momentum through bouncing movements to stretch the muscle beyond its normal range of motion. This is not a recommended type of stretching because it may lead to injury.

- Dynamic: Dynamic stretching consists of controlled movements within your body's normal limits. You can gradually increase the speed of movement. This should not be confused with ballistic stretching. Ballistic stretching is fast, jerking movement that exceeds the normal range of motion, which can lead to injury. Dynamic stretching should be part of your daily preworkout or precompetition routine.

• Active: Active stretches are commonly done in yoga. Active stretching requires moving a body part into a stretch position and using the strength of your muscles to hold it in place. This type of stretching can improve your strength and balance.

• Passive: Passive stretching involves moving your body into a stretch position and holding it with another body part or an object. This slow and relaxed type of stretching is beneficial in helping improve range of motion and doesn't require a partner.

• Static: The most common method of stretching, static stretching is almost the same as passive stretching except it involves stretching the muscle to the farthest point and holding it in that position. This type of stretching is commonly used because it can be done anywhere without a partner and can help improve range of motion.

• Isometric: Isometric stretching involves contracting the muscle you are stretching and using a body part or an immovable object to prevent your limb from moving. An example is lying down and putting your leg up against the wall and pushing as hard as you can for 15 seconds, then relaxing the muscle for 20 seconds. This is done to distract the muscle so that it doesn't tense up when you are putting it in a stretched position. This allows you to move the body part being stretched a little further than with static stretching.

• PNF stretching: PNF (proprioceptive neuromuscular facilitation) is a great way to increase flexibility. It combines passive and isometric stretching to improve flexibility. PNF stretching requires a partner and is done by contracting the muscle while your partner holds the body part and keeps it from moving (usually for 10 to 15 seconds). When your partner says to relax, you relax the muscle while your partner moves the body part further through its range of motion. With this type of stretching, you can really see some noticeable changes in your flexibility.

All of these stretching techniques, with the exception of ballistic, have a place in a good flexibility program. Some types of stretching may work better for different people. Dynamic, passive, and static stretching are good choices for goaltenders. PNF can be beneficial if proper technique is taught.

HENRIK LUNDQVIST

Recently the NHL has seen a dramatic rise in European goaltenders. One reason for this is the Europeans' commitment to off-ice training, which includes speed, quickness, and agility training as well as flexibility. Henrik Lundqvist is one of the top European goaltenders to make his presence felt in the NHL. One of his best attributes is his flexibility and his ability to reach out and get to pucks most goaltenders would not be able to reach. Increased flexibility is not something that happens overnight. It is the product of a long-term commitment to increasing flexibility and therefore improving your game.

Born March 2, 1982, Lundqvist is still developing and expected to be on the NHL's list of top goalies for a long time. His only NHL team thus far has been the New York Rangers, and he has helped transform the Blueshirts into Stanley Cup contenders. In the 2007 playoffs, he surrendered two goals or fewer in 7 of 10 postseason games. Although he has played in the NHL since only the 2005-2006 season, Lundqvist has twice been named a finalist for the Vezina Trophy. A Swedish national-team goaltender, Lundqvist won an Olympic gold medal for Sweden in 2006.

© Icon SMI

STRETCHING PROPERLY

Goaltenders can see great benefits from a good stretching program that is done on a consistent basis. Note that you should never stretch cold muscles—this could lead to a muscle strain. Perform a general 10-minute warm-up (e.g., stationary bike, treadmill, stair stepper, or elliptical) before you do any stretching. This raises your core temperature a couple of degrees. Next is dynamic stretching (dynamic warm-up), and this should last 10 to 20 minutes, followed by either static stretching or sport-specific movements. This is a personal preference. At the bare minimum you should do a general warm-up and dynamic warm-up before exercise and static stretching at the end of the workout. Some dynamic and static stretches are described in the next section.

There is sometimes a fine line between a goal and a big save. Just think about the impact it would have if you had that extra inch of flexibility to make the big save. Making the save would be well worth the time you put into stretching.

COACHES' TIP

Guidelines for Stretching

1. Never stretch cold muscles.
2. Perform a general aerobic warm-up for 10 minutes before stretching.
3. Follow the general warm-up with a dynamic warm-up for 10 to 20 minutes.
4. Use smooth, controlled movements; do not bounce.
5. Inhale before you stretch, and exhale as you move through the stretch.
6. Stretch until you feel tension in the muscle or mild discomfort, not pain.
7. Hold the stretch for 15 to 30 seconds to allow the muscle adequate time to stretch.
8. Stretch after your workout and cool-down.
9. Stretch every day, not only to help prevent injuries but also to improve your flexibility.

STRETCHES

The dynamic warm-up stretches and static stretches listed here are specific to goaltending and helpful for improving overall flexibility. These stretches are easy and effective for goalies of all ages, but there are many more stretches that you can add to your flexibility program. If you have stretches that you like and work well for you, then keep them as part of your routine.

When crunched for time, most athletes today will usually neglect stretching. We have all done it. You get to the rink 10 minutes before practice starts, rush to get on the ice, skate around the rink twice, and stretch for 5 minutes on the side. Or you get to the gym and have to squeeze your workout into 45 minutes, so you get on the bike for 5 minutes and then start lifting.

If you do this too often, you are asking for an injury. Also, if you neglect your flexibility, you cannot perform at your highest level. Flexibility may be more important for goaltenders than for any other position and is one of the most critical components of a good training program. Always make time for stretching. When the season comes, you'll be glad you did.

Dynamic Warm-Up Stretches

These exercises should be done over a distance of 20 yards (18 meters) and performed two times. The movements should be fluid and through a full range of motion. Playing goal requires many different fluid and controlled movements. All these dynamic stretches were chosen to prepare the different muscles of the lower body for the demands that will be placed on them. The real areas of focus for goalies are on the groin and the hip flexors, which are used so much with the integration of butterfly slides and pushes into goaltending. Because of how the position has evolved over the past 15 years, there are more groin and hip flexor injuries in goalies than ever before.

LUNGE WALK

Muscles Worked: Hip Flexors, Groin, Hamstrings, Gluteals

Procedure:

1. Start with both hands at your sides.
2. Take a step forward with your left leg. Keep your chest and head up. Don't allow your left knee to extend over your toes, and don't allow the right knee to hit the floor (see photo).
3. Alternate the left and right feet.

LATERAL LUNGE WALK

Muscles Worked: Groin, Hamstrings, Gluteals

Procedure:

1. Take a lateral step to your left about twice your shoulder width. Keep your right leg stationary.
2. Flex the left knee, allowing for a stretch of the right groin (see photo).
3. Pull the right leg in toward the left. Make sure to keep good posture.
4. Repeat this for 20 yards (18 meters), then move to your right on the way back.

SHUFFLE

Muscles Worked: Groin

Procedure:

1. Start in a squatting position, with the knees and hips bent (see photo *a*).
2. Shuffle to the left, making sure not to cross your legs (see photo *b*).
3. Continue for 20 yards (18 meters), then go back the opposite direction.

RUSSIAN MARCH

Muscles Worked: Hamstrings

Procedure:

1. Start facing forward, with your arms extended in front of you.
2. Keeping your legs and arms straight, kick your leg as high as possible, alternating legs (see photo).

SPIDERMAN

Muscles Worked: Hamstrings, Groin, Gluteals

Procedure:

1. Start bent at the hip, with your hands on the ground next to your feet (see photo *a*).
2. Walk out to a push-up position, then drop your hips to the ground (see photo *b*).
3. Bring one foot forward at a time until it is even with your hand (see photo *c*).

 **HIGH KNEE**

Muscles Worked: Hip Flexors, Hamstrings, Calves

Procedure:
1. Run forward, picking your knees up as high as they can go (see photo).
2. Keep your forward arm bent at 90 degrees, and keep them moving.

 BUTT KICKS

Muscles Worked: Hip Flexors, Quadriceps, Calves

Procedure:
1. Run forward, kicking your heels to your butt as fast as you can (see photo).
2. Keep your arms bent at 90 degrees, and keep them moving.

CARIOCA

Muscles Worked: Groin, Hip Flexors

Procedure:

1. Start facing laterally (see photo *a*).
2. Cross the right leg over the left (see photo *b*), then move the left leg so that you are back in the starting position. Next, cross the left leg behind the right.
3. Continue repeating as quickly as you can for 20 yards (18 meters), then go back the opposite direction.

Much like strength training, the effects of stretching will come over time. Work consistently at improving—not just maintaining—flexibility, and your game will certainly improve.

COACHES' TIP

Static Stretches

Static stretches can be done individually or with a partner. Both ways are beneficial and can help improve flexibility. Individual static stretches are useful because they are easy and can be done almost anywhere. Partner stretches are valuable because your partner can help push the body part being stretched beyond where you can stretch it by yourself. Both methods should have a place in your daily training routine.

Individual Static Stretches

When performing individual stretches, make sure you are doing the stretches properly and that you stretch all the muscles. It is important that you do not neglect certain body parts. When playing goal, at some point all your muscles come into play, so make sure you do a thorough stretch.

NECK AND TRAPEZIUS STRETCH

Procedure:

1. Place your left hand on the right side of your head, and gently pull your head down to your shoulder (see photo).
2. Repeat on the other side.

SHOULDER STRETCH

Procedure:

1. Walk your hand up a wall, and reach to its highest point, leaning into the stretch (see photo).
2. Repeat on the other side.

CHEST STRETCH

Procedure:

1. Bring your arm out to your side, parallel to the ground with your elbow bent at 90 degrees.
2. Place your elbow and forearm on a solid object, and lean into the stretch (see photo).
3. Repeat on the other side.

TRICEPS STRETCH

Procedure:

1. Move your right arm straight across your chest.

2. Pull the arm across with your left hand positioned at the elbow.

3. Repeat on the other side.

BICEPS STRETCH

Procedure:

1. Raise your arm straight out to the side until it is parallel with the ground.

2. Grab a solid object, and rotate your body away from the object that you are holding (see photo).

3. Repeat on the other side.

HIP, GLUTEAL, AND LOW BACK STRETCH

Procedure:

1. Sit on the floor, with your right leg out in front of you and your left leg flexed.
2. Place your left foot over your right leg on the floor, about even with your knee.
3. Put your right elbow on the outside of your knee, and rotate your trunk to the left (see photo).
4. Repeat on the other side.

GROIN STRETCH 1

Procedure:

1. Sit upright on the floor and flex your knees, bringing the heels and soles of your feet together.
2. Holding your feet together, place your elbows on the insides of your knees and apply pressure downward, pushing your legs to the floor (see photo).

GROIN STRETCH 2

Procedure:

1. Get into a full-squat position, with your toes slightly pointed out.
2. Put your elbows on the insides of your knees and push outward (see photo).

HIP STRETCH

Procedure:

1. Start lying on your back with your legs extended.
2. Flex one knee, grab it with the opposite hand, and pull it across your body, keeping your head and shoulders flat on the floor (see photo).
3. Repeat on the other side.

HIP FLEXOR STRETCH

Procedure:

1. Start kneeling on one knee, with the other leg flexed out in front.

2. Lean forward, pushing the hips forward until there is tension on the front of the upper thigh and hip (see photo).

3. Repeat on the other side.

QUADRICEPS STRETCH

Procedure:

1. While lying on your side, flex your top leg toward your buttocks, grab your ankle, and pull your foot back toward your buttocks while keeping the knees in line (see photo).

2. Roll over and repeat on the other side.

HAMSTRINGS STRETCH

Procedure:

1. Stand facing a bench, and put your heel up on the bench.
2. Bend forward at the waist, trying to lower your chest down to your knee (see photo).
3. Keep the leg that is in contact with the ground slightly flexed.
4. Repeat on the other side.

CALF STRETCH

Procedure:

1. Stand upright, a couple of steps away from the wall.
2. Extend your arms straight out in front of you, and place your hands on the wall.
3. Flex one leg and move it forward while extending the other leg back.
4. Keep both feet flat on the floor.
5. Now lean forward into the wall, until there is tension in the calf muscle (see photo).
6. Repeat on the other side.

Having a good relationship with your goaltending partner can make a good season great. By doing partner stretches with your goalie partner, you can help make each other better as you share the common goal of team success.

COACHES' TIP

Partner Static Stretches

Partner stretches can help improve flexibility because your partner can move your body parts through a greater range of motion. Some goalies prefer stretching with a partner because having someone to talk to can take the boredom out of stretching. Just as with working out, you can also make each other work harder instead of just going through the motions.

HAMSTRINGS STRETCH WITH PARTNER

Procedure:

1. Lie on your back with your arms out to the side.
2. Your partner straddles one leg while grabbing the opposite leg, placing one hand on the heel and the other hand on the front of the knee.
3. The partner then stretches your leg to the point of mild discomfort while you keep the opposite leg and the hips on the floor (see photo).
4. Repeat on the other side.

HIP FLEXOR
AND QUADRICEPS STRETCH WITH PARTNER

Procedure:

1. Lie on your abdomen, and flex the knee of the leg to be stretched.

2. Standing at your feet, your partner grabs just above the knee of the flexed leg.

3. The partner lifts up on your leg until you feel mild discomfort (see photo).

4. The partner can hold your hip down with his free hand.

5. Repeat on the other side.

GLUTEAL, HAMSTRINGS,
AND LOW BACK STRETCH WITH PARTNER

Procedure:

1. Lie on your back with your arms out to the side.

2. Kneeling in front of you, your partner grabs your knee, pulls the leg across the hips to the other side, and pushes upward until you feel mild discomfort (see photo).

3. Repeat on the other side.

GROIN STRETCH WITH PARTNER

Procedure:

1. Lie on your back with your arms out to the side.

2. Kneeling in front of you, your partner puts her hand on the inside of your knee.

3. Keep your leg flexed while your partner pushes down on the inside of your knee until you feel mild discomfort (see photo).

4. Repeat on the other side.

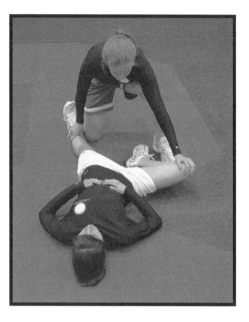

CHEST AND SHOULDER STRETCH WITH PARTNER

Procedure:

1. Kneel on the ground with your arms out to the side.

2. Standing behind you, your partner grabs your forearms and pulls the arms back until you feel a stretch (see photo).

chapter 4

IMPROVING QUICKNESS AND AGILITY

Dave Flint

Quickness and agility have always been important for the position of goaltending. With the increased speed of the game because of bigger, stronger, and faster players, these attributes have become even more crucial. If a goalie lacks quickness and agility, it may be difficult for him to be successful. It's true that there have been some big, blocking-style goalies who weren't overly quick or agile yet had great careers. Those goalies were very good at reading plays, playing their angles, and controlling rebounds. There have also been great goalies who haven't been good at reading plays, playing angles, and controlling the puck and have relied on their quickness and agility. Ultimately, if you want to be a top-level goaltender, you should train to be as good as you can in all of these areas.

A goaltender's quickness is measured by how fast or explosively she can move into a save or react to a shot. Hand and foot quickness can be improved through a variety of training methods, such as plyometrics, reaction drills, agility ladder drills, cone drills, sprints, and various footwork drills.

Some goaltenders are blessed with great quickness and agility because of genetics, but everyone can get better in these areas with proper training. When training quickness and agility, it is very important to learn proper form and technique before trying to improve quickness. If you try to perform the movement quickly with bad form, then you are not getting the full benefit of the training. Once proper technique is achieved, you can increase the rate at which you perform the exercise. By doing a specific movement over and over again, you develop muscle memory, and it becomes second nature. Before you know it, you will be able to perform the exercise or movement at a high rate of speed. This goes for on-ice drills and off-ice drills.

OFF-ICE DRILLS

Off-ice drills are beneficial because they can be performed almost anywhere. With the cost of ice time, goalies need to find ways to train themselves away from the rink. Different things you can do off-ice to develop quickness and agility include reaction drills, agility ladder drills, agility footwork drills, and plyometrics. All of these can help a goaltender develop speed, quickness, agility, and eye–hand coordination, which are important aspects of goaltending.

Reaction Drills

Goaltending is a unique position that requires a unique training regimen. Eye–hand coordination and quickness may be two of the most important aspects of a goalie's game. Whether or not a goalie has been blessed with great eye–hand coordination and quickness, every goalie can get better by performing reaction drills and making them part of his training program. Reaction drills can be performed throughout the year (preseason, in-season, and off-season). All that is needed is 10 to 15 minutes, two or three times per week. Equipment can vary from three tennis balls for beginners to a stability ball and a slide board for more-advanced drills.

Perform reaction drills at different times in your workout. Do them at the end when you are tired so you can teach your body to concentrate and react even when you are tired and stressed. Also perform them at the beginning of a workout when you are fresh and can work on your quickness. Another use of the drills is as part of your pregame warm-up to prepare your muscles and your eyes for action. These drills should not replace your dynamic warm-up but be used as part of it.

MIIKKA KIPRUSOFF

To be successful today, a goaltender must be quick on his skates and quick down on the ice. Miikka Kiprusoff, one of the best goalies in the world, possesses lightning quickness whether he is moving spot to spot on his skates or utilizing butterfly slides and pushes. Kiprusoff is another of the European goaltenders who have made their mark in the NHL. He possesses very high athletic ability and has committed himself to off-ice training, which improves speed, quickness, and agility. He has tremendous ability to transition from slides to pushes, reverse direction on a dime, and regain his feet quickly, and with the NHL opening up the east–west game, these skills are essential.

It took five years in the minors for the Finnish Olympic goaltender and Calgary Flame to find a starting job in the NHL, but this tireless worker has blossomed into an NHL superstar. Despite being a fifth-round draft pick, Miikka Kiprusoff is regarded as one of the elite goaltenders in the world. A Vezina Trophy winner, he appeared in the 2007 NHL All-Star Game. His postseason heroics have become legendary, as he seemingly won games single-handedly to lead his team to the 2004 Stanley Cup finals. Kiprusoff's 18 home shutouts in his first four seasons with the Flames are the most by any NHL goalie, which has made him a fan favorite in Calgary.

© Dave Reginek/NHLI via Getty images

Juggling

Juggling can be done with two balls for beginners, progressing to two balls and one hand, then three balls and two hands. Elite jugglers can try three balls against the wall or four balls and two hands. If you have a partner, you can work on juggling three balls between the two of you, trying to keep two balls in the air at the same time. Juggling is a great way to work on your catching ability and eye–hand coordination. Here are the steps for learning basic juggling.

Step 1: Standing erect, hold a tennis ball in your throwing hand. Place your elbows to your sides, with your forearms out in front of your body and parallel to the ground. Using your wrist, toss the tennis ball underhand to your opposite hand, creating a high arc (see figure 4.1a). This arc should pass just over your forehead. After catching the ball, place it once again in the hand that threw it. Practice getting a feel for the ball and the proper throwing height.

Step 2: Place one ball in your right hand and one in your left. Toss the ball in your right hand toward your left. As the ball reaches the top of the arc, toss the second ball inside the path of the first (see figure 4.1b). Catch the balls and stop. Repeat the exercise again, throwing the right ball first, until you are comfortable. The most common mistake is to rush the second ball. It may help to count "one and two and . . ." to help get the rhythm.

Figure 4.1 To juggle, first start with one ball *(a)*, then two *(b)*, then finally progress to three balls *(c)*.

Step 3: Once you have perfected step 2, place a third ball in your right hand with the first ball. Rest one ball on two fingers, with the other in your palm. Do the same exercise as in the last drill, but with one extra throw. Toss one of the balls from the right hand toward your left. As this ball hits its peak, toss the ball from your left hand to the right (see figure 4.1c). As this ball hits its peak, you should have caught the first ball (with your left hand) and be throwing the third (from your right hand). You will end with one ball in your right hand and two in your left. Make no more than these three tosses until you can consistently control all three balls. Then place one of the balls in your left hand into your right and repeat the sequence.

Step 4: If you can complete the last step, you are ready to juggle. Simply follow the last instructions, but continue by throwing for a second time with your left hand. Count how many throws you can make before you lose control. It won't be long before you are juggling.

Drop Drills

For these drills you need a partner. Drop drills are beneficial for developing eye–hand coordination, peripheral vision, and reaction time. The drills listed progress from easy to more difficult.

UNDERHAND CATCH

Procedure:

1. Start by facing your partner about 2 to 3 feet (0.5 to 1.0 meter) apart with your hands at your sides and your knees slightly flexed.
2. Your partner holds a tennis ball in each hand straight out in front of him at your eye level.
3. He then drops one of the tennis balls, and you have to catch it underhand before it hits the floor (see photo).

Variation: When your partner drops the ball try to catch it overhand. *Tip:* Bend your knees as the ball drops in order to move with the ball. Don't slap at it—try to have soft hands.

GOALIE EXPLOSIVENESS

Purpose: Teaches explosiveness as well as recovery technique (correct leg).

Procedure:

1. While kneeling, face your partner, who is standing 10 feet (3 meters) away with his arms out to his sides at a 90-degree angle, a tennis ball in each hand.

2. When your partner drops one of the balls, stand up and sprint to try to catch the ball before it hits the floor twice (see photo). The most important part of the drill is that you get up with the correct leg. If you need to sprint to your left, you must get up on your right leg and drive toward the ball; recover with your left leg when you are going to your right. This is important because it helps develop muscle memory, which will translate on the ice. When goaltenders recover on the ice, they always use the opposite leg of the direction they are going in order to get a strong push that will take them where they need to go. If they get up with the incorrect leg, they lose the ability to get an explosive recovery.

Wall Drills

Wall drills are easy to perform because all you need is a wall, tennis balls, and a partner. These drills are great for developing eye–hand coordination and improving reaction time and catching ability. As you become better at these drills, have your partner challenge you by throwing the ball harder.

WALL BALL

Purpose: To develop reaction time and catching ability when the ball is deflected off a surface (the wall) and changes direction. This translates in a game as seeing a shot at the last second when the puck is deflected off a screen.

Procedure:

1. Stand about 6 to 10 feet (2 to 3 meters) away from the wall, and have your partner stand behind you with tennis balls (see photo).
2. Have your partner throw a ball off the wall, and try to catch it before it gets by you.
3. Make sure that you stay square and don't open up your shoulders or your lower body. Drive into the ball just as you would on the ice, looking the ball into your hand.

180-DEGREE TURN

Purpose: Works on foot quickness, reaction time, catching ability, and moving your body as a unit to get square. In a game situation, it approximates when you need to get your feet set quickly, pick up the shot, and react to it.

Procedure:

1. Stand facing the wall, with your partner about 10 feet (3 meters) behind you. Get in your normal stance that you use on the ice.

2. When your partner says, "Go," she will throw the ball. Turn as quickly as you can 180 degrees, and try to catch the ball before it gets by you (see photo).

3. As you get good at this, have your partner move closer or throw the ball quicker.

Slide Board Drills

Slide board drills can be done with a partner or against a wall. Slide boards are a great tool not only for reaction drills but also for conditioning.

DRIVE AND CATCH GLOVE AND BLOCKER

Purpose: To mimic driving into the shot, whether it is to the blocker or glove side; to develop anaerobic conditioning and leg strength.

Procedure:

1. Start on the right side of the slide board if your catching hand is your left.
2. Get in your stance and drive across to the left side of the slide board, pushing off with your right leg. While you are doing this, your partner throws a tennis ball toward your glove hand (see photo).
3. Catch the ball and throw it back to him while using your left leg to stop your momentum, then push back across to the right side.
4. Keep repeating this for 30 seconds as fast as you can go.
5. Rest for 90 seconds and repeat three times. Challenge yourself to see how many balls you can catch in 30 seconds.
6. As you become more fit, you can increase the time and the number of repetitions.
7. Repeat this for the blocker side. Make sure to catch the balls. Even though in hockey you do not catch with your blocker, you can always work on your catching ability and eye–hand coordination.

DUELING SLIDE BOARD CATCH

Purpose: To mimic driving into the shot, whether it is to the blocker or glove side; to develop anaerobic conditioning and leg strength.

Procedure:

1. You and your partner get one slide board each and set them up, facing each other about 5 feet (1.5 meters) apart. Start with one tennis ball.

2. Slide back and forth as quickly as you can in your stance, and start tossing the ball back and forth to each other, seeing how many you can catch in a row.

3. As you get confident, you can add another ball (see photo), working your way up to three.

Stability Ball Drills

The stability ball is a great tool not only for these reaction drills but also for developing core strength, which is very important for the success of a goalie. Goaltenders need to recover from saves quickly or change direction in a split second, all while trying to keep good body position and technique. Core strength is critical for being able to do this. Good core strength also helps decrease muscle injuries.

KNEELING ON THE BALL

Purpose: This exercise is used as the first step in learning to stand on the ball. It will develop core strength while also allowing you to work on eye–hand coordination.

Procedure:

1. Start by putting both knees on either side of a stability ball, with your feet off the floor. Keep your butt off your heels so your knees are flexed 90 degrees. Keep your abdominal muscles tight, and try to stay balanced on the ball.
2. Once you can balance, have your partner toss you a tennis ball. See how many you can catch before you fall off or drop one.
3. Have your partner throw the balls a little farther away from you so you need to reach for them while maintaining your balance.

Variation: Have your partner kneel on a ball also, and play catch (see photo). Try to challenge each other by making the other one fall off.

STANDING ON THE BALL

Purpose: Once you have mastered kneeling on the ball, you can attempt standing. It will develop core strength while also allowing you to work on eye–hand coordination.

Procedure:

1. Start in the kneeling position, with your hands on the ball just in front of your knees.
2. Bring one foot up under yourself, and place it on the ball.
3. Bring the other foot up, and place it on the ball. Make sure that all this time both hands remain on the ball to stabilize it.
4. Once you have both feet on the ball, try to stand upright, using your arms for balance. It may take a while to perform, but it is not impossible. When trying this, make sure you do it on a somewhat padded floor and you have a reliable spotter.
5. Once you are up standing on the ball, you can start playing catch with the tennis balls.

CARD TOSS

Purpose: This drill works on eye–hand coordination more than quickness. It is difficult at first, but after some practice it gets easier. Have some fun by competing to see who can catch more.

Procedure:

1. Get a partner and a deck of playing cards. Stand about five feet (1.5 meters) apart, facing each other.
2. One person holds the cards, and the other person puts one hand behind her back.
3. The person holding the cards throws them like a Frisbee at the other person, and he tries to catch them (see photo).

Learning to control your body is essential for goaltenders. Making that extra save because you have improved your dexterity will be very gratifying. Adding technique to an athletic goaltender is the best recipe for success.

COACHES' TIP

Agility Ladder Drills

An agility ladder is basically a rope ladder that lies on the ground. Each box made by the ladder is approximately 1 foot by 1 foot (0.3 meter by 0.3 meter). If you don't have access to one of these, you can put tape on the ground or draw one with chalk. Ladder drills are a great training tool for goaltenders. The purpose of these drills is to work not only on agility but also on foot quickness. You can incorporate the ladder into every training session for about 10 to 15 minutes, whether it is at the beginning, as part of the warm-up, or as part of the general workout.

Many athletes who have not used an agility ladder before may struggle at first. Beginners should perform the drills at a slow pace until they get the movements down. As they get comfortable with the movements, they can increase the speed at which they perform the exercise. Try to step outside your comfort zone and challenge yourself each time to get quicker, but make sure you are still performing the correct pattern. Here are several agility ladder drills, but there are many others. See if you can come up with new ones that will challenge you.

FORWARD ONE IN

Procedure:

1. Start facing the length of the ladder.
2. Move quickly straight ahead, alternating each foot in the squares (see diagram). This is an easy drill to get started.

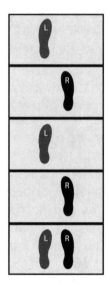

FORWARD TWO IN

Procedure:

1. Same as for the forward one in, but touch both feet in each square.
2. Lead with the right foot the first time and then with the left the second time (see diagram).

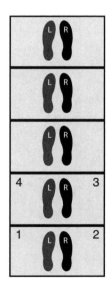

CLOSE THE FIVE HOLE

Procedure:

1. Stand facing the length of the ladder, straddling it.
2. Quickly bring both feet together inside the square, then advancing ahead, jump so both feet are straddling the next square (see diagram).
3. Repeat the process the length of the ladder.

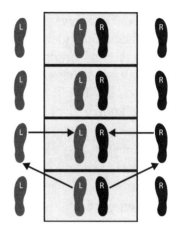

THREE-POINT SHUFFLE

Procedure:

1. Start standing to the left of the ladder, facing the length of it.
2. Step with your right foot into the square followed by your left, then step out the right side of the ladder with your right foot (see diagram).
3. Reversing the steps, go back the other direction in the next square.

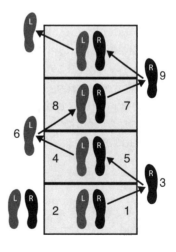

SCISSORS

Procedure:

1. Start standing on the side of the ladder, facing the ladder with your shoulders parallel to its length. Start with your left foot in the first square and your right outside the square. Your right arm is forward and your left arm is back (running position).

2. Switch the feet and the arms at the same time, moving the right foot in the square and the left foot outside the square and reversing the arm position (see diagram).

3. Repeat this movement the length of the ladder.

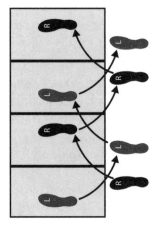

 # CARIOCA

Procedure:

1. Start with your left shoulder facing the length of the ladder. Have your left foot inside the first square.

2. Cross your right foot behind your left, and put it in the next square.

3. Place your left foot in the next square, and cross your right foot over your left, placing it in the next square.

4. Alternate crossing over in front and then behind (see diagram). It is the same as regular carioca except you are using a ladder.

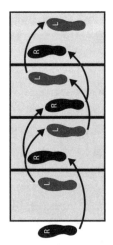

COACHES' TIP   The first thing many scouts evaluate is a goalie's skating ability. Footwork is the foundation of goaltending, and without proficient skating ability, potential is limited. The ladder is a tremendous way to improve the most important aspect of your game.

Cone Drills

Cones are excellent tools for developing quickness and agility. The following drills can be used when training goalies of all ages. If you have a drill that you like, then you should add it to your routine. Don't be afraid to try new drills or come up with some of your own.

T-TEST

Purpose: This drill can be used for testing purposes to measure a goalie's quickness and agility in all directions.

Procedure:

1. Set up three cones in a straight line, each cone 15 feet (4.5 meters) apart. Then put a fourth cone 15 feet (4.5 meters) away from the middle cone, forming a T.
2. Starting at the bottom of the T, sprint forward and touch the middle cone, shuffle to the left and touch the cone, shuffle all the way across to the right and touch the far cone, shuffle back to the middle cone, and then backpedal to the starting point.

PRO AGILITY

Purpose: This drill is primarily used to develop a goalie's quickness and ability to change direction.

Procedure:

1. Set up three cones in a straight line, each cone 15 feet (4.5 meters) apart.
2. Starting at the middle cone, sprint to the right and touch the cone, sprint to the left and touch the far cone, and finish by sprinting through the middle cone.

LATERAL CONE HOPS

Purpose: To develop lateral speed and quickness, which is an important part of goaltending.

Procedure:

1. Set up 10 to 15 cones in a straight line, each cone 18 inches (45 centimeters) apart.

2. Align your right or left shoulder with the first cone.

3. Hop laterally over the cone (see photo), touching both feet in the space between. Repeat this through all the cones as quickly as possible.

4. Once you reach the end, quickly change direction and hop over the cones back to the starting point.

chapter 5

MAKING THE SAVES

David Alexander

Whether you are a goaltender, a coach, or a hockey fan, you know that goaltending is one of the most difficult positions in all of sports. There are a number of reasons for this, but one that stands out is the technical complexity of the position. Goaltenders have an extensive save catalogue that when broken down to a science can be talked about in terms of angles or even frames per second. But what is more interesting is that a goaltender can be called on to perform accurate technical execution within the matter of a split second during competition. Having the ability to react athletically with a sound repertoire of saves is vital for the success of any elite goaltender.

Very few goaltenders make it to a high level of hockey without developing proper save techniques. These rare goaltenders have superior reaction skills and a tremendous ability to anticipate plays and read the release of a shot. Most goalies need a strong system of play as well as solid save mechanics. These mechanics go a long way in developing the base a goaltender needs in order to focus on the puck and make saves when it counts. This chapter focuses on honing your existing save techniques or developing new ones.

BASIC STANCE

The stance is your foundation for success between the pipes. In today's game of lightning-fast shots, curved sticks, and big bodies blocking your vision, the quality of your stance is vital. You cannot afford to rely solely on reflexes.

A quality stance begins from the feet up. There are three important things to keep in mind for your stance:

1. You must be solid on your skates in order to be able to react with correct form as well as hold your position in traffic.

2. For optimum balance, distribute your weight on the balls of your feet (see figure 5.1*a*). Too much weight on your toes or heels leaves you in poor balance, diminishing your ability to perform saves and control rebounds.

3. Bending your knees allows you to sit comfortably and play with confidence fostering control of your body (see figure 5.1*b*). It's imperative that you be comfortable in your stance while at the same time be in the best position to react quickly to the action.

Figure 5.1 The basic stance from *(a)* the front *and (b)* the side.

Skate Position

The base of the stance comes from the position of the skates. A good place to position the skates is a little wider than shoulder-width apart. Some goalies have success with a much wider base, but the risk of an extreme base width is a decrease in power when moving laterally and a tendency to have a loose plant for recovery techniques. A narrower base is not conducive to dropping quickly into a butterfly and so is suitable for goaltenders who like to stay on their feet more.

Pad Position

Years ago, coaches used to tell goalies to stand with their legs together. Today, goalies play with a triangular opening between their legs, allowing them to go down faster and cover the low corners better than with the stand-up style. Of course this leaves an opening at the five hole, but it is a calculated risk. The benefits of covering the low corners better and facilitating the butterfly move outweigh covering the five hole. Ninety-five percent of all shots are to the left or right of a goalkeeper's center point. Whether the shots are high or low, you must react with lightning quickness. On those rare occasions when the puck is heading directly down the pipe, you must reverse your outward movement and pull your body inward.

Knee Position

Many goalies have a bad habit in the way they position their knees. With the triangular stance, the pads meet at the knees. Some goalies press their knees together to create support for their bodies so that it is the structure and not the thigh muscles (quadriceps) that support the weight of the body. This makes completing drills less tiring, but it also slows a goaltender's reaction time and severely slows muscular development. The feet become like suction cups on the ice, and the goalie is trapped by his own stance. To react to a shot with the knees squeezed together, the goalie must first come out of his position by popping up and then go into the save—making two movements instead of one. You should work on an open stance where the knees are not pushing against one another. This will open up the hips and allow for more fluid movement and quicker reaction time.

Glove Position

Glove position is important in covering as much net as possible and in maintaining proper balance. With the ability of the shooters to pick the top corners, most goaltenders have switched from holding their gloves at a 3:00 o'clock angle and now have their fingers at a 1:30 to 12:00 position. By having the fingers facing up, the glove can take away a greater angle of flight and create better blocking coverage. Remember that the shot usually originates from ice level. If the glove is turned up and slightly forward, it will block more of the net that the puck can enter. Therefore, the angle of flight that a puck takes to score top shelf will have to be steeper if the goalie holds his glove in the right position.

Holding the glove upright also allows a goaltender to keep his shoulder in good blocking position. With a lower glove position, the tendency is to roll the shoulder back when making a glove save, thus exposing more net. With the higher glove position, the tendency is to keep the shoulder in place. The glove should be forward and not at the same depth as the body.

Many goalies employ two stances: one as they are setting up for the shot, the other at the moment the shot is released. By holding the glove high in your initial stance, you can visually take away more net from the shooter. As he is shooting, the glove will move back down to be in line with the trajectory of the shot, which of course originates from ice level. Playing bigger early (rather than too compact) may give you a perceived advantage. The initial stance is meant to visually take away as much net as possible, but the moment the shot gets released you must be in optimal position to make the save. Sometimes a goalie will not only raise his glove a little high but may also be slightly more upright, once again creating an intimidating visual for the shooter.

You should not hold your gloves directly at your sides. This takes away blocking coverage as well as the possibility of shifting your center of balance back toward the heels of your feet. Move your hands forward, as if asking for the puck. With your hands back, any inward movement of the gloves will be hampered by the pads, causing a slight delay or even "handcuffing" you (i.e., keeping you from moving your gloves into position to make the save). You want to cover as much net as possible. The catching glove must remain open. Make sure the glove and blocker are fully facing the shot.

Blocker Position

The blocker should be held off the goal pad and facing the play. If the blocker is locked to the side of the pad, then the movement of the pad will dictate the movement of the blocker. For example, if the blocker is locked on the pad and the pad shifts to the right, the blocker will automatically shift to the right as well. If the blocker moves, the stick will obviously follow, which could create an opening in the five hole along the ice. By contrast, if the blocker is off the pad and slightly ahead, the pad movement will not dictate the movement of the blocker, and it can move independently.

Stick Position

Hold the stick firmly, with a little pressure on the ice. The blade should lie between the legs, 12 to 16 inches (30 to 40 centimeters) in front of the skates. This leaves room to cushion the shot and minimizes the rebound. It also leaves the stick free to make a quick movement in the path of an arc to steer pucks to the corner. If the stick blade is tight to the pads, then there will be no way to "give" with the stick blade to cushion the puck. This creates big rebounds. Also, with no extension of the stick, the blade will be able to move only forward and sideways. To steer a puck, the stick blade must follow the movement of an arc. The blade should have a slight backward tilt in order to direct pucks high toward the corners while steering.

Elbow Position

The elbows should be comfortably touching the chest protector at the lower part of the ribs. With the elbows in this position, pucks should not be able to squeeze through the arms and the body. It is important not to have the elbows back as this would cause the hands to come back as well. If the elbows are back then the gloves are not blocking enough space, and your balance is being pushed away from the puck and not over it. Having the elbows too far forward will create a gap between the arms and the torso, in turn leaving the goaltender susceptible to a goal that goes through the body.

Posture

Your chest and shoulders must be square to the puck, not the opposing player. Your chest should stick out in a convex position (imagine a rooster). You should be able to draw a straight line from the chest down to the pads. Make sure your shoulders don't droop, as such a position can decrease coverage of the net an extra inch or two.

If it is difficult or tiring to hold your head back, it is probably because your shoulders are hunched over. From head to toe, your body should be in perfect symmetry and balance. A goaltender must be able to explode out of his stance and recover with sound mechanics. You must cover as much of the net as possible, while at the same time remaining compact enough not to show many holes.

DEFENDING LOW SHOTS

Now we'll focus on the save fundamentals necessary to be a consistent force in the nets. The ability to steer and smother pucks proficiently is essential for controlling rebounds, and your goals-against average will reap the benefits. First, the techniques involved in stopping low shots will be the priority, and then save tactics for higher shots will take precedent. Proper use of the butterfly and pads allows you to stop low shots without giving up any holes, and the paddle down will assist you in jam situations and scrambles. With higher shots come standing smothers and glove saves, which allow you to control the play. Blocker saves are another form of steering pucks away from the net, and center shifting into a puck allows you to maximize coverage and protect against soft goals.

In saves, being efficient in your movement is essential. Combining center shifting and butterfly basics with progressive techniques, such as the butterfly slide and the butterfly push, allows you to add mobility to the butterfly and drive into shots. With the new rule changes opening up the east–west (side to side) play, the techniques covered in this chapter will improve your ability not only to make the routine save in perfect form but also to get side to side with better lateral movement.

In the past, coaches used to tell shooters that the best place to shoot on a goaltender was down low. This is no longer the case as butterfly techniques have made it difficult for players to beat the goalies along the ice. In this segment you will learn not only how to stop a low shot but also how to control the rebound.

Stick Saves and Steering Down Low

The stick save is usually the first save that goaltenders learn. Stick activation, using the stick blade to control rebounds and steer pucks, is a valuable skill and a must for any goaltender who is looking to improve his game.

Getting Ready to Make a Stick Save

To fully utilize the stick, whether standing or in a butterfly, you must start with it in the proper position. The stick should be out in front of the tip of your skates by about 12 to 16 inches (30 to 40 centimeters). There are several reasons for this. First, if the stick is pressed firmly against the pads, the likelihood of generating an unwanted rebound is higher; having the stick away from the pads allows you to cushion the puck. Second, having the stick out front allows you to rotate the stick in a semicircle or an arc with minimal hindrance from the skates or pads. Third, if you want to deflect the puck high and wide to a desired location, the stick blade must be at an angle; having the stick in close would eliminate any possibility of generating a high rebound out of harm's way.

Making a Stick Save While in the Stance

A low shot along the ice should be steered to either corner using the blade of the stick. This can be done while standing up or going down into a butterfly, which will be covered shortly in the butterfly segment. In the first scenario, the goaltender is on his feet with his shoulders and hips square to the puck. With the puck moving along the ice, not dangerous enough to warrant a butterfly, the goalie moves his stick along the path of an arc in order to steer or angle the puck toward the corner.

Stick activation in making a stick save has two key execution points. First, a good wrist, and second, proper upper-body positioning. You can significantly improve your stick technique by using your wrist. Essentially, the wrist acts as a hinge in which the stick rotates, allowing the stick to move in a semicircle. This type of motion allows for optimal puck control toward the corners. Additionally, using the wrist gives you greater blade control. The wrist is used to tilt the blade forward or backward to get leverage on the puck. With that comes the ability to pop pucks up high off the glass if desired. Another positive feature of using the wrist is that it keeps the stick blade on the ice longer; thus, the heel or toe will not lift off the ice.

Also important is the position of the upper body. Ideally, the upper torso should turn slightly toward the direction of the puck but not so far that it exposes too much of the net (see figure 5.2 *a* and *b*). Many goaltenders who fail to properly activate their sticks when steering pucks, whether in a drill or in a game, tend to have incorrect upper-body positioning.

For example, imagine a shot directed at the left corner of the net. A goaltender with weak mechanics will either lean away from the puck or keep his body facing forward. There are a few ramifications here. First, if the goaltender leans away, there is a high probability that the stick will not remain flat along the ice. Lifting either the heel or toe minimizes the goalie's ability to direct the puck as well as the amount of blade available to effectively steer it. The stick will also be less likely to extend to the side to its fullest capability, which shortens its range of motion. Second, if the goaltender remains facing forward, again, the stick's range of motion will be limited. Ideally, it is best to turn slightly in the direction in which the stick is moving. So, if you execute a stick save to the left, your upper torso should turn slightly in that direction. Please note that it is essential to watch the puck throughout the save and into postsave recovery.

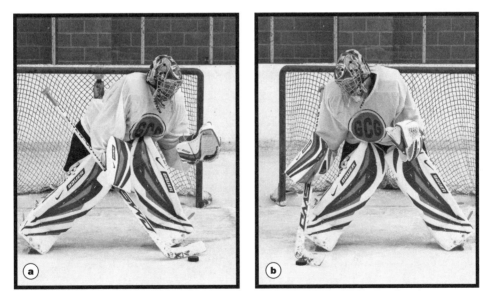

Figure 5.2 Stick save from the stance to *(a)* glove side and *(b)* blocker side.

Butterfly Save

Without question, the butterfly has become the focal point of the modern-day goaltender. At first, it was about playing the percentages, but now it has become the starting point for many save executions. The butterfly allows a goaltender to take away the bottom portion of the net and the middle as well. This forces the shooter to pick a high corner in order to score a goal. With the design of modern goaltending equipment, a goalie can block much of the net fearlessly and leave very few, if any, holes. To some extent the butterfly has almost become a secondary stance.

Butterfly Stance

The butterfly has many variations, but it is basically an inverted V-type spread with the pads flush along the ice. It is the flare of the butterfly that allows for the greatest coverage of width protecting the bottom of the net. This also includes having the knees shut tightly to eliminate the five hole (see figure 5.3 a-b). When in the butterfly, keep your chest and shoulders high. A slight break at the midsection allows for torso mobility. Elbows and triceps should be snug to the outside of the rib cage.

It is important to have the stick blade in the five-hole region but not to have it pressed too firmly against the pads, as this will generate unwanted rebounds. The best place to have the stick is out in front by 8 to 12 inches (20 to 30 centimeters). By having the stick here, you are creating a cushion of sorts for oncoming shots. With the correct gap between your pads and stick blade, you can freely move the stick from side to side to steer pucks to the corners.

Glove position is also very important in the butterfly. When executing the butterfly for a shot coming from the perimeter, the hands should be up and

Figure 5.3 Butterfly position from (a) the front and (b) the back.

active (see figure 5.4*a*). Doing so allows the hands to move freely, to either direct pucks with the blocker or catch pucks with the trapper. The same can be said for the slot. So, in these two areas, a goaltender almost assumes a reactionary position with the hands. However as the puck moves closer, into the tight zone, the hands should move closer to the body and lower to form better blocking coverage (see figure 5.4*b*). This provides maximum coverage for the areas along the body, which is important in tight situations. In addition, having the hands in tight allows the whole upper body to move as a single unit, which is more efficient for a goaltender.

Figure 5.4 *(a)* Loose butterfly and *(b)* tight butterfly.

Dropping Into the Butterfly and Staying Big

Dropping into the butterfly is a very simple maneuver. Simply allow your skates to flare outward while driving your knees toward the ice. You should land in perfect balance on the inside of your pads. Staying big while dropping into a butterfly is one of the most important parts of the move. Make sure your buttocks do not drop. This is a major area of concern. Dropping the buttocks causes two major issues. First, you lose coverage of the upper portion of the net, and second, recovery becomes much more difficult. To resist dropping the butt too low, concentrate on a higher knee flexion when your pads hit the ice. It is to your advantage to keep the buttocks up and remain tall. The shoulders should also remain high to maximize coverage. With the butt and shoulders up, it becomes very difficult to be scored on over the shoulders.

Butterfly Steers and Smothers

The butterfly steer is used to deflect pucks to the corner of the rink by using your stick blade and backing up your stick blade with the butterfly. From a butterfly, position the blade of the stick to move along the path of an arc from the midline so that when the puck hits the blade, it is the angle of the blade that dictates where the puck is heading. Most goalies find it helpful to have the blade slightly tilted back so the puck will deflect high toward the glass as opposed to along the ice. Too much ramp on the blade will cause the puck to come up at a sharp angle, and you run the risk of not having enough leverage to direct the puck to the corner.

Avoid punching the blade of the stick forward or along a parallel path, as this will increase the odds of the rebound staying above the goal line extended. When steering with the stick blade, your shoulders should turn slightly into the direction you are angling the puck but not so much that it exposes the net. Your upper body and gloves should remain compact, but slightly rotate as well so the stance remains intact (see figure 5.5 *a* and *b*).

A butterfly smother allows a goaltender to swallow up the puck in a butterfly position and not allow the rebound. When the puck is shot 12 inches (30 centimeters) or higher off the ice and between both armpits (goalie's midline), then the butterfly smother is used to trap the puck in the body pocket. In a butterfly position, and as the puck enters the body pocket, make sure your elbows are tight to your core so nothing gets through you. As the puck makes contact with your body, bring your glove in, under, and up your midline so as to trap the

Figure 5.5 Butterfly steer to *(a)* glove and *(b)* blocker sides.

puck (see figure 5.6). Do not bring your blocker across the midline, but lock it tight to the body along with the blocker elbow. When making the in, under, and upward movement with the glove, do not release the glove-side elbow from being tight to the core (so the puck can't squeeze through), and remember to keep your upper torso high in order to stay big. If you collapse too soon on a smother before the puck enters the body pocket, then you will have limited blocking coverage if a puck is tipped or deflected. To help deaden the puck you can roll your shoulders forward, as this will separate your chest protection from your body and create an air pocket to cushion and deaden the puck.

The smother can be used in a variety of situations, whether a save from a point shot or even a player streaking down the wing. It is important to note that having the puck hit you dead center illustrates that you are in control and in position. Most important, it can slow the play down by forcing a whistle and does not allow for a potential flurry of shots.

Figure 5.6   Butterfly smother.

The ability of a goaltender to smother the puck is so important because it eliminates second and third attempts, which are generally the most dangerous. The goalies who smother the best are the ones who square up early and get their feet set.

COACHES' TIP

ROBERTO LUONGO

The ability to control rebounds is one of the most important skills a goaltender can possess. Controlling the puck decreases the amount of second and third chance scoring opportunities by the opponent. One of the best in the NHL at controlling rebounds in Roberto Luongo. He has exceptional positioning and any puck that is shot at him has a high likelihood of either ending up toward the corner and beneath the goal line extended or smothered in his body. When smothering the puck it is important keep your chest up, elbows in, and your hands forward. When a puck enters Luongo's body pocket it is as if it sticks to Velcro.

In 1997 Roberto Luongo was a first round draft choice of the New York Islanders and has played for the Florida Panthers before joining the Vancouver Canucks. In the 2006-2007 season he set the NHL record for most shots faced by a goaltender and most shots faced in his first Playoff game (76), His 47 win season tied Bernie Parent's former league record with most wins in a single season and was recognized with the Cyclone Taylor award for Canucks MVP, the Most Exciting Player Award and the Molson Cup Trophy winner as well as representing the Canucks at the 2007 All-Star game. Luongo is now depended on by the Canadian Olympic team and as a junior was named the best goaltender at the 1999 World Junior Championships.

© Icon SMI

Butterfly Position Pad Saves

The butterfly is an excellent technique for utilizing your pads to make saves on low shots. The modern-day style sees a lot of goaltenders using the butterfly as the save of choice. To further that, many goaltenders have adopted a drop and block style. This style, in short, is based on the premise that the goaltender finds optimal positioning and drops into a butterfly.

To perform the save, simply drop with authority into the butterfly and allow the puck to carom off your pads (see figure 5.7 *a* and *b*). The back diagonal angle in which the pads lie on the ice allows the puck to ricochet off the pads and toward the corner of the ice. The butterfly pad save is used when getting the stick blade on the puck is not a viable option. Either the puck is too quick to get the stick blade on it or the shot is just over the stick blade. Another reason to use the butterfly pad save is in the event a puck may get tipped or deflected toward the five hole. In this case you may not want to remove your stick from the five hole. As pads get better at securely blocking the five hole, this risk continues to get smaller.

One of the issues that many goalies have with their pad saves is that for every save they make, the butterfly is the starting point. For instance, a player takes a shot from the slot region, and the puck is traveling toward the top right corner. During shot release many goaltenders will initiate a butterfly save—to play the percentage—then execute the desired save once the puck's direction is determined. There have been some bad habits developed through this approach that need to be rectified.

Figure 5.7 Butterfly position pad save *(a)* to glove-side and *(b)* to blocker-side.

One reoccurring tendency that causes ineffective rebound control is the directional approach the leg takes to make a save in the lower corner when releasing from that butterfly position. First let's understand the problem and then devise a solution.

The initial problem is the inverted V position the legs assume when in a butterfly. This position is good if the puck hits the pads; the inverted V is geometrically advantageous to steer the puck to the corner. But very few goaltenders have legs long enough to reach both posts all the time. Thus, the goaltender must leave the butterfly position and extend the leg to reach any pucks going to the low corner of the net. It is here where the problems start.

The problem is in the directional angle the leg takes to make a save in the low corner. What most commonly occurs is that the goaltender, upon recognition that he must extend the leg, swings the foot out from the butterfly and forward to make the save. This creates a punching effect. Basically, the puck is coming at the corner, and because of the force required to react quickly, the pad punches the puck forward back in front of the goaltender. Although there are times when having a rebound back in front is not a bad option, these situations are limited. Thus, the goaltender must learn to make a leg extension rather than a leg kick to ensure the rebound goes to the corner and out of harm's way.

The problem is handled by properly executing a leg extension, which is rather simple. Think about this: If you were to assume your basic stance and to draw a perpendicular line on the ice from the middle of your skate blade outward, this would be the directional line that your foot should follow. This directional line will provide the geometric ability for the puck to be steered away from the front of the net using the pad. So, for proper execution, the goaltender drops into the butterfly and just prior to full completion of the butterfly, the goaltender extends the desired leg along the aforesaid directional angle (see figure 5.8 *a* and *b*).

Figure 5.8　Butterfly pad save extension *(a)* to glove side and *(b)* to blocker side.

Half Butterfly

The half butterfly nearly became extinct in the French Canadian lock and drop era but is now creeping back into play in a much more compact form. The reason is that with the new rule changes, goalies must stay up a little longer than in recent history and combine reaction saves with their blocking techniques. The half butterfly save is used on low and high shots, and goalies may also use a tight half butterfly when steering the puck with their stick blade as well.

The principles that apply to the butterfly also pertain to the half butterfly. In this move, the goaltender drops like in the butterfly but keeps one pad slightly raised (see figure 5.9 *a* and *b*). On the side in which the pad makes contact with the puck, or backs up the stick blade if the shot is along the ice, the foot is extended and slightly back diagonal to the knee. This allows the puck to be deflected to the corner as opposed to out front. The weak-side leg is flared and flush to the ice, while the glove and blocker maintain a compact position within the upper part of the stance. The goal is to lift the pad off the ice as little as possible and keep the five-hole exposure to a minimum. Only when absolutely necessary should you open up to make this save.

When you perform this move, be sure you have a bend in your extended leg. With a straight knee, your pad will be exactly square to the shooter, causing the rebound to go straight out and back into a dangerous position. A bent knee allows you to direct pucks to the corner and out of harm's way and will also not get in the way of a puck steered with the stick blade.

Hip rotation is extremely important in the half butterfly. Rotate the hips and chest slightly in the direction in which the puck is headed. This allows your torso to pivot while your chest goes toward and then over the puck. If you don't slightly rotate your hips and shoulders, you will be unable to follow the complete path of the puck and are likely to be left with a rebound that you are not in position to stop.

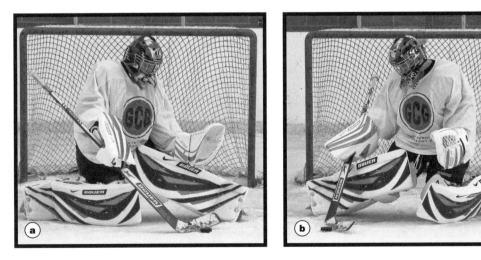

Figure 5.9   Half butterfly *(a)* to glove side and *(b)* to blocker side.

Paddle Down Technique

The paddle down can be a positive attribute or a major detriment to your game depending on its use. The paddle down execution is rather simple. From a butterfly position, all you must do is lean forward and drop the paddle (see figure 5.10 *a* and *b*). To build coverage, you can extend your glove-side leg with the stick in front as this allows the upper torso to be raised as well as the glove. The glove should be over the extended pad as well, and the blocker-side pad should be extended.

There are a few ramifications of raising your left pad while in the paddle down. First, extending your trapper leg shifts your center of gravity and your upper-body coverage to the blocker side, leaving the glove side exposed. Second, it creates an opening between the ice and the trapper knee, which is not beneficial for pucks in close because they can slip through. Essentially, the technical execution of the paddle down is not that difficult. Rather, its complexities are found in understanding when and when not to use the paddle down.

The paddle down is most effective when the play is very tight and opposing players are trying to jam the puck through the goaltender because they are too tight to get the puck over the coverage. First, with the butterfly paddle down, you still gain that lower-net coverage that you seek. But second, when you drop the blocker down to the ice, your upper body shifts forward. As a result, your head gets closer to ice level, providing for improved tracking on pucks that are in tight or in scrambles. It is here, in tight, where there are a number of advantages.

We do, however, lean on the side of caution for paddle down use on shots outside of scrambles and tight play. The reason is that a number of deficiencies

Figure 5.10 Paddle down technique to *(a)* glove side and *(b)* to blocker side.

can arise in this type of situation. By having the paddle down, your blocker and upper body are closer to the ice, exposing the top half of the net. Moreover, the ability to effectively control rebounds with the paddle down is diminished. This is due to the fact that the paddle down is limiting to rebound control techniques. For instance steering, leg extensions, and so forth are limited by the paddle down position. Finally, with the blocker hand down on the ice, you have limited the ability to recover to the glove side. If your blocker is down and your body is shifted forward, it becomes rather difficult to pick that blocker leg up and push in the direction of the trapper side. This becomes difficult because there is very little room for that blocker leg to get all the way up with equipment such as the blocker in the way.

DEFENDING HIGH SHOTS

Now that you have a good handle on stopping low shots, it is time to look at stopping shots up top. Shooting high is now the preference of goal scorers because goalies are so solid down low. Stopping high shots while staying on your feet or going down in the butterfly will depend on the play.

Standing Smother

The stand-up smother save is used for a high shot down a goaltender's midline. Once you have identified that a smother save should be initiated, the first movement is to roll the shoulders. This pushes the chest pad out from the body, creating a cushion for the arrival of the puck.

Next, tighten up your elbows to the rib cage, and move the trapper hand under and up the front of the body on impact of the puck (see figure 5.11). The blocker moves in but does not disrupt the glove's movement to smother the puck. The blocker does not come across the midline, so the stick stays centered and in position for a rebound. The save is complete when the puck is smothered inside your body pocket.

Figure 5.11 Standing smother.

Glove Saves

For many goaltenders, the glove save is what initiates the urge to play goal. Many see on television a miraculous glove save and someday dream of doing that on the big screen. The fact of the matter is the pros who are making these types of "big-wheel" saves are making them as a last resort to get to a puck. If they could make the save more technically sound, they would. The big-wheel glove save might look good, but simplifying your glove save, although it might be less flashy, allows you to get to those hard-to-reach shots to the top corner.

Executing a glove save is very similar to catching a baseball. From the stance you want to look the puck into the glove and catch it cleanly in the webbing. Shoulders and hips should rotate slightly, allowing the chest to get up over the puck for easier tracking. The glove will move slightly back in order to cushion the puck. Try to keep the glove-side shoulder in the shot, and try not to let it roll back. Pulling the glove-side shoulder out will expose more net and affect the path of the glove. Glove saves can be made standing up (see figure 5.12a), using a butterfly (see figure 5.12b), or using a half butterfly, and all three circumstances follow the same principles.

The main thing to remember is that the glove save is basic geometry. Essentially, you want to get from point A to point B in as short a distance as possible. That being said, your glove hand should travel in a straight line when you make a glove save. Many goaltenders try to make a big swinging loop. However,

Figure 5.12 Glove save from (a) standing position and (b) butterfly position.

this path of movement takes more time and becomes costly as you move up the hockey echelons. As you progress in hockey, the better goaltenders are fractions of seconds quicker, and this is just one example of how to gain these fractions of a second in your game.

Another important feature of the glove save is ensuring that you catch the puck with your glove forward and not off to the side of your core or behind you. A glove save should be to the outside of your midline, with your elbow against the bottom of your rib cage. To understand why this is so, it is best to look at the ramifications of not catching the puck in front. There are two major issues. First, by catching the puck behind you, your trapper finds itself at an angle that allows the sight line of the puck better access to the net. So, instead of cutting off the trajectory of the puck, you are opening it up. Second, when you move the glove behind to make a save, your glove-side shoulder falls out, which in turn pulls the glove hand away from the side on which the save is being executed. This is very problematic in that you can lose valuable inches of coverage.

We know that the trapper should move in straight lines, which might be easier said than done, but this can be simply self-taught. However, what about catching pucks in front? What about not pulling the trapper shoulder out? This also has a simple solution, and the solution can be found in the trapper's starting point, the stance. By rotating the trapper in the stance to a fingers-up position, you can eliminate many problems. Assuming a fingers-up position allows you to position the glove so that it cuts off the trajectory of the puck as it approaches from the ice. Also, this position allows the glove to travel in a straight path with more ease. But most important, it will decrease the likelihood of your shoulder pulling out of a glove save. This is due to the fact that the glove and shoulder are connected. That being said, if the shoulder pulls out of the shot it is inevitable that the glove will also pull out. Again logic tells us that if the glove is pulling out of the shot, the coverage is decreased minimizing the goaltenders ability to stop the approaching shot.

Lastly, you should look at the final save process. With good visual tracking, the goaltender aims to catch the puck in the glove. Ideally we see the goaltender catching the puck in the pocket portion of the glove. Again, this type of accuracy requires tremendous focus.

The beautiful glove save has changed over time. It used to be an acrobatic swing of the arm that would make the crowd go crazy. Now, the ultimate glove save is the one with very little movement, and the goalie makes it look as if it were a piece of cake.

COACHES' TIP

Blocker Saves

Although the blocker save does not receive as much attention as the glove save, the two are very similar in many aspects. The major points of the glove save are all critical for the blocker save as well. For instance, traveling in a straight line, making the save in front of the body, and not pulling the blocker shoulder out all apply. What does differ is the final save process. The blocker, unlike the glove, is designed to steer or redirect pucks to a desired location. Therefore the save process is more complex for the blocker. Once you identify the blocker save as the save of choice and the blocker is traveling in a straight line, you now need to understand how to properly steer the puck.

From the stance you want to look the puck into the blocker and steer toward the corner. The shoulders and hips should rotate slightly, allowing the chest to get up over the puck for easier tracking. The wrist should tilt the blocker slightly back diagonally so the rebound does not end up above the goal line. The blocker arm movement should come with the puck as opposed to punching toward it, causing bad rebounds. Try to keep the blocker-side shoulder in the shot, and keep the chest in the shot as opposed to pulling back. Pulling the glove-side shoulder out will expose more net and make it difficult to track the puck. Blocker saves can be made standing up (see figure 5.13a), using a butterfly (see figure 5.13b), or using a half butterfly, and all three circumstances follow the same principles.

The blocker save is essentially a steer or a redirect. It is important that you do not punch at the puck. Punching at the puck decreases the probability of directing the puck to the desired location. In most cases, punching will cause

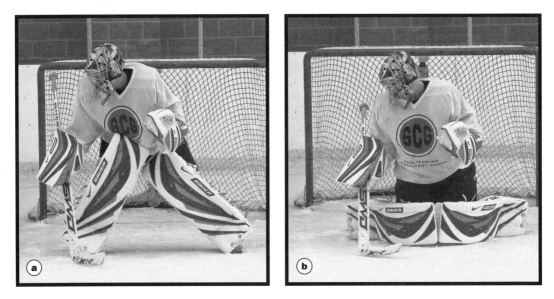

Figure 5.13 Blocker save from *(a)* standing position and *(b)* butterfly position.

the puck to end up above the goal line extended and possibly in a harmful location. So, even though the save should be made in front of the body, it should be done in guiding fashion.

Steering or redirecting can be done in a number of ways. Ideally the goaltender should redirect the puck into the corner of the rink. The easiest way to achieve this is to break the wrist at the moment of contact between the arriving puck and the blocker. The breaking action has two major advantages. First, it directs the puck to the corner of the rink. But second, it cuts off the trajectory of the puck, similar to the fingers-up position of the trapper.

Poke Checks

Recently, the use of the full poke check has diminished greatly. Today you see more quick stick plays in tight rather than the power pokes of old. The reason you see fewer aggressive poke checks is the success of goaltenders playing within a compact stance, not wanting to get extended and therefore opening up holes. There are circumstances when the poke check can come up big, such as when the element of surprise is on your side, and it can be very effective. A poke check can also be used to knock a puck out of a dangerous area before the opposition gets to it.

There are two ways to propel your stick out for a poke check. You can propel the stick by pushing out at the top of the paddle. As the stick slides forward, the shaft will glide through your hand. Just as you approach impact, catch the stick at its knob (see figure 5.14). This approach is best used to camouflage the ensuing poke check.

Figure 5.14   Poke check throw.

For a power poke check, you slide your hand up the shaft of the stick and grab firmly at the knob. Propel the stick toward the puck with control. Although this approach allows you to throw your stick out with power and confidence, it may tip off the shooter.

The keys to a successful poke are the elements of surprise and timing. If an opponent has his head up he will see the poke coming and walk around you. Try to catch the shooter with his head down. Time your poke so that the blade thrusts through the interception point. If you throw it too early, the player will walk around you and tuck the puck into the empty net. The wider the angle that the forward is cutting to the net, the better chance you have to take the puck. If you try to poke check a player coming down the middle, he can easily maneuver left or right, giving him a high probability of beating the move. If the shooter is sweeping in at an angle, his momentum is set, and he will have a hard time adjusting his path—thus giving the goaltender the advantage.

To perform a blocker-side poke check, from a stopped position, generate momentum by turning your blocker-side foot out in an open T-glide position. Bend at the knees and waist, exploding toward the puck while staying low. Propel the stick forward, landing on the ice with your body extended and your head up while following the course of the puck.

The glove-side poke check is very risky and should not be used with any regular frequency. This move is successful most often when the player is cutting toward the middle of the net on his off wing (backhand). Your ability to execute this tactic will require timing and a lot of practice. From a T-glide, execute a two-pad stack. The stick should be facing the center of the ice; the glove should be over the pad, ready to react if a quick shot is released. Unlike with a poke check to the blocker side, when going to the glove side you should leave the stick along the ice to block the path of the puck rather than to intercept it at a particular point.

Half Poke Check

The half poke check is a very effective tool because it allows you to maintain a compact butterfly as well as be proactive with the stick. The half poke can be used when the shooter gets in too tight. You do not want to break your knee flexion in your butterfly using the half poke, as this will put you in a vulnerable position if you don't get all of the puck.

You can use the half poke from either side by staying on your feet or in the butterfly and poking, generating the power from a firm grip on the paddle. In this move you do not slide your hand up the shaft of the stick—your goal is to quickly shoot the blade at the puck (see figure 5.15*a*) and remain on your feet so that you are prepared to follow the puck. Execute the exact same move when an opponent attacks on your glove side, except turn the blade over so that it is facing out instead of in (see figure 5.15*b*).

Figure 5.15 Half poke check to *(a)* blocker side and *(b)* glove side.

Although the use of the poke check is now much more limited than in the past, it can still be an effective tool to surprise the shooter. The key is timing and recognizing when the attacking player has his head down.

COACHES' TIP

DESPERATION SAVES

We've all seen the scenario a hundred times . . . a player staring at a wide-open net only to have the goalie come out of nowhere and get enough of the puck to make the save. These saves are desperation saves, and even though most people think they are just instinctual movements by the goalie, desperation saves have a methodology all to themselves.

The first rule of thumb is that in general you do not want to be making desperation saves. Your goal is to stay compact and in control as much as possible, but there will be times when you have to sell your soul to the goalie devil and break out of your controlled movements. In the following paragraphs, you will learn how to go about "selling out" in a calculated manner.

COACHES' TIP   When making desperation saves, the first goal is to cover the lower part of the net as fast as possible and then build coverage up.

Long Body Save

The long body is a technique used on backdoor plays. It can originate from a standing position or from your knees. The long body is simply an extension of the butterfly slide and used when the butterfly slide will not give you enough lateral coverage to make the save. Picture standing in your stance at the top of the crease at a 45-degree angle. The opposition is standing all alone off to the weak side of the net and about to insert the puck, and if you use a butterfly slide you will never make the stop.

In the long body, the key is to extend the skate toward the target and get the lead pad flush while sliding along the ice. Your momentum comes from the drive off of your weak-side leg. Your upper body does not rotate toward the puck until extension is achieved, and your chest actually ends up on the ice in order to achieve that extension. In this case your weak-side leg will end up creating a V with the lead leg. Once you have achieved maximum extension with your lead pad, your upper body can rotate toward the puck. Although you still may be sliding, the rotation of the upper body toward the strong side will pull the lead pad back in so it does not overshoot the target.

If you are sliding to your glove side (see figure 5.16 *a-b*), you should build coverage up from your pad with your glove, and your stick can either come in front to the pad or you can leave it out in front to take the passing lane. If you are using a long body to the blocker side (see figure 5.17 *a-b*), you can build up from your low coverage by bringing your blocker and stick up over your pad

Figure 5.16 The long body save to glove side *(a-b)*.

Figure 5.17 The long body save to blocker side *(a-b)*.

and using your glove to take away the passing lane and smother rebounds. When building coverage with your blocker, you can keep the blocker facing forward or turn it over and utilize the back of the stick paddle for coverage. One other method you can implement while using the long body to the blocker side is to drop your stick along the way while rotating your torso. This allows you to move your blocker freely without being inhibited by your stick.

Dive Save

Diving to make a save is a dramatic play that couldn't be farther away from compactness and control. The principle of the dive is similar to the long body— take away the ice quickly and then use your hands, arms, and torso to build coverage up. The dive is usually used when you are totally out of position and there is no other chance to make the stop. The key to a successful dive is the drive you get from your plant leg. If you are standing up, make sure the skate you are driving off of is positioned at the proper angle in order to generate the most power. You do not want to be adjusting the angle of your plant skate while driving off of it. If your dive originates from a down-low position, you should rotate in the butterfly and plant before you dive so your drive skate is at the right angle.

When diving to the glove side (see figure 5.18 *a-b*), you should lead with the paddle of your stick in order to take away the ice. The time and distance that needs to be covered will dictate the power of your drive. The paddle should also be angled toward the corner of the ice so that a hard shot will carom off the paddle and go toward the corner and out of harm's way.. The glove should be used to build coverage over the paddle and be ready to catch high shots.

When diving to the blocker side (see figure 5.19 *a-b*), the stick is utilized to take away the ice by turning the paddle over. The time and distance that needs to be covered will dictate the power of your drive. Once the ice is covered with your blocker arm and stick, bring your glove over in order to stop any high shots.

Two-Pad Stack

The two-pad stack used to be a valuable save in a goalie's repertoire but has been replaced with the butterfly slide and butterfly push. The stack is now used randomly as a desperation save and is seen sometimes as a continuation of the butterfly slide. The two-pad stack can get your two biggest pieces of equipment across the ice to cover an unprotected net. The move requires timing and precise fundamentals.

To perform a two-pad stack to the glove side, begin in a strong stance and begin a butterfly slide to the glove side. After the drive with your blocker-side leg, throw that leg under your body and along the ice as your body moves in that direction. Stack the pads one on top of the other, forming a wall, and lie

Figure 5.18 Dive save to glove side *(a-b)*.

Figure 5.19 Dive save to blocker side *(a-b)*.

on the side of your upper torso. Your glove should build coverage from the top of the pads and should face the shooter. Your stick can be used to either take away the ice in front of the pads or be laid out to intercept a pass.

To perform a two-pad stack to the blocker side, begin in a strong stance and begin a butterfly slide to the blocker side. After the drive with your glove-side leg, throw that leg under your body and along the ice as your body moves in that direction. Stack the pads one on top of the other, forming a wall, and lie on the side of your upper torso. Your blocker and stick should lie on top of the pads and should face the shooter. Stretch out your glove arm to prevent the forward from cutting to the middle and to quickly smother rebounds. Keep your armpit in contact with the ice.

Sometimes after performing a butterfly slide more range is needed. At this point you can choose to either long body or stack. If the puck is in tight with very little time, a butterfly slide into a long body is probably your best choice. If the puck ends up a little farther out and there is time to execute a stack from a slide, this will build some additional coverage that a long body cannot deliver.

Don't allow yourself to fall back during execution of this save. If your pads are tilted back, the shooter will have a better trajectory to lift the puck over you. A common problem is too much or too little bend in your waist when you're down on the ice. With too much bend, too much area is left uncovered; insufficient bend delays reaction time and recovery.

As in all saves, it is important to keep your eye on the puck. You can also use your head in this save to remind yourself to cover the hole underneath your armpit. As you hit the ice, lay your head, while still watching the puck, on your shoulder. This should force your armpit onto the ice.

MOVING INTO A BLOCKING POSITION

Dropping into a butterfly is primarily a blocking maneuver. The actual save can come as a result of the butterfly or through a reaction made during the drop or from the butterfly technique. This section will teach you how to take the benefits of the butterfly and add movement. These techniques allow you to benefit from all the blocking coverage produced through the butterfly and permit you to move that blocking coverage from point A to point B. Moving efficiently, with power and while allowing very few seams for a puck to find its way into the net, are the benefits of these progressive techniques. After you have maximized your net coverage, saves can be made with the butterfly or a reaction from the butterfly.

Center Shifts

A great tool to add to your arsenal, center shifts illustrate how much our position has changed in the past 10 to 15 years. In previous years, goaltenders tended to rely on their extremities to make saves, and a more reactionary approach was taken. Goaltending has now developed into an exact science, with an understanding of how the body can be used to block space. For instance, coaches and goalies alike are recognizing that the upper body and core form an impenetrable surface that if positioned correctly can cover more area than any other body part. In addition, by moving your body into the puck, you can gain more inches if an extremity is needed to make the save versus if you were stationary. One of the best examples of this is 2007 Stanley Cup winner Jean-Sebastien Giguere. J.-S. Giguere uses a geometrical approach combined with the power of center shifting to win night in, night out. After reading this segment, you too will hopefully take the initial steps toward applying the center shift to your game.

So what exactly is a center shift? As the name suggests, it is a goaltender's ability to move the body into the direction of the puck versus using the limbs to make the save. Thus, in turn, more pucks are stopped with the upper body and core, which both possess positive attributes for rebound control.

Any of the save techniques described in this chapter can be used while center shifting. The shift itself can be done while standing to handle a high shot, while in a butterfly to handle a low shot (described next), or while in a half butterfly to the glove. To execute the center shift, you must recognize the puck's path of travel. This requires seeing the puck right off the shooter's stick blade and reading where it is headed. For example, if you note that the released puck is heading at the blocker side, you would slightly shift to that direction. To create momentum for the shift, place weight on the weak-side leg (see figure 5.20a). This leg provides the power to shift to the opposite side. Do not overextend the shift; overextending can cause problems with angles and balance as well as increase seams the puck may be able to squeeze through. To ensure that you do not over shift, remember that your push for the shift should not be as hard as a butterfly slide would be. Remember the center shift should only have you sliding about a foot or two depending on how far from the puck you are (see figure 5.20b). A major flaw with over pushing is that it will leave you out of position.

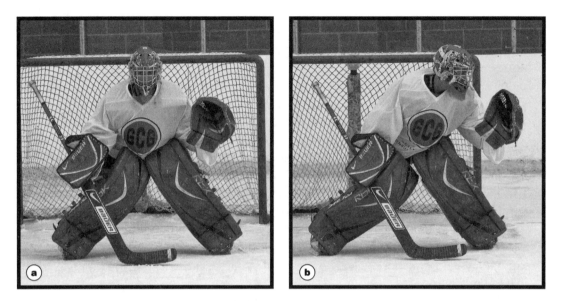

Figure 5.20 Center shift to standing glove save *(a-b)*.

 COACHES' TIP Being able to center shift is extremely important. If we allow goalies at a young age to lock and drop into the butterfly and then reach for pucks, then they will never learn to read a shot release. Young goalies must learn to have patience and not rely on blocking techniques early in their development.

Butterfly Slide Saves

The butterfly slide is a great example of center shifting. Imagine a shot headed to the low stick side of the goaltender. Twenty years ago the only save choice would have been a skate save, which opened up a bunch of holes for the puck to enter, let alone if the shot was deflected along the way. Now we can maximize the compactness of the butterfly by shifting it toward the puck.

The butterfly slide originates from the stance. The weak-side leg generates power toward the side of the ice the puck is heading. The lead leg immediately gets flush to the ice. While sliding into the shot, the drive leg tucks in down and tight to form the butterfly. The glove and blocker remain in perfect form throughout the save, moving only if necessary to stop the puck. The stick remains in the five hole during execution of the slide. Once you have arrived in position, the save is made from the butterfly. After the save, stop the slide by planting the lead skate and initiating recovery. The lead pad is quickly followed by the drive leg in regaining an upright stance.

The butterfly slide is a great way to build coverage in saves. Smothers and glove, blocker, and steering saves can all originate from the slide. Sometimes a butterfly slide is not practical because a shot release is too quick, and there is only enough time to extend and get a piece of the puck. A detailed breakdown of the butterfly slide in a blocking or zoning situation follows.

Butterfly Slide as a Blocking or Zoning Technique

The butterfly slide has become a critical element of a goaltender's arsenal. Its purpose and design allow the goaltender to get from point A to point B while covering the lower portion of the net. The butterfly slide is perfect for handling cross-crease plays, backdoor passes, and pass-outs. The goal is to block as much of the net as possible while tracking a play or pass. Please note that the same fundamentals apply to moving to either side and are slightly different than for the butterfly slide save. For this example, we assume that you wish to slide to the right.

Two major components of the butterfly slide occur from the start. First is visual recognition. Many goaltenders execute their slide while gaining visual recognition of the puck. To execute, first turn your head and find the puck (see figure 5.21*a*). Second, apply what we call a momentum cut or momentum build. This is done by making a tiny C-cut, as covered in chapter 6, with the skate that will lead the slide, or the skate on the side to which you wish to move. (Please note that a momentum cut is not necessary when performing a butterfly slide save.) So a slide to the right would require a momentum cut from the right skate. This tiny cut will give you some momentum to initiate the movement and will gain the line of travel for the slide. This line of travel is very important. It provides the pathway or direction for the slide, and it also allows you to be square through the slide and when arriving to the puck. If the momentum cut is not made, you may not be able to get square. As a result, you might try to get square during the slide, which can be hazardous to your balance and to the slide itself.

After you make the momentum cut, it is important that the lead leg hit the ice first. The design of the butterfly slide is to ensure lower coverage. So for instance, if the direction desired is to the right, make the momentum cut with the right leg, then after the momentum cut, drop the right leg to the ice. Having the lead leg on the ice provides the lower-ice coverage you are seeking from the slide. With regard to the lead leg, ensure that it remains flared out and on the ice. In some instances, goaltenders tend to let the lead leg creep back under them, which minimizes coverage.

With visual recognition, the momentum cut made, and the lead leg down, it is now time to drive (see figure 5.21*b*). Driving hard with the inside edge of your left skate will get you sliding to the right. However, the drive leg is not done. If you were to leave the drive leg extended it would create drag, which would slow you down. Also, it would expose the five hole, minimizing that lower-net coverage you seek. So, it is important to bring that back leg in quick. Neverthe-

Figure 5.21 When performing a butterfly slide save, start with strong positioning *(a)*, visually track the puck while sliding *(b)*, then shift your butterfly to cover the shooting lane to the net *(c)*.

less, this does more than just prevent drag and cover the five hole. It actually provides you with some additional speed because it is another force pushing you in the direction you want to go. Once that back leg is in, the technical part of the slide is complete. From here, hopefully you used a strong enough drive to get you to the desired location.

Glove and stick positioning is key when executing the butterfly slide. The job of these pieces of equipment is rather simple: to stay stationary. Similar to when dropping into the butterfly, the gloves and stick should not move. Keeping the blocker still will keep the stick still and vice versa. This is important because five-hole coverage is key. It is here where many intermediate goaltenders have difficulty. Although the legs perform the required movements, the hands tend to move a lot. This can cause difficulties for balance and coverage. Even some pros find this difficult, and keeping the hands still is something that every goalie has to work at. A way to work on fixing this problem is to watch yourself executing the movement. So, how do we do that? On the ice go to a section that has a dark colored advertisement on the boards. Execute the slide a few feet from the boards. This should allow you to see yourself in the reflection of the advertisement. This idea is a good way to see yourself doing a variety of movements, not just this one.

Once you have slid to where you want to be, you are technically in a blocking position as you have used the butterfly slide to shift your butterfly into a position to cover the shooting lane to the net (see figure 5.21c). Making the save at this point may require no extra movement, or you may be called on to react based on the location of the shot.

Butterfly Slides on Breakaways

The butterfly slide is currently regarded as the best save selection to stop a breakaway deke. It allows the goalie to move with the attacker while taking away the ice and maximizing blocking coverage. After gaining initial depth, the goaltender recoils to the top of the crease when the shooter makes his move. The goalie then utilizes the fundamentals of the butterfly slide in order to protect the lower portion of the net and has his hands ready in case the shooter tries to get the puck up over the pads. If the shooter is too quick for the goalie, he can always extend into a long body from the butterfly slide, which is covered in the segment on desperation saves.

Butterfly Push From a Down Position

The butterfly push technique is very similar to that of the butterfly slide and can be used both as a blocking technique or a save. The sole difference lies in its beginning. Here, the goaltender is starting from a down position. So, if you have gone down to make a save, or the puck has changed direction, whatever the case may be, you need to move your butterfly in a particular direction starting from a down position to cover a shooting lane.

The process starts with a visual recognition. You must turn your head and find the puck (see figure 5.22a). In unison with the turn of the head, you should perform what is simply called a butterfly rotation. Here, you rotate your body so that it is in line with the directional path you wish to pursue.

As your body rotates in the desired direction, the push foot should come up and rest next to the lead-leg knee and should be angled in order to push along the correct path (see figure 5.22b). The plant skate is very important and is the source of power and direction. Performing what we call "a tight plant" allows you to get the most power out of the push. A tight plant is when you position the plant skate close to the lead pad, allowing you to use leverage to get a great push. In a loose plant, your skate leg is away from the body, and you cannot get your chest over the drive skate to produce power.

Figure 5.22 Butterfly push from a down position *(a-c)*.

With the butterfly push, you have essentially met up with the halfway point of the butterfly slide. The lead leg is down, the direction has been determined, and the push leg is about to push. Now, all that is left to do is push and bring the back leg in, again keeping the hands static, the stick in the five hole, and the body upright (see figure 5.22c).

As in the butterfly slide, once you have pushed to where you want to be, you are technically in a blocking position as you have used the butterfly push to shift your butterfly into a position to cover the shooting lane to the net. Making the save at this point may require no extra movement, or you may be called on to react based on the location of the shot.

PERFECT PRACTICE MAKES PERFECT

Certainly technique is a major part of a goaltender's game. It is something that needs to be continually developed, and we say this for two reasons. One, techniques themselves are continually being refined or changed, and goaltenders must adjust accordingly. Second, we are all human, and honing our skills is something we should all do on a daily basis. Even the pros take time to work repeatedly on technique. By doing so they create the muscle memory required to execute movements in a split second during pressure situations. There is a cliche in the world of sports that says, "Perfect practice makes perfect." Well, we don't think anyone can be perfect. But what we do agree with is that when practicing your technique, take your time and do it right. Having a solid technical foundation can be the base for years of success between the pipes.

COACHES' TIP

Although many of the save techniques described in this chapter are almost in a step-by-step sequence, the ultimate goal from a technical standpoint is to make all these techniques one fluid motion. This is something everyone can work on. What is nice is that fluidity can be worked on without a goalie coach. A lot can be done on your own. You are the designer of how good you can become, so make productive use of your ice time.

chapter 6

CREASE MANAGEMENT

Terry Barbeau

T he foundation of goaltending is the ability of the goaltender to be in the shooting lane before the puck gets there and to do so as efficiently as possible. Without the skating skills necessary to quickly move from spot to spot, whether standing or on the ice, a goalie will have limited success. Being on the correct angle, square to the puck, as well as having the proper depth is key to increasing your probability of stopping the puck. Therefore, it is essential to build a solid base and then battle to stop every shot without thinking about the mechanics necessary to get you there. The previous chapter detailed save techniques. In this chapter, you will learn how to get in position to make the save.

The goalie with the best fundamentals will make fewer mistakes under pressure based on muscle memory. The ability to get to the correct spot quickly without excess movement and therefore with total control of the body is a great advantage. During practice, concentrate on working on the skating techniques needed to handle game situations. Whether it is moving from your post to the top of the crease while on your skates or using a butterfly push from the top of your crease back to your post, it is essential that you train hard consistently so in a game your focus can be on the puck and reading the situation.

Many of the things you do during a game without making a save may not show up in the game summary or on the highlight reel but do show up in the win column. It could be tipping a pass from behind the net, leaving the puck in a good position for your defense, making a great angle play that forces the shooter to miss the net, or clearing the zone for your team with a hard shot off the glass. Setting up on the right angle, taking the net away from the shooter, and adjusting your depth based on reading the position of the opposition are just as important as making the big save. You play a special position and must pay attention to these and many other details during a game. That is what separates the average goalies from the best goalies.

Skating skills, being square to the shooter, and the amount of depth you can attain are essential no matter what style you play. This chapter illustrates the skills necessary to give you the foundation to make a save, and it will be your passion and dedication that will determine whether that puck is going to cross the goal line.

SKATING SKILLS

A goalie needs to have good balance and quick feet in order to keep up with the puck carrier. With the increase in the east–west or side-to-side action that the new rules have fostered, staying on your feet longer is essential. A successful goaltender must be able to move quickly from side to side, to the center of the crease and back to the post, and from the post out into the shooting lane. Today's goalie also needs to be able to go down and return to his feet quicker as well, and this is what we refer to as recovery, covered in chapter 7.

The recently regulated smaller equipment should help make for quicker feet and legs. Goalies have a greater say in the outcome of the game now because so much is required of them, not just simply stopping the puck. Often it is what is left or created after the initial save that is of greater importance. Because of their need for increased responsiveness and speed, goaltenders have always had to be the best skaters on the ice, but with the new rules in place, this is more important than ever.

As mentioned in chapter 1, it is imperative that goaltenders keep their skates sharp enough to be able to perform butterfly-style saves and recovery techniques as well as movements along the ice. The inside edge of the blade needs to be sharp enough to stop their slides and possibly to quickly head in another direction to make a rebound save without having to get back up into the standing position. It is a goalie's preference as to how sharp his blades need to be (see chapter 1 for more information). Skate sharpening is all part of preparedness, and every goalie needs to take care of this in order to practice and play at his maximum. It's just another part of his toolbox of skills.

SKATING TECHNIQUES FROM THE STANCE

The primary techniques a goaltender uses to move while on his feet are the T-glide, drop step, and shuffle. C-cuts and step-outs are used to give and take away gaps. The T-glide is used to cover greater areas, and the shuffle is used to make small positional adjustments. The drop step is a slight variation on a T-glide and allows the goalie to get more on the inside edge of his lead skate. Using C-cuts is what gives goalies the ability to move backward and forward in their crease, and step-outs allow goalies to quickly cover a good chunk of ice.

The Goalie's Base

To move efficiently and in control when driving from spot to spot, your feet need to be parallel to maximize power and speed. Your skates should be a little wider than shoulder-width apart in order to get a good lateral push (see figure 6.1). A base that is too wide will result in a decrease in explosiveness, as not enough body weight will be loaded on the drive skate.

Most goalies have a dominant leg and are usually quicker pushing to their glove side. To equalize the strength in your legs, you need to constantly work on both legs on the ice and in the gym (see chapter 2 on strength training). Whether you are doing a T-glide, the goalie variation of the T-glide (called a drop step), or the shuffle, your stick remains centered to cover the five

Figure 6.1 The goalie base.

hole. When pushing to your catching-glove side, your stick often leaves its five-hole position or trails the play. When moving to the blocker side, sometimes the stick can drag or get locked by being tight and to the side of the blocker. It is important to work on leading your movement with the stick but through the middle of your stance covering your five hole.

 ## T-Glide

The T-glide is used to cover a lot of distance quickly (e.g., after a cross-ice pass), and the shuffle is used to follow an opposing shooter (e.g., in tight situations with the puck or when tracking the shooter). A generalization is that you should use a T-glide or drop step when there is a pass. When the shooter carries the puck, the shuffle technique is most effective.

To execute a T-glide, begin with a strong stance (see figure 6.2a). First, you need to turn your lead-skate toe out in the direction you are going and bring the heel back in toward the body. Your drive skate and lead skate form a T. Make sure that your shoulders, gloves, and stick stay square to your target, and do not rotate with the hips because your hips will not be square in this movement. Your drive skate makes a good hard push in that direction (see figure 6.2b). One thing to think about while trying to stay square is to imagine a string from the logo on your jersey to the puck when moving laterally. The biggest part of your body and equipment needs to be square to the puck before it is shot. It is essential that you stop to T-glide before the shot is released so that your feet are set.

Figure 6.2 The T-glide *(a-b)*.

Drop Step

The drop step is very similar to the T-glide and for the most part has replaced the T-glide in most instances. The only significant difference is that when a goalie drop steps, the lead skate is a little farther back than in a T-glide. This allows

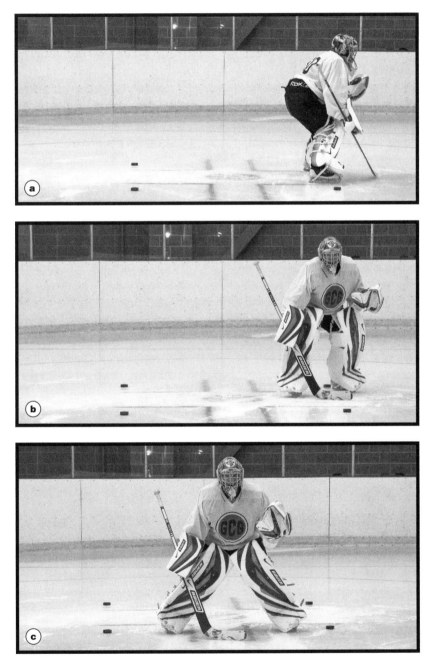

Figure 6.3   The drop step *(a-c)*.

the goaltender to get on his inside edge and move toward his target from the center. The execution is the same as for the T-glide except for the initial placement of the lead skate. From a strong stance (see figure 6.3*a*), use a C-cut (see page 138 for information on how to perform a C-cut) to move your lead skate in and back of the drive skate. The drive skate provides the momentum, and the lead skate will open and close in a narrow C-cut (see figure 6.3*b*). The opening of the toe allows the body to square up to the puck. Once the body is square to the puck, then the toe closes back in until the movement is stopped (see figure 6.3*c*). By adding pressure to the lead skate you can increase the depth attained.

The T-glide gets you to your spot quickly because the lead skate allows you to go in a straight line. A drop step allows you to fill the angle quicker than the T-glide. By dropping the lead skate back and getting on the inside edge in the initial stages of the movement, an arc is created. This arc allows you to fill the shooting lane quicker, and the T-glide enables you to get to your desired set point. The set point is where you want to be stopped and ready to make a save.

Shuffle Step

The shuffle is a more compact move than the T-glide and therefore used when a shorter area needs to be covered. To execute the shuffle, begin with a strong stance (see figure 6.4*a*). With both skates facing forward, use the inside edge of one of your skates to drive your stance either left or right (see figure 6.4 *b-d*). There should be no movement in the hips, chest, or hands, with the objective being staying square to the puck. Your feet will stay parallel to each other. Both feet are on a bit of an inward slant, allowing you to work your inside edges in

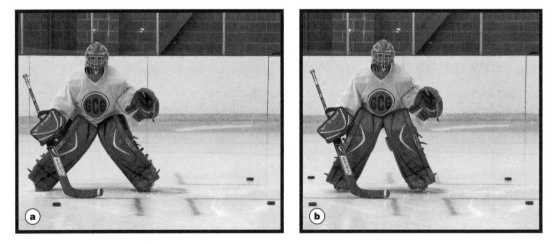

Figure 6.4 The shuffle step begins with a strong stance *(a)*. When executing the shuffle *(b-d)*, there should be no movement in the hips, chest or hands, with the objective being staying square to the puck.

order to stop, make the save if needed, and be able to make a good push in either direction for a recovery. Remember that you never break from your set stance while shuffling square to the puck. The puck is centered in the middle of your body at all times. You need to pull the pushing foot over quickly to close the width of the five hole.

In the shuffle your stick blade is covering the five hole and your hands are out front and to the sides of your pads, covering more of the net. You are always looking out at the puck so that your upper-body weight is over your knees and the balls of your feet, allowing you to keep your balance and maximize speed. If you look down at your feet your balance will tip forward, taking away from your foot speed.

Remember, your hands and legs work together to maintain balance when moving and making a save. They do not work as well or as quickly independently of each other. When shuffling, both skates remain on the ice as well. If not then your body weight will bob up and down, not allowing you to be ready to make the quick save if need be. Through this whole sequence your shoulder height should remain the same.

COACHES' TIP

Whichever skating technique you use, you should not allow your stick or glove to trail as you move. You must maintain the compactness of your stance within your movement in order to keep seams closed and maintain balance. This is why the blocker must not be locked on the side of the pad, as the pad movement will then dictate the path of the blocker and therefore the location of the stick blade.

Figure 6.4 *(continued).*

C-Cut

Backward and forward movements are the result of a technique called the C-cut. To move forward from your stance, propel yourself by putting pressure on the heel of one of your feet while it is angled slightly to the outside. Then push your foot through the path of an arc and then transfer your weight to the other foot at the same time. The skating motion should not affect the quality of the stance. The stick should remain on the ice; the hips, shoulders, and chest should face constantly forward; and the head should remain high, facing the puck. The only significant body movement you should see is in the feet and pads. If the rest of the body is bobbing up and down, there is something wrong. Recently the step-out has taken precedence over the forward C-cut, but there are still situations when it is applicable.

A similar motion to the forward C-cut is created when you move back toward the net. The only difference here is that you transfer your weight to the ball of the designated pushing foot to begin the C-cut or arc. This technique is used when skating backward, or recoiling, when the shooter approaches. Tight C-cuts keep the five hole closed as much as possible as you try to match the shooter's speed.

Step-Out

Goaltenders use step-outs to close the gap between themselves and the shooter as quickly as possible. To execute a step-out, you must start with a strong stance (see figure 6.5a). If you are moving straight ahead, turn your glove-side toe out. Your blocker-side skate should be facing forward. Drive yourself forward off the inside edge of your drive skate (see figure 6.5b). Stop your momentum by placing slightly more weight on your blocker-side skate, and square up (see figure 6.5c). If you are stepping out to either side, then your weak-side skate should be your drive skate and your lead skate becomes the set skate.

Figure 6.5 The step-out *(a-c)*.

SKATING TECHNIQUES WHILE IN THE BUTTERFLY

Although butterfly slides and pushes are covered in the saves chapter (chapter 5), it is essential to review the fundamentals of both as they apply to movement. The slide and push can be broken into steps to better work on the execution. Slides and pushes should be practiced at every training session as they are now as important as performing skating techniques from the stance. It is important when performing these techniques that your hands and stick have no movement and maintain proper form. Here are the steps to follow.

Butterfly Slide

The easiest way to describe the butterfly slide is putting the butterfly in motion. When moving from an upright position to a butterfly and moving to the left or right, the butterfly slide is implemented. There are four steps in performing this technique.

Step 1. Start with a strong stance (see figure 6.6*a*). Keep the inside of the lead pad flush to the ice as you drive the weak-side pad in the direction of the lead pad.

Step 2. Once propelled in the direction of the desired coverage, tuck the drive leg in tight to close the five hole and form the butterfly (see figure 6.6 *b-c*).

Step 3. After the slide, stop your momentum by planting the skate of the lead pad, toe forward (see figure 6.6*d*).

Step 4. Once the momentum of the slide is stopped, then the recovery to the skates is complete when the drive leg returns to an upright position (see figure 6.6*e*).

Please note that there is no momentum build in these steps. A momentum build is implemented when initiating a butterfly slide as a blocking technique as opposed to a save, where there is little time for a momentum build. A momentum build starts the goalie in a backward motion before executing a slide. The butterfly slide is very important when covering lateral or backdoor plays. The slide allows you to cover the lower part of the net quickly, therefore making the attacking forward put the puck upstairs to score. By putting the butterfly in motion, you are able to block a large portion of the lower and middle part of the net in one fluid movement that also maintains efficiency and control. Butterfly slides help a goalie center shift on shots as well as move the butterfly in a blocking position on backdoor plays and pass-outs. The butterfly slide is also the optimal way to stop a deke.

Figure 6.6 The butterfly slide *(a-e)*.

Butterfly Push

When you are down in the butterfly after making a save, rebound control is not always what you would like it to be. If you were not able to smother the puck, you will need to be ready to move in another direction. As always you must watch the puck come into your body and then watch in what direction the puck goes off your body. If you do not have time to get back up on your feet, then you need to follow the following steps.

Step 1. From the butterfly (see figure 6.7a), lift your weak-side leg and plant your skate at the necessary angle for maximum power (see figure 6.7b). This may require a rotation.

Step 2. Explode off the inside skate of your drive leg and then tuck it tight to close the five hole and form the butterfly (see figure 6.7c). Make sure your lead leg remains flush to the ice and flared.

Step 3. After the butterfly, stop your momentum by planting the skate of the lead pad.

Step 4. Once the momentum of the slide is stopped, then the recovery to the skates is complete when the drive leg returns to an upright position.

Should the rebound glance off into a backdoor angle situation, then you must rotate your body and push toward the outside post of the net. It is essential that you square your body to the puck before you push. If you do not get square early in the push, your body will rotate out of position in relation to the puck, and therefore the rebound on the second shot could deflect into the net, out to the slot, and proper recovery may be made problematic. It is much harder to get square to the puck when in motion than from a stationary position. Your body always seems to overrotate, even in the standing position. This whole sequence is made much easier if you are ready for the play early and have read it properly.

Figure 6.7 The butterfly push *(a-c)*.

Getting Square During the Push

Getting square begins with your eyes finding the puck, then a full shoulder turn, followed by your hands and stick. It is virtually the same as long as your eyes, upper body, and hands and stick are all squared up in the same direction and at the same time. The only thing you need to do then is clear your hips and push in the direction of the puck or angle needed. To do this, you simply rotate the inside edge of the pushing foot in the same direction as the upper part of your body. If you do not do this, then your push will take you out from the puck rather than to the puck. Once again, being a good skater with excellent balance and sharp inside edges is necessary to perform this move correctly.

COACHES' TIP The butterfly push is a great technique for in-tight rebounds. You must use your goalie sense when deciding to stay down or get back to your feet. This will depend on the proximity of the puck and the amount of time available.

 ### Momentum Changes

Momentum changes are used when a goaltender has to stop moving in one direction and then go in the opposite direction. This is also referred to as transitions for goalies. With today's emphasis on opening up the offensive end of the game and progressive butterfly techniques goalies are using more momentum changes than ever and the transition abilities of goaltenders are a big part of having success between the pipes. A momentum change can occur while in the upright stance or while sliding and/or pushing. A momentum change while standing would take place when you are following the play with a shuffle or drop step and then have to go back against the grain as the puck moves in the opposite direction. A momentum change while in the butterfly can occur when a goalie slides to one side and then must recover quickly to the opposite side. You can either recover to your feet following the slide or stay in the butterfly and implement a butterfly push. Staying down or recovering to an upright stance will depend on the amount of time you have to reposition yourself. Another possible scenario would be a butterfly push in one direction followed by a second butterfly push in the opposite direction. You can also change your momentum from a push with a recovery to your feet in either a drop step or a shuffle as well.

Regardless of whether you are on your feet or down in the butterfly there are two key ingredients to momentum changes. The first is when you decide to change directions, it is important to use a hard stop with the inside edge of your plant skate as well as have the plant skate positioned tightly and at a 90 degree angle to the direction you want to head. The second key is to maintain control of your upper body. If on the momentum change planting of the inside edge there is excess movement of the arms it will cause a lack of efficiency and therefore a trailing of the stick and/or glove as well as secondary balance adjustments. When performing a momentum change you cannot allow your glove and/or blocker to come into the midline (armpit to armpit) of the stance. Figure 6.8 *a-g* illustrates how to perform a momentum change using a drop step. Figure 6.9 *a-g* illustrates the technique using a push.

Momentum Continuations

Momentum continuation is when a goaltender continues along the same path while tracking a puck. This terminology is most commonly used when a goaltender initiates a butterfly slide and/ or push and then continues his momentum with a butterfly push. A common example would be a butterfly slide while tracking the puck on a pass out followed by a butterfly push toward the opposite post. Momentum continuation can also be used for continuous butterfly pushes. As with momentum changes, the key points to remember are to get solid plants with good angles as well as maintain control of your upper body.

Figure 6.8 Butterfly momentum change using a butterfly push with a drop step recovery *(a-g)*.

Figure 6.9 Butterfly momentum change using a butterfly and a butterfly push recovery *(a-g)*.

Reverse Rotations

The reverse rotation is used from the butterfly (see figure 6.10a) when the momentum of your body dictates how to follow the puck. A great example of when to utilize a reverse rotation is when you are in a butterfly, off angle, and the shot misses the net and continues off the boards or glass to the opposite corner. In this case you would continue watching the puck while rotating with your inside skate and pad. Normally you would rotate with the outside skate to move through the middle of the net, but since your momentum is already moving to the outside, you simply continue the recovery. Using the inside edge of your plant skate, begin your recovery to your feet while at the same time driving to your destination point in order to finish square to the puck (see figure 6.10b). When you get to your spot, stop your recovery and then set using the same skate that initiated the recovery (see figure 6.10c). This is one of the few times that your drive skate is the same as your set skate.

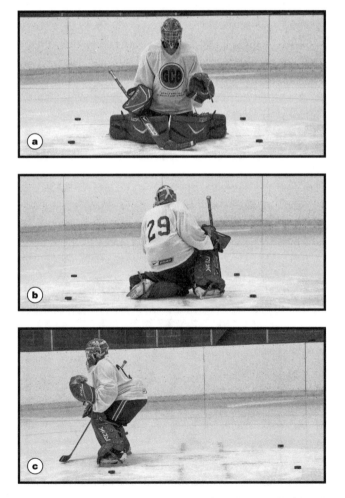

Figure 6.10 The reverse rotation is used from the butterfly *(a)* and simply follows your momentum to the outside *(b-c).*

CAM WARD

In the past it was easy to tell who the best goalies were. They were the ones making the acrobatic saves demonstrating their athleticism and skills. Today's goaltenders are judged by their ability to position themselves so that acrobatic saves are not necessary and to make saves look easy through body control and proper mechanics. Cam Ward of the Carolina Hurricanes is a great example of a goaltender who can play at a high level and make it look easy. Any coach today will tell you that he doesn't want a goaltender who flops around diving for pucks. When watching Cam Ward make a save, notice how efficient he is and how little movement goes into stopping the puck. This is a skill that is learned through training and repetition.

Cam Ward took the goalie world by storm when he led the Carolina Hurricanes to the NHL's promised land, winning the Stanley Cup in 2006. A member of the AHL all-rookie team the season before, Ward has won his fair share of awards, such as WHL goaltender of the year in 2002 and 2004 as well as WHL player of the year in 2004. One interesting note is that Cam Ward was actually a player in youth hockey and converted to full-time goalie at the age of only 12.

© John Russell/NHLI via Getty Images

SQUARING ON ANGLE AND RANGE OF DEPTH

To cover as much net as possible, goalies need to be square to the puck at all times. You want the largest part of your body facing the puck and centered in the net. Getting into position early allows you to square up to the puck, often before the shooter is ready to execute. Once you are square, then the next task is gaining proper depth. Proper depth is achieved when you are blocking as much of the net as possible without leaving yourself too far away from the net if there is a rebound. Working to be square at the right depth takes place long before the shot is taken on the net. Being at the right place at the right time is the final product. For more consistent rebound control, being square to the puck is essential so you can read how the puck consistently comes off the body. That includes the stick as well.

We just detailed skating technique, and here is where we put it into action. The first thing is understanding the shooter illusion, what it means to be square, and adjusting your range of depth. The use of reference points will also be a big help in being on angle.

The Shooter Illusion

You need to set your angle on the puck rather than on the shooter's body because the puck is what will do the damage (see figure 6.11 *a-b*). A shooter's head is either off to the right or left of the puck, so his vision will show more net to that side. If he is a left-handed shooter, then he will see more net off to the right of the goalie and may shoot there. If he is a right-handed shooter, then he will see more net to his left. If you center on the puck, then it does not matter whether the shooter is a left-handed shot or a right-handed shot. Look at a shooter and you will see that the puck is at least 2 feet (0.5 meter) away from his feet, which line up with his head, so he is well away from the puck, as is his vision in relation to the angle. The most common mistake that young goalies make is lining up—getting square—to the shooter instead of the puck. It is because of this that the goalie will get off angle and give up goals that he has the skill to stop.

Figure 6.11 The shooter illusion. Get square to the puck *(a)* not the shooter *(b)* to stay on angle and give up fewer goals.

Starting Point

The starting point is where a goalie positions himself before the play approaches. You should be positioned in the middle of your crease and close to the goal line (see figure 6.12a). The middle of your back should be lined up perfectly with the T-bar of the net. When the play comes through the neutral zone, use a step-out to establish initial depth (see figure 6.12b), which is generally at the top of the crease or 2 to 3 feet (0.5 to 1.0 meter) above the crease depending on the situation (see figure 6.12c). After you establish initial depth, use the previously detailed skating drills to track the puck and stay square. Please note that when the puck moves left or right on the other side of center ice, you should remain at the same spot. Resist the temptation to move side to side. The benefit of using a designated spot as a starting point is that when the play does come your way, only a minimal adjustment is necessary to get on your angle. Since you are already in the middle of the crease, it should be easy to be on the proper angle.

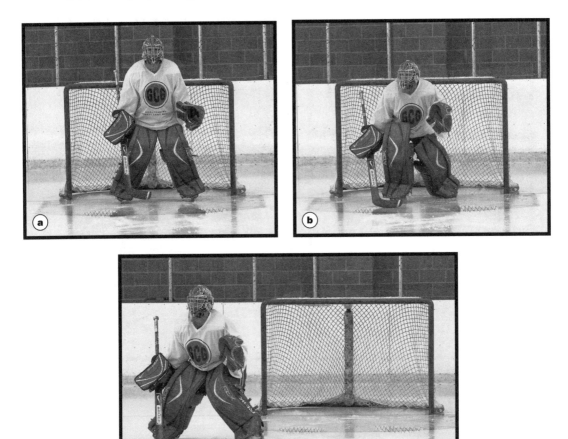

Figure 6.12 The starting point is where a goalie positions himself before the play approaches. Move from the middle of your crease close to the goal line (a) using a step-out (b) to establish initial depth at the top of the crease (c).

Squaring Up

When square to the puck, a goalie's shoulders and hips are directly facing the puck. If you were to draw a triangle from the puck to the right shoulder, to the left shoulder, and then back to the puck, the sides would be identical. Drawing a straight line from the puck to the middle T-bar of the net should end up cutting right through the center logo on your jersey. If these lines are where they are supposed to be, then you are squared up.

Getting ready early allows you to square up to the shooter as he crosses the red line, and then you merely have to follow the puck, either with a shuffle or T-glide. Stepping out from the crease allows you to establish strong positional depth. The movement of the opposition and puck determines which skating skill you will use. As the shooter approaches the net, you will perform backward C-cuts, a shuffle if he carries the puck east–west, and a drop step on a pass. No matter which technique you are using, the key is to picture that perfect triangle, with the puck and the line that goes right through your jersey's logo.

Reading the play is very important, and you want to be "ready early, ready longer." This means that the earlier you get square to the puck, the longer you will be square and therefore in good position. Again, you should square up as the puck crosses the red line and stay ready until the puck leaves your zone or the grade-A scoring zone. You should never put yourself in a position to be surprised by a play.

Using Reference Points

As a goalie you have the luxury of using points of reference to help set the proper angles when the puck is far away from the net or when there is a flurry of scoring opportunities and you find yourself far away from the goal crease. Sometimes when committing to leaving the net, you can lose your bearings. This is a scary time for a goalie because you need to scamper back quickly while facing the play.

Start again, in the middle of the net, close to the goal line, and look out at all the visual aids at your disposal. These aids include both face-off circles in your end (the dots), both blue lines where the paint goes up the boards, the face-off circles outside the blue lines, the center-ice face-off circle, your own hash marks in your end (middle of or left and right of the middle of the hash marks), and the opposing net. Any visual aid lined up with the middle of your net can be used as a point of reference—whatever works for you. Remember though, that a reference point is to be used in relation to the puck, the middle of your body, and the T-bar in the middle of your net.

To practice this concept, simply start in the middle of the net, square up to the point of reference, and move out on your angle in the set or ready position. To aid you in this, you may want to use cones or pucks located at the reference points. When struggling in a game or practice with your angles, it is always good to go back to these basics. Do this while moving out and receding or recoiling back to the net, facing the point of reference at all times. You may make this part of your pregame warm-up drill.

> **COACHES' TIP** The key to great angle and reference point play is being ready early. This cannot be stressed enough. Be in position with your feet set before the shooter takes the shot. It makes for better awareness, more first-save capabilities, and easier rebound control.

Angles and Depth

Every goalie's angles should begin from the middle of the net. If you look at the net, the crossbar is joined in the middle by a shorter piece of steel running to the middle back of the net, giving the net its strength and forming a T. Simply put, you should square up to the puck from the T-bar with your belly button (middle of your body) to the puck. You always set up to the puck and the puck only. You then move out into the shot lane square to the puck from this position.

A good way to teach goalies about angles is with the use of a rope. Drill a hole through the middle of a puck, slip a 50-foot (15 meter) rope through the hole, and tie the ends to each post, creating a V out to the hash marks. From the middle of the net at the T-bar, move out to the end of the V in a set position. If you are square, you should see equal space between you and the rope on either side. By moving forward and backward, you can see the effect that gap has on the amount of net covered (see figure 6.13 *a-b*). The perfect triangle is now very apparent.

Figure 6.13 Shallow depth *(a)* exposes a lot of the net. Strong positioning *(b)* takes away more of the net.

Next you should move from the T-bar out to the top of the crease in a squared position using a step-out or C-cuts. Have a teammate slide the puck to your right, creating a very tight V. Shuffle along the arc of the crease, keeping the puck centered on the middle of your body and the middle of the net, holding the same angle until you reach the goal line. You will notice one side of the rope gets shorter while the other gets longer. This is where the terms *short side* and *far side* originate. The farther from the middle of the ice the rope gets, the tighter the sides will squeeze in on your shoulders. This is where you really get an advantage on the shooter.

Movement Along the Arc

When tracking a player with shuffles, you should always move along the plane of an arc. By moving along an arc you remain square to the shooter as he moves from side to side. If you move sideways, you will eventually not be square to the shooter and be at a severe disadvantage to make the save or control the rebound. The arc of the crease is a great guide for goalies. Whether you are at the top of the arc, higher, or deeper, you should shuffle along an imaginary arc. Always being square gives you a chance to stop the puck regardless of your depth.

Gap Control

Proper depth, otherwise known as gap control, is critical on odd-man rushes, backdoor plays, screen shots, deflections, and a number of other situations that occur during a game. Depth, or gap, can describe either the distance between the goalie and the shooter or the goalie and the posts behind him. You must be able to adjust this gap based on the speed of the attack and the location of the opposing players. You must also be able to regain your gap or depth when the play moves from a down-low area to up top in the zone.

Gap is initially established as the play approaches. You step out of your crease to establish position. That position is generally at the top of your crease or 2 to 3 feet (0.5 to 1.0 meter) outside the crease. Depth is determined by how you read the play. In the case of a breakaway, you will come out aggressively in order to have room to build momentum with backward C-cuts to combat the deke. If there is a backdoor option, you will not be as aggressive so as not to get caught too far out of the net. Ideally, you would like to make the save at the top of your crease.

After the save is made, you will need to use recovery techniques to respond to the puck. The farther you are out of your net, the less chance you will have of stopping a rebound. The range of using efficient recovery techniques is at the top of the paint, and any farther depth than that may require desperation saves. A rule of thumb is that a smaller goaltender will have a greater range of depth because a bigger goalie does not have to come out as far to cover as much net.

Backdoor Plays

When talking about depth and gap control, it is not always in relation to the shooter. Sometimes it is in relation to the backdoor players or in relation to the posts and net behind you. When the shooter has a backdoor option, you cannot challenge as aggressively. By being too far out in this situation, you leave yourself vulnerable for the backdoor goal. Also, when making a save, like in billiards, it is often what you leave your opponents that causes you the most trouble. If you have a man positioned on the backdoor and you are too aggressive, then the effectiveness of your postsave recovery techniques will be limited.

Short Side

Many coaches consider short-side goals bad goals. From here the shooter should see only the five hole as a possible scoring option. If a shooter scores on the short side, the goalie usually has made a mistake. This typically happens when the goalie gives the shooter too much room between his body and the post; drops in the butterfly save position too soon, exposing the top of the net; or is not aggressive enough on the shot. A goalie needs to practice short-side patience. You really only need to have the proper angle on the puck, and the player should simply have no place to shoot.

A good strategy is to stay up as long as possible, forcing the shooter to make a mistake. A goalie who drops too soon on the shot exposes both sides of the top of the net. Why give back to the shooter what you have already taken away with the perfect angle? An early butterfly drop does that. The idea is to force the shooter to shoot to the far side of the net, giving you a longer time to react to make the save. The shooter may also miss the net because he is shooting at a smaller target. Often when missing the net on the far side, the puck will clear the zone, making an easy transition for the defensive team. Another tactic, called loading, is used on attackers down low with a bad angle. Loading can be used during off angle down-low attacks and walkouts.

When you are squaring up to the shooter on a side angle, stop your step-out using your outside leg but also square to the shooter. This puts a little weight on the outside leg so that if the puck moves toward the middle of the net, you have the ability to push quickly from the set or save position. This will save you the extra move later of having to plant your outside foot in order to move in a reverse direction. Should there be a rebound, it will hopefully be directed into the corner away from the net.

Up the Middle

Let's say you need to drive straight out at the puck while holding the proper angle, whether it be for a shot or breakaway up the middle. To do this, you must get your drive leg, preferably the glove side while moving forward, in a parallel position to the puck and push straight out while remaining square to the shooter. If you make a push more off to the side than out, you may push yourself off angle, exposing more net to one side than the other for the shooter. If the situation is a breakaway and you must recede back toward the net, you need to move in straight lines while maintaining the angle on the puck. Being ready early lets you set your angle without panic. There are no surprises, and you learn sound angle and positional play.

Playing the Angles to Your Advantage: Knowing the Percentages

For a veteran goalie or one who knows the shooters around his league, cheating on angles can work to your advantage. You can play off the strong points of a shooter's game while trying to fool him to go for a certain spot of the net, perhaps glove side. In leading the shooter, you purposely position yourself off angle to bait him to shoot for the open area, and then you take it away at the last second. We do not recommend this tactic for all goalies, however.

Remember too, when the face-off is in your end, check to see which hand the opposing center shoots from. If he is taking the draw on his backhand, you might play the recipient of the pass off the draw. You should also communicate with your center to find out what his intentions are when taking the face-off. You do not want to expose the net in case he wins the draw back in that direction. It could prove most embarrassing if the puck goes in the net because you cheated on the play.

Does Size Matter?

You always want to make yourself look as big as possible in the net. There is an advantage to being bigger in today's game as long as you also have the skating and foot-speed skills necessary to keep up with the play. If you are a smaller goalie, you obviously need to be more aggressive on the puck and be more mobile. Being an exceptional skater is critical. All goalies need to share most of the same skills, but in some cases angles and depth are more critical for a smaller goalie.

Unfortunately, smaller goalies are at greater risk when it comes to depth and gap control and sensing the danger behind them. A smaller goaltender needs to challenge the shooter more on his angles to cover the same amount of net as a bigger goalie, therefore making covering the backdoor play more difficult. A smaller goalie has to work harder to make the same save as a bigger goalie. Again, smaller goalies must be great skaters to allow them to recover back to the posts or make a backdoor save off a pass or rebound. Goalies of all sizes can have success at every professional level, including the National Hockey League.

Each goalie must use his natural attributes to his advantage and work hard to achieve the skills that will make up for his natural or physical shortcomings, no matter what they may be. Obviously a bigger goalie does not have to leave the net as far on his angle to cover the same amount of net as a smaller goalie, but he still needs to realize his strengths or weaknesses for recovery. His size, though being a natural asset, does not allow him the luxury of being a poor skater. He still needs to be aware of the dangers around and behind him.

International Competition and Playing the Angles

Because of international competitions held in European ice rinks, it is more important than ever for goaltenders and their coaches to pay special attention to depth and gap control because of the larger playing surface. There is a huge adjustment factor here, not just for angles but also for the proper time for the goalie to square up on the short side and head toward the post rather than out to the shooter out of the square position. With European ice surfaces larger than their North American counterparts, a goaltender has to be more patient in staying on his feet because there are bigger passing lanes and therefore more options for the shooter. If you leave your feet early to go into a butterfly, you may end up being beaten by a backdoor play. You must wait out the shooter in this scenario. Also, because of the wider rink, we often see short-side goals at the beginning of international competition until a goalie can make the adjustment to his angles. This is when you can use reference points to help figure out your angles.

chapter 7

POSTSAVE RECOVERY PLUS BLOCKING, TRACKING, AND REACTING

Brian Daccord

In the previous two chapters you read the word *recovery* several times. Postsave recovery is the action or actions that a goalie takes to prepare himself for a second shot or a flurry of shots. As progressive techniques have changed the way goaltenders now stop the puck, new techniques and strategies have also had a profound effect on postsave recovery. This chapter looks at postsave recovery from a stance, or upright position, and from a butterfly, or down-low position. In addition to postsave recovery, momentum changes, otherwise know as goalie transitions, are also analyzed.

After the postsave recovery segment of this chapter is complete, you should have a solid grasp of save techniques, skating techniques to get you in position to make the save, getting square to the puck, and recovery techniques to use after the save. With this in place, tracking and reacting to pucks is the next step to build on your progression. The distinction between saving a puck and blocking a puck is detailed to help you maximize your net coverage and probability of making the save.

POSTSAVE RECOVERY

Although most saves are now made from a down-low position, the foundation of a goaltender will always be his stance. The better the coverage, balance, and mobility in the stance, the better that goaltender will be able to play. Whether a goaltender makes a save from his stance or the butterfly, the following are the key elements of postsave recovery.

• Tracking the puck with your eyes. Your eyes and your ability to track the puck will have the greatest influence on your ability to make the initial and second save. When scouting goaltenders, scouts always pay close attention to their ability to maintain visual contact with the puck at all times. If this is a weakness, it will be tough for that goaltender to be successful as it becomes increasingly more difficult to track the puck as a goalie moves up levels. The eyes and head are the first part of starting a chain of events in which the goaltender will move to get prepared for the second shot.

• Deciding how to play the situation. With a visual of where the puck is, or where it is heading, and the awareness of where the offensive and defensive players are, you must choose how to move. The first decision is whether to stay on your feet, go down, or stay down in a rebound situation. The general rule of thumb is if the puck is in close proximity, and you are now facing a quick shot, you should be down on the release of the shot, utilizing strong blocking techniques. If the puck moves away from the net, it should allow you the luxury of being on your feet. Having the patience to stay on your feet is an important attribute for a goaltender. Following are a number of situations that require holding your feet—in other words, staying up on your skates after a save. These situations range from no adjustment to adjustments of angle and depth.

MARC-ANDRE FLEURY

It isn't very often that a player will beat an NHL goaltender with the first shot. It is the second or third opportunity that nets the goal. This is why the best goaltenders are the ones who can stay in control after the first shot and put themselves in position to make the save off the rebound. A great example of a goalie who has tremendous postsave capabilities is Marc-Andre Fleury of the Pittsburgh Penguins. Fleury's ability to move while on the ice is second to none, and he possesses the skills to make a flurry of saves . . . no pun intended. One reason for his success is his quickness in performing butterfly pushes as well as filling up the lower part of the net with a flush lead pad. His outstanding performance in the 2008 Stanley Cup finals demonstrated that all the hype about his ability while in junior was right on the money.

Marc-Andre Fleury was the first player selected overall in the 2003 entry draft. High expectations were placed on the young goalie when he was drafted, and he spent time between the Penguins, his QMJHL team in Cape Breton, and Wilkes-Barre in the AHL. It wasn't until the 2006-2007 season that Fleury settled in and fans saw the bright future ahead of him. His 40 victories in 2006-2007 are the second-highest win total in Penguins history. With a young and talented team and a potential superstar in net, the Pens are going to be a force in the NHL for years to come.

© Icon SMI

Holding Tight

When the rebound ends up in a position that lets you stay square to the puck, and you already have good gap and a good chance to react to the release of the shot, you should hold tight. Simply hold your position so the rebound does not catch you moving and your feet are set.

Taking Gap

If you are square to the puck and have a second to take some gap (close the distance between yourself and the shooter), you can most effectively do so with a quick step-out. Stepping out allows you to take the most gap possible and allows you to get your feet set for the shot. When stepping out straight forward, point your glove-side skate at a 90-degree angle and your blocker skate straight ahead. Power forward by driving off the inside edge of the glove-side skate and stopping with more weight on the blocker-side skate while setting in your stance. When stepping out, it is important to keep your stick centered.

Shuffling Into Position

If the puck moves to the left or right, you will need to shift your body to get square for the anticipated shot. You can use either a shuffle or a drop step. In either case, before you move, it is essential that your drive skate, the skate opposite the side you are moving toward, be at the proper angle to move you where you want to go. If the angle of the drive skate is not perfect, then adjust the angle before the move.

As described in chapter 6, a shuffle should be used for short-range lateral adjustments that do not require adjustment in depth. Therefore, if the puck requires an adjustment of 12 inches (30 centimeters) and there is a probability of a shot as soon as you arrive at your destination point, the shuffle is the correct call. A shuffle maintains the compactness of your stance, and you maintain a good position to react to the shot. The shuffle is limited, however, when there is a lot of real estate to cover, such as going cross-crease. Another limitation is the lack of ability to gap out after you arrive. If you wish to gap out after a shuffle, you will require an additional move. Therefore if you wish to make a lateral move that requires an adjustment of depth, then the correct skating technique is the drop step.

Drop Step for Maximum Lateral Coverage

When you are moving side to side, the drop step allows you to maintain a strong stance, take away gap, and also cover a larger area. The drop step is very similar to a T-glide, with the difference being the lead skate is at a 90-degree angle off the heel of the drive skate (see page 135 for a full explanation of how to perform the drop step). This allows you to drive east–west but maintain your weight on the inside edge of your lead skate (see figure 7.1 *a-c*). Using the

Figure 7.1 When moving east to west, the drop step (a-c) allows a goalie to maintain a strong stance, take away gap, and also cover a larger area.

drop step allows you to C-cut your lead skate and adjust your depth once you are square to the shooter. The drop step also allows you to move through the center of your net, thus taking away angle, getting square, and then moving forward. You will stop the movement with the lead leg, also known as the set leg, depending on how much lateral area you wish to cover and then how much gap you wish to close.

Tips for the Hips, Shoulders, and Hands

When you are preparing for a second shot, the hips and the shoulders must work together in a shuffle and apart in a drop step. In a shuffle the shoulders line up with the puck at the exact same angle as the hips. In the drop step the shoulders need to stay square to the puck, but the hips will have a greater rotation. If you allow your shoulders to stay with your hips as the hips rotate in the drop step, you will lose efficiency as well as require a greater balance adjustment when arriving at your destination point. You must practice making this movement without throwing your shoulders into it.

Your hands play a significant role in your ability to stay square in both your shuffle and drop step. When goalies move laterally, they have a habit of trailing with their hands. For example, if a goalie moves from his glove to blocker side, the tendency is to throw the glove away from the body, and the blocker will come toward his midline. With the glove moving away, as opposed to with the movement, it will hold the hips back from moving to a square position. The blocker will have a tendency to move toward the same side and add to the strain on the hips. Also, with the blocker trailing on the play, the stick will now trail the opening of the five hole. What this all leads to is a bad angle, open shooting lanes through the body, and then a significant adjustment when arriving at the destination point. This adjustment will affect the goalie's balance—taking up valuable fractions of a second as he readjusts—as well as open up seams the puck can penetrate.

The same is true for a goalie moving to his glove side. The blocker will trail, therefore fighting against the rotation of the hips as well as leaving the five hole unprotected by the stick. The glove will come across the goalie's midline toward the blocker side, making it difficult to square the hips as well as minimizing coverage on the glove side. You must work hard on your mechanics so you move with efficiency. The stronger a goalie gets through core stability training, the more efficient these movements will become.

Moving to a Load

Sometimes a goalie is in a spot where he does not need to move laterally or leave his feet while at the same time would like to maximize his blocking coverage. This usually occurs when the rebound is off angle and in close proximity to the goaltender. In this situation, you can use a load, which involves keeping your strong-side pad upright but flaring the weak-side leg. This position allows you to stay big and take away the short side but also be ready to push to the weak side as well. For more information on loading, see chapter 10.

POSTSAVE BUTTERFLY

The butterfly is utilized after a save from an upright position when the puck is directly in front of the goaltender and the shot is imminent (see figure 7.2a). Also, in this scenario, the shooter does not have the time or space to move laterally. Utilizing the butterfly in this situation allows you to take away the lower and middle part of the net with a strong blocking technique (see figure 7.2b). The timing of the butterfly drop is usually the key to its effectiveness. You should drop on the release of the shot if it is too close to read and react to. Also, a step-out in order to gain depth can be used to maximize butterfly blocking coverage, time permitting.

Figure 7.2 A tight butterfly slide *(a-b)* is paramount for postsave protection.

Postsave Butterfly Slide

A butterfly slide is used as a postsave recovery when a goalie needs to move laterally and take away the bottom of the net quickly and in control (see figure 7.3*a*). The rule of thumb is you should stay on your feet, time permitting, but in this situation you will utilize the butterfly slide as a block. To start the slide, the drive skate must be at the proper angle (see figure 7.3*b*). The proper angle of the lead skate is dictated by the angle you want your slide to be. As you drive off the weak-side skate, the lead pad becomes flush with the ice and the drive leg tucks in to form the butterfly (see figure 7.3*c*). Perfect timing is when you arrive at your destination point in the perfect butterfly just as the shot is being released and you are perfectly square to the puck.

Figure 7.3 Postsave butterfly slide *(a-c)*.

From a Butterfly Position

Once you have gone down to make the save, there are a number of postsave responses you can make. Your response will be dictated by where the puck is and the chance of receiving a shot. You will need to decide whether to regain your feet or stay on the ice. Whether you stay down or get up, there are many techniques you will employ. Here are a number of situations you will be faced with along with the correct postsave response.

Staying Down

If the puck ends up directly in front of you with an impending shot, there will be no time to get up. Maintaining a strong butterfly with no seams under the arms will help you block as much space as possible. Having your glove and blocker out and building blocking height off your pads will allow you to cover the lower portion of the net with your pads and the upper portion of the net with your torso, arms, and hands. If the puck is very close, feel free to be active with your stick in order to poke the puck away or to pull it in and cover it.

Staying Down and Gapping Out

If the puck is close, directly in front of you, but you have a fraction of a second to take some gap away, then use a butterfly push. While maintaining your butterfly, plant your glove-side skate at a 90-degree angle and propel your body forward. This allows you to take a few more inches away from the shooter as well as maintain your down-low coverage at the same time. Using your glove-side skate to propel yourself forward is highly recommended, as using your blocker-side skate can make it more difficult to maintain contact between your stick blade and the ice. A very aggressive move in this situation, time permitting, is to use an extended poke check to knock the puck away. This play is risky because it involves stretching out on the ice to make a play and will leave you in a vulnerable position for a follow-up shot.

A good rule of thumb is to be active with your stick in tight while maintaining your knee flexion. Once you change your knee flexion, then you have diminished your positioning for stopping a second shot. Therefore, using your stick without breaking the compactness of your stance allows you to be active with your stick while at the same time being in good shape to react to a shot.

COACHES' TIP

Staying Down and Adjusting Your Angle

If the puck position forces you to move right or left, you can utilize a butterfly push (see figure 7.4*a-c*). The butterfly push allows you to stay in the butterfly and move along the ice in order to get square to the puck. To utilize a butterfly push, maintain your butterfly, and by raising your weak-side pad, use the inside edge of that skate to propel your butterfly in the appropriate direction to block as much net as possible. A rule of thumb is that you should always use the leg opposite to the direction you are going to power your push. For example, if the rebound is to your blocker side, you should initiate the push with the glove-side skate and vice versa.

Remember, using a butterfly push allows you to get square without getting up. A common mistake goalies make is to push toward the puck as opposed to choosing a path that would take away the shooting lane of the opposing player. If you are at the peak of your crease and the shot is expected to go to your blocker side from the face-off dot, the correct angle of the push should be back diagonally. To position the drive skate at the proper angle, a rotation is required to put the skate at the desired angle to push back diagonally. Conversely, if you propel yourself to the face-off dot, you are choosing to try to get maximum depth before filling up the shooting lane.

The key to the correct path of the push is in planting your drive skate at the proper angle. If the angle of the drive skate is planted properly, then you will get maximum power on your push. If the angle of the drive skate is not at the correct angle, then the path you are pushing will not be right or you will need to use a last-second C-cut with the drive skate to get on the right path. This C-cut will cause a balance shift and decrease efficiency in the movement. If you are in the butterfly and need a very small lateral shift to get square to the puck, then a knee shuffle can be used as opposed to a push. To knee shuffle, simply extend the lead knee and pull the trailing knee in to close up the butterfly.

Figure 7.4 From the butterfly *(a)*, a back diagonal butterfly push *(b-c)* is an excellent response to a tight rebound.

Blocker and Glove Extension

Sometimes during a butterfly push, a goaltender blocks the lower part of the net with his lead pad but not the upper part. To provide coverage in this situation, you can extend your strong-side glove or blocker forward and toward the puck during your push (see figure 7.5 *a* and *b*). By closing the gap with your gloves, you decrease the scoring lane that the puck must travel to enter the net.

Figure 7.5 *(a)* Glove extension and *(b)* blocker extension during a butterfly push.

COACHES' TIP When you use the butterfly push, the power will come from the inside edge of your drive skate. To maximize power, you must plant that skate under your body in order to utilize the leverage you receive from your body weight. Sharp skates are necessary.

Regaining Your Stance and Adjusting Your Angle

If the postsave recovery allows you the time to regain your feet, this is generally the preferred course of action. If the rebound is in front of you while you are in the butterfly (see figure 7.6a) and you have the time to recover, quickly get back to your feet using your glove-side leg first (see figure 7.6b). If you have time to get to your feet but not take any gap away, then your toes should be facing forward when planting your skates. By having your toes facing forward and not out to the side, you will not need a secondary movement to get your pad square to the puck and therefore not affect your balance. If you have time to take some gap when recovering to your feet, then point your glove-side skate at a 90-degree angle and drive yourself forward while regaining your stance (see figure 7.6c). Recovering and stepping out in conjunction takes two movements and synchronizes them into one.

Figure 7.6 Getting back to your feet after the save *(a-c)*.

Get up from a butterfly position while moving forward with your glove-side skate. Raising your blocker-side pad with this recovery technique may force the blocker up and therefore lift the stick off the ice.

If the puck position forces you to move right or left (see figure 7.7a) while allowing you time to regain your feet, then you should be using either a shuffle or a drop step in your postsave recovery. A good rule of thumb is if there is a short distance to cover and you only have time to fill the net and not take gap, then a shuffle should be implemented. If there is time to take gap as well as move laterally, then a drop step is the correct technique to use. It is imperative that you synchronize the recovery into a shuffle or a drop step with the actual movement of getting to your feet in order to save time (see figure 7.7 b-c). Do not wait until you get to your stance and then start moving east or west.

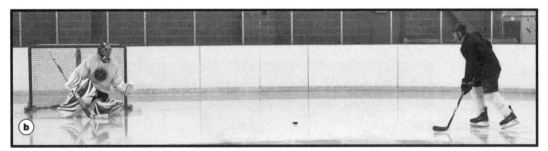

Figure 7.7 Getting back to your feet and out to a 45-degree angle (a-c).

Once again, the angle of the plant skate will determine the path you take to your destination point. You may need a rotation before your plant skate is in position. Also, the key with recovery is taking as much of the net away as quickly as possible, and therefore your path should be through the middle of the shooting lane. Take your gap from that point. When using the drop step or shuffle recovery from the butterfly, be sure to keep your stick in the five hole and your hands in their proper position. When a goalie goes in one direction, his stick and hands tend to lag behind, which does not optimize net coverage.

TRACKING, BLOCKING, AND REACTING: ANTICIPATION AND PREDICTABILITY

Since the original *Hockey Goaltending* book was published, the ratio of blocking versus reacting saves has changed dramatically and has even fluctuated lately. It is important for a goaltender to be able to recognize when to implement blocking techniques, when to have patience, and how to anticipate. Predictability is also a topic we examine, as well as how the ability to understand timing and read the play will help you stop pucks.

Tracking

Tracking the puck is the cornerstone of goaltending. If you can't see the puck, the chance of stopping it is decreased dramatically. Tracking involves simply following the puck with your eyes and body. Some goalies who do not have the best technique are the best in the game because of their ability to keep focused on the puck and stay square. Being efficient and controlled in your movement will make it easier to track the puck as well as fight through screens. Following the puck into your equipment is part of tracking, as well as keeping your eyes on the puck if there is a rebound. The goal is to always maintain focus and not lose attachment.

Without a doubt, saves all start with the eyes. Visual tracking in its own right is not a save technique, but it is still an imperative part of the save process that must not be overlooked. A goaltender must be able to watch the puck all the way into the body. This will ensure precision of the selected save, allowing you to put the puck where you want. In late 2006, a study by researchers in the University of Calgary's kinesiology department found a major difference in visual tracking between the novice goaltender and the high-performance goaltender. More so, many goaltenders have good tracking until about 12 inches (30 centimeters) from the body, and then they lose the puck.

You can tell how good a goalie is at tracking the puck by watching his mask. If his mask is always following and directly facing the puck, it's a good bet that his eyes are zeroed in. When a goalie gets surprised by a quick play, it usually means he wasn't working hard enough watching the puck. It sounds simple to do but requires the utmost in concentration and determination. There are obviously times when a goalie will lose the puck, but the great goalies find a way to reconnect with the puck quickly. When the puck is in a quiet zone and not a threat, a goalie must be able to take his eyes off the puck and survey where the danger is in the zone. When returning focus on the puck a fraction of a second later, his ability to once again lock in on the puck is critical.

Visual tracking can be improved in many ways. One of the best is the long-standing practice of eye–hand coordination. Eye–hand coordination drills can be done simply with tennis balls. You can bounce balls off a wall, simulating an approaching puck, or can use reaction balls that provide unpredictable bounces off the rebounding surface. This requires you to be quick and to have acute visual tracking. Whether you use tennis balls or reaction balls, it is a must to watch the ball all the way into the hand. Numerous drills are available in chapter 4 to help develop tracking skills.

On the ice it is simple to enhance visual tracking. One of the best ways is to overexaggerate watching the puck into the body. By doing so, not just the eyes but also the head will turn and follow the puck. This action makes a goaltender more conscious of watching the puck and improves visual tracking very quickly.

Blocking

Blocking is when a goaltender positions his body, generally in a butterfly, load, or paddle down position, to block as much net as possible. A goaltender uses his size, equipment, and depth to block the potential shooting lanes into the net. A block is usually implemented when a goalie thinks he will not have sufficient time to react to a shot, which usually translates into close-range situations or screens. A goaltender can also react from a blocking position.

Because of tremendous strides in equipment protection and functionality, a goalie can play the percentages (i.e., if he is in the proper position, the shooter is going to have to make a great shot to beat him). Blocking generally starts with taking the lower part of the net away and then building up coverage, essentially through the midline. This leaves only a slight chance that a shooter will be able to score on a high shot to the right spot.

With the success of the French Canadian blocking style through the late 1990s, many goaltenders adopted these winning strategies and techniques. As always in this cat and mouse game, the shooters adapted. Their ability to score up high has improved as well as their patience to get the goalie to drop so they can adjust the angle of the shot. With the scaling back of the size of goaltending equipment, the opening up of the game, increasingly more east–west play, and the adaptation of the shooters, today's goaltenders cannot rely solely on blocking techniques and must learn to use blocking techniques in the correct situations.

Goalies who run into trouble are those who go to a blocking technique too early and when a player has time and space. You should block when a player is in tight, and hold your feet and have patience if he is farther out. If you are screened and anticipate the shot, you can align yourself in a block to protect as much space as possible. You can also butterfly slide and butterfly push into one-timers where you wish to fill up as much net as possible.

Reacting

Making a save is different from blocking a shot, although a save can come from a blocking position. Generally, saves are when the goaltender reads the shot and reacts to it in order to stop the puck. Reading and reacting to a shot comes with experience and relies on focus and reflexes. Saves come in many different forms, and the correct save selection comes from reading the shot. Chapter 5 discusses save techniques and implementation.

Today's goaltenders have to find the right mix of blocking and saving techniques without relying too heavily on either. Before the recent rule changes, blocking percentages were higher, as the play was more north–south with less cross-crease play. With a higher likelihood of needing to move from side to side, you must hold your feet longer in order to have a greater chance of getting into position to make a save. This translates into having more patience and trusting your ability to react to the shot.

Patience

Having patience is extremely important for a goaltender. If you drop too soon, you leave yourself vulnerable to the shooter's passing at the last second, adjusting the angle of the shot, or beating you upstairs. Patience usually stems from confidence. If you are confident in your ability to make the save, you can wait the shooter out. If you lack that confidence and leave your feet too soon to block, you sometimes make it too easy for the opposition.

You can work on patience in practice. Take advantage of the fact that a goal does not count in practice, and challenge yourself to wait that extra second before dropping. Don't get in the rut of dropping early because of lack of focus.

COACHES' TIP

Anticipation

Anticipation is the ability to read the play and determine what the shooter is going to do with the puck. This is a skill that is developed from playing and analyzing the game. By watching hockey games on TV, playing hockey games, and studying plays and the tendencies and habits of offensive players, you can teach yourself how to anticipate what is going to happen next. By being able to read the situation, you will then be quicker to react.

You can improve your anticipation skills in several ways. Know the team you are playing and their tendencies. Know who the opposition's top players are, and be ready for them. Know the habits and tendencies of your own team as well as the strengths and weaknesses of your players. When you have the opportunity, look away from the puck and scan the defensive zone, picking up where opposing players are lurking. Get set on the puck early by moving spot to spot with power as opposed to gliding in your crease. The sooner you get set, the more time you will have to analyze the attack.

Predictability

One of the greatest goaltenders of this era is Martin Brodeur of the New Jersey Devils. He will tell you that one of the most effective tools a goaltender can have is his lack of predictability. He believes you should keep the shooters guessing by not letting them know what you are going to do, thereby giving you the upper hand. It is important for you to know your game and be confident in your choice of save techniques and strategies. Many goaltenders find success by sticking with a small arsenal of techniques, while others use several different techniques and strategies depending on the situation. It is up to you to find what works best and what gives you the best chance of being successful.

chapter 8

SHUTTING DOWN OFFENSIVE ATTACKS

Brian Daccord

Having a feel for the game and reading the situation are truly what will help you decide the best strategy to use in a given situation. That being said, goaltenders should have a thought process in mind as to how they wish to handle offensive attacks so that their reaction is not strictly instinctual but is grounded in a well laid out plan. That plan can be used as a base and then be adapted as the play develops. This chapter goes through a series of attacks as well as strategies you may wish to utilize in order to improve your game.

STAY ALERT AND FOCUSED

Making smart decisions is the sign of an experienced goaltender. The only way to make these correct decisions, however, is to always know the situation of the game as well as the personnel. When a quarterback lines up to take a snapped football on a passing play, before he gets the ball he knows what all his players will be doing and what his options will be when he drops back to pass. This allows him to read the defense and make the right choices. Imagine what would happen if that quarterback didn't know what patterns his receivers would be running when he got the ball. The same rationale applies to the goaltender and his teammates in respect to how to play certain situations. Be prepared!

You should always be aware of what's going on throughout the game. Continuously focusing on the game situation will allow you to concentrate better and not have lulls when your mind starts to drift. Your head for the game will show your teammates and scouts that you are alert and ready. Here's a good coaching tactic for helping goalies become more mentally alert: After a goal is scored in a scrimmage, have the goalie give you a detailed verbal description of where everyone on the ice was when the goal was scored.

You should know which way each of your defensemen shoots. This will help you place the puck conveniently for them and aid in the breakout. For every action there is a reaction. If you and your teammates are prepared to handle the numerous situations that may exist within a game, chances are your reactions will come more quickly and be made with more confidence.

THE STARTING POSITION

Before the play enters your zone, it is important that you always start from the same spot. This way you will always be on your angle when you get set for the attack. Most goalies like to position themselves deep and in the middle of the crease. When they identify the play coming toward them, they step out to the top of the crease or 2 to 3 feet (0.5 to 1.0 meter) above the paint depending on the attack. Stepping out should be a hard drive and set as opposed to a swizzle and glide. The quicker you can get to your spot, the more time you will have to read the play.

When the play is at the opposite end of the ice, you do not need to be in your ready stance because you know it is not a shooting situation. Understanding when you can play with a higher knee flexion and when you need to be in a stance with your stick on the ice will come with experience. A higher knee flexion will save leg strength, and there is no need to be in a full stance when you don't have to be. As the play gets closer to the net or a shot is anticipated, it is clearly imperative that you be ready. On the initiation of the attack and when the puck is in the "quiet areas" or nonscoring-threat areas, then you can relax your stance and play big and comfortable.

DEFENDING THE BREAKAWAY

After identifying the breakaway, position yourself in front of the crease in order to be able to move backward as the player approaches. You must be far enough out not to show too much of the net, but not so far as to allow the shooter an easy deke (see figure 8.1*a*). Your depth will be determined by your skating ability as well as the speed of the opposing player. The goal is to match the attacker's speed so that when you arrive at the top of the crease, he is one stick length away (see figure 8.1*b*). Use C-cuts (see chapter 6 for an explanation of how to execute a C-cut) as you move backward, and be ready to move right or left, making a save on the shot or deke. A cardinal rule for a goaltender is never to make the first move; but a smart goaltender can sometimes use his positioning and tactics to dictate the actions of the shooter.

Figure 8.1 On a breakaway, begin in a strong position *(a)* and match the attacker's speed so that when you arrive at the top of the crease *(b)* he is one stick length away.

The depth of your initial gap should depend on your skill in skating backward. If you can skate well, there is no reason to show the shooter a lot of the net to begin with. Challenge him so that when he picks his head up, he sees an opponent with confidence—this gives you the psychological advantage.

If you are coming out to face the shooter, you are also challenging him to beat you with a deke. You are one step up on him, because just by your positioning you are coaxing him into your trap. If you are not a great skater, don't come out too far from the crease—the most important factor in this situation is timing.

Wherever you position yourself, anticipate the timing of your backward motion in accordance with the speed of your opponent's approach. You are trying to time it so that when you arrive at the peak of your crease, you are in perfect position to stop a shot or play the deke. If you arrive at the peak of your crease too soon, chances are that when your opponent shoots or dekes, you will be too deep in the net.

To learn exactly what your rhythm is, take a lot of breakaways in practice. Don't let the players approach at half speed when you're doing drills—this will hurt you in a game. Practice both coming way out and playing shallow. If you are comfortable in practice, your confidence will lead to big saves during games. If you spend little time and thought on your approach during practice, a breakaway in a game will become a crisis rather than an exciting challenge.

Taking Charge

Occasionally the goaltender makes the first move and poke checks the puck carrier (see chapter 5 for execution of poke checks). Use this move in a breakaway situation only if you have the angle on the shooter and primarily when he is attacking on your stick-hand side. You should poke check only if the shooter has his head down and you are looking for the element of surprise. Don't attempt the poke check if he is coming down the middle; the odds are too low in this situation, and if you miss you'll look very bad. If he comes from your glove side, poke check only if you have supreme confidence in your ability to perform this difficult save.

KARI LEHTONEN

One of the most overlooked aspects of goaltending is a goaltender's ability to read the play and anticipate what is going to happen next. If a goaltender can do this, he will be right on top of the puck. One of the hottest goaltenders in the NHL is Kari Lehtonen of the Atlanta Thrashers. Although still very young, he showed his goalie sense at an early age by playing with composure and not overplaying situations. Composure is an important ingredient because it allows a goalie to stay calm and analyze potential options as the play moves quickly around him. Lehtonen's international experience from playing in three World Junior Championships has helped him, and as he matures in the NHL he is destined to be among the best.

Kari Lehtonen proved he was in the NHL for keeps when he played in 68 out of 82 games in 2006-2007 and led the Atlanta Thrashers into the NHL playoffs while boasting a 34-24-9 record. He set single-season records and career highs with 68 games, 66 starts, 34 wins, 4 shutouts, 3,934 minutes, 2,075 shots, and 1,892 saves and a team record with a .912 save percentage. Lehtonen holds the Thrashers' all-time franchise record for games played (158), wins (75), and shutouts (11). In Europe, he was voted the Finnish Elite League's best goaltender and league MVP in 2002 as well as being named First Team All-Star.

© Icon SMI

Handling Dekes

If a player dekes, then ideally you will be at the top of the crease when he does so. This gives you the initial depth to move back diagonally or make the save. The best option in terms of save selection is the butterfly slide. This technique allows you to take away the bottom of the net and slide your butterfly along the ice with the player (see figure 8.2 *a-b*). If you think he has a step on you and will beat you to the post after the deke, you can always try a desperation save and extend fully into a long body.

Figure 8.2 Handling dekes *(a-b)*.

DEFENDING PENALTY SHOTS

After a penalty shot has been called, concentrate on your breathing. The excitement could trigger you to breathe too fast, which will diminish your effectiveness. Slow down your breathing pattern by taking long, deep breaths and exhaling slowly; this will improve your coordination and your poise. Next time you watch a basketball game, pay close attention to a player preparing to take a free throw. He has been running up and down the court, so he must settle his nervous system down in order to have the poise to make the foul shot. He does this by controlling his breathing pattern.

As soon as possible after the penalty shot is called, sweep the snow that has built up on the side of the crease toward the slot area. This may make it difficult for the shooter to control the puck as he approaches the net. If you are heading into a shootout at the conclusion of a tied game, sweep the snow out front right after you hear the siren and before you skate to the bench. The linesmen will clear the snow from the posts and check the netting just before the shootout begins.

The penalty shot is the most exciting play in hockey. Having confidence in your ability to make the save in this pressure environment is just as important as your technique. Control your breathing, focus on the puck, and make the big save!

DEFENDING THE ONE ON ONE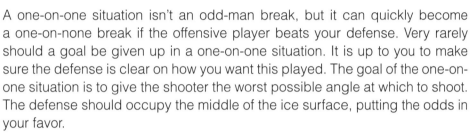

A one-on-one situation isn't an odd-man break, but it can quickly become a one-on-none break if the offensive player beats your defense. Very rarely should a goal be given up in a one-on-one situation. It is up to you to make sure the defense is clear on how you want this played. The goal of the one-on-one situation is to give the shooter the worst possible angle at which to shoot. The defense should occupy the middle of the ice surface, putting the odds in your favor.

Gap control is an essential element of this strategy. If your opponent is angled to one side but given lots of room, his percentages are increased. If shooter has no passing options, you can be aggressive. You must trust that your defenseman will prevent the attacker from cutting back to the middle of the ice, and you must fill the shooting lane (see figure 8.3). Fill the shooting lane aggressively by taking an extra step forward when you know the shot is his only option and there is no weak-side threat.

Figure 8.3 Defending the one on one.

DEFENDING THE TWO ON ONE

A two-on-one break requires confidence and communication between the goaltender and the defenseman. The objective is for the defenseman to take responsibility for the pass and the goaltender to play the shooter. The defenseman tries to place himself between the open man and the puck carrier (see figure 8.4). He must try to stay in the middle of the ice surface, forcing the shooter to release on a bad angle. The farther the shooter is away from the midline of the ice, the greater your chance of stopping the shot.

Challenge the shooter within reason, trusting that your teammate will intercept an attempted pass. The more the defenseman covers the open player and allows the puck carrier more room in the middle, the greater the disadvantage to the goalie. If a pass is made close to the net on a two on one, you can use either a butterfly slide or, in the case of desperation, a long body.

You must recognize whether the puck carrier is on his strong side or off-wing. If the puck carrier is on his off-wing, then his stick is toward the middle of the ice and therefore his shooting angle is better. There is a tendency for this player to take the shot. If the player is on the strong side, then the puck is further off angle, decreasing his percentages to score and therefore promoting the pass.

In the event of a pass, you must also recognize which way the second opposing player shoots. If he is on his off-wing, be ready for the one-timer; if he is on his strong side, you may need to cover more real estate, as the puck could be released from the opposite side of his body. You must also keep in mind that the player on his strong side may elect to collect the puck and cut back against the grain, calling for a momentum change.

Teams must spend time practicing the two on one so the defensemen can get to know the goaltenders. There is a big difference between how an aggressive

Figure 8.4 Defending the two on one.

goalie and a patient goalie will play this situation. When an aggressive goaltender identifies the shooter, he will immediately come out and challenge—which means that an early pass in the zone could trap him, leaving an empty net for the pass recipient. The defenseman must know in advance how his goalie will react. If he knows the goalie is aggressive, he will quickly take responsibility to cover the pass; if he knows his goalie is more patient and waits longer for plays to develop before challenging a shooter, he will take more time to force the shooter to a tougher angle.

Be aware of a common mistake made by defensemen close to the net in two-on-one situations: Once defensemen get close to the crease, they often peel off to tie up their man. The problem comes when they peel off early, allowing the shooter the option of cutting in front of the net. The defenseman must stay in the middle all the way to the top of the crease, thus forcing the shooter to release at a tough angle and giving the goalie a greater chance of making the stop. The shooter must not be given the option of cutting across the net to the far side because this will increase his scoring percentages. It is much better for the goalie to face the shot from the angle.

As a goalie, you must take the responsibility of explaining to your teammates how you want the two on one played. Don't let your defense make the same mistakes over and over without being corrected. In the end, you are the one who could pay the price.

COACHES' TIP

DEFENDING THE TWO ON NONE

Facing two attackers can be an intimidating situation for a goaltender, but you are not without recourse. The most important point to remember is not to let one player isolate you, leaving an empty net if the second player receives the pass. This is often a tough job for aggressive netminders who like to challenge the puck carrier.

When facing a two on none, resist the temptation to play too aggressively. Come out of your net and position yourself conservatively based on where the attackers are, ready to skate backward with the right timing, as in the breakaway situation. The old rule remains intact: "Always play the shooter." But don't let him pull you so far away that you'll be unable to play the second opponent if the shooter passes. Always be in position to react to the shot, deke, or pass. Reading which way the puck carrier and his teammate shoot is the same as for the two-on-one scenario.

DEFENDING THE THREE ON TWO

Playing a three-on-two situation requires preparation and anticipation. The goaltender must rely on many different skills because there are many possible scenarios. Your first priority, as always, is the puck carrier. He has the option of shooting or going hard to the net and trying to drive by the defenseman. Play the angles as if he will shoot; but don't come out too far or he will pass the puck behind you, leaving an open net for his teammate on the weak side.

Usually the second opponent to gain the blue line will be driving hard to the net, while the third attacker positions himself in an open area as the trailer or high man. If the puck goes to the high man, you should adjust and get square to the puck by executing a quick drop step in order to take away the angle from the shooter. If the puck carrier tries to pass it to the second forward driving to the net, then you must be aggressive. Don't back away from the confrontation, allowing him to deflect or one-time the puck into an open net. Intercept the pass if you can, or get right on top of where the tip or redirection may come from with a butterfly slide. This player should also be taken by the weak-side defenseman. It is imperative that you know your defensemen and that you all understand how you will play any situation as a group. Don't be afraid to shout instructions to your teammates.

If your defenseman takes the opponent going to the net, you are in a two-on-one situation; as in any two on one, you want the player with the lowest percentages to shoot the puck. If you have the puck carrier isolated on a tough angle, shout this to your teammates so they know that the pass is their responsibility because you are aggressively playing the carrier. In practice, don't just run through a bunch of three-on-two situations without talking and strategizing with your defensemen. Make sure everyone, from the coach to the sixth defenseman, understands and is in agreement on the strategy you are using. Reflexes can take you only so far. A smart goaltender playing in synchrony with his teammates can significantly diminish the number of big opportunities for his opponents.

DEFENDING THE POWER PLAY

Special teams have become a huge part of hockey with the rise in penalties due to tougher regulations. The clubs with the best special teams have a distinct advantage over the competition. No disrespect to the other players on a team, but the most important penalty killer is, and always will be, the goalie. Whether it is a five on four, a five on three, or a four on three, the philosophy for a goaltender stays the same. You must always play the shooter but be ready for the backdoor pass. This means you cannot be as aggressive as in a five-on-five situation, and therefore your depth will be shallower than normal to allow you to get cross-crease. When considering the possibility of an uncovered opponent, you must be very aware of where you leave your rebounds. A sloppy rebound with an open forward in front means a quick goal.

All in all, the goaltender who is great at defending against the power play is the goaltender who can read the play and determine what the opponent is trying to do. You must identify what power-play formation the attacking team is in and what threats come with that formation. This means you must be able to look away from the puck when it is in a quiet area or when you know you have a second to scope out where everybody is. Good goalies steal glances and take their eyes off the puck when they know they can. If you know where the opponents are and what they are trying to do, then your reactions will be that much quicker.

There are two basic power-play formations: the umbrella and the overload. When the opposing team is in the umbrella, there will be one defenseman positioned near the center of the blue line, with shooters on both sides above the top of the circles. Usually the umbrella is designed to get a one-timer from these two shooters, and therefore you must be ready for the quick release as they are generally on their off-wings. There will likely be a man in front to try to screen you and another who is floating on the backdoor looking for a cross-ice feed. It is your responsibility to find the puck through any screen and know which side the open forward is on.

With the overload, there are generally two players on the blue line, one on the half-board, one in the corner, and one in front of the net or backdoor. Many overload plays are designed to generate scoring opportunities from down low. They come in the form of a give and go with the half-board player and the player in the corner, or a give and go with a pass to the backdoor opponent. Versus the overload you not only have to be prepared for a shot but also may need to intercept a pass or get cross-crease quickly to cover a backdoor pass. Once again, communication with your own players is important as well as understanding and anticipating what the opposing team is trying to do.

SUPPORTING THE POWER PLAY

The goalie can be a tremendous asset to the power play. The number one way to do this is to be active in playing the puck. Valuable seconds can be saved when a goalie stops a clear by the opponent and transitions his team back on offense with a good pass. A quick transition by the goalie could mean the opponent's tired penalty killers don't have enough time to get off the ice. One thing to be aware of is forcing a pass because the team might be best served by setting up the breakout and moving up the ice as a unit. You must learn to recognize when to move the puck and when to set it up. This decision will be based on where teammates are, the availability of a passing lane, and simply if it would be wiser to set the puck rather than play it.

A major backbreaker for a team is to be on a power play and give up a goal. A shorthanded goal can occur because the power-play unit is taking chances and most of the time is the result of a breakaway or odd-man rush. A goalie's mind-set cannot be that the power play is a time to relax. You must be ready for a turnover and possible scoring opportunity. If you relax your focus, you are susceptible to being beaten. Your role on the power play is to be alert to move the puck as well as bail out the power-play unit if they give up a turnover.

chapter 9

BEHIND-THE-NET COVERAGE

John Alexander

One of the most difficult situations for a goaltender is when the puck ends up below the goal line. The goalie's body is facing up ice, but his head is looking in the opposite direction. Unfortunately, many people consider wraparounds and walkout goals as soft because of the proximity to the net, but in fact they can be very difficult to play. It is very important that goalies have a comprehensive system to handle all situations that originate from behind the net and understand the timing necessary in utilizing these techniques. In this chapter, you will read strategies and techniques that will help you be successful in down-low attacks.

POST POSITIONING

Post positioning, or post "integration" as it may be referred to, is the basis for all play that takes place below or near the goal line. Whether the play involves tracking the puck behind the net, a wraparound, a walkout, a pass out front, or a low net attack from this area, the fundamental skill of proper and functional post positioning allows a goaltender to repel any attack on the net in the most proficient manner.

Proper post positioning today involves a seamless integration of the skate and lower portion of the pad to the near-side post and not total body integration, as was the case in the past. This position allows a goaltender to move smoothly, without hesitation, and as part of a transition from another location in or around the crease or the opposite post. In other words, you must be able to arrive at the post in proper position and not arrive and then adjust to the correct position. Because a myriad of scoring opportunities exist depending on the position of the low puck carrier, the importance of this tactic cannot be overemphasized.

Today's post positioning has evolved to deal with changes in the opposition's attack tactics as well as changes in the rules and the game itself. Now goaltenders must be more prepared to repel speedy low attacks and shots from unobstructed players in primary scoring areas. The concern is far less on intercepting the puck or seamless body–post integration because of new tactics at the net. In the past, defensemen were given greater latitude by the officials to control players in front of the net. Now this is tightly controlled, and attacking players have more time and space in front of the net than ever before. This leads to more time to change shooting angles on the goalie as well as to dish pucks to open teammates. The opponent with the puck is no longer as predictable, and therefore the goalie has to be prepared for several scenarios.

Here are the keys to a goaltender's post positioning on each side.

Glove-Side Post Positioning

1. The outside heel of your near-side, otherwise known as the strong-side, skate should be in firm contact with the post (see figure 9.1*a*).

2. Align your back-side skate at approximately 30 degrees to the goal line and a little more than shoulder-width apart from the other skate.

3. The alignment of the back-side, otherwise known as the weak-side, skate may fluctuate based on the location of the puck carrier. If the puck carrier is off to the side of the net and below the goal line extended, then your back-side skate positioning will depend on the passing angle of the puck carrier. The strong-side skate needs to be positioned to drive out to where a pass out front might be made. The smaller the passing lane is for the

passer, the more the back-side skate can be off the goal line. Therefore, the more the net cuts off the passing lane, the farther out your back-side skate will be.

4. The heel of your stick should extend from the toe of your near-side skate when the puck is below the goal line.

5. Reposition the stick, with the toe of the stick to the toe of the skate, when the puck moves above the goal line or deeper toward the corner.

6. Tuck the glove-side elbow inside the post, with the glove up, palm facing forward. The glove will cover the gap that opens up with knee flexion of the strong-side pad. By having the palm facing forward and not turned over, your stance can remain compact, and the glove is in a better position to block space in the various blocking techniques available.

Blocker-Side Post Positioning

1. The outside heel of your near-side skate should be in firm contact with the post (see figure 9.1*b*).

2. Align the back-side skate at approximately 30 degrees to the goal line depending on the location of the puck carrier and the width of his passing lanes.

3. The alignment of your back-side skate may fluctuate based on the location of the puck carrier, identical to the glove-side post integration.

4. The heel of your stick should extend from the toe of your near-side skate.

5. Your stick arm is free from the post with the elbow bent. This gives you the ability to freely use your stick to intercept pass-outs.

6. Position your glove just a little away from the body, open and at a 45-degree angle to the goal line. The glove does not cross your midline but remains compact in the stance and ready to catch a saucer pass out front if necessary.

7. Your elbow is bent and the arm relaxed.

On both sides the weight distribution is approximately 60 percent on the near-post skate and 40 percent on the back-side skate. This allows you to rapidly transition into another position or tactic depending on how the situation evolves. Except for the dominant weight-bearing leg, your body should remain relaxed, with your head turned as you track the puck and puck carrier. At opportune times, you should look off the puck to determine the presence and location of opposition attackers. Because of its simplicity, the method of positioning presented here gives you the greatest degree of flexibility for handling all types of goal-line attacks as well as plays that originate from near or behind the goal line to the front of the net.

Figure 9.1 Post integration for *(a)* the glove side and *(b)* the blocker side.

Moving into a lateral butterfly slide, loading, puck tracking behind the net, or just simply repositioning to another location in the crease is facilitated by using this method. Because the position mirrors a goaltender's stance, you can transition quickly, smoothly, and easily to the proper post position. Note that you will be a little more erect, with less hip, knee, and ankle flexion, than in your normal stance. Also, adaptation to this post positioning eliminates issues of balance and allows you more time to read the play as it develops because it is less complicated to set up.

PUCK TRACKING BEHIND THE NET

In the previous section, we cover proper post positioning. It follows that we now move to tracking the puck behind the net. This is the natural progression from post positioning for plays that develop below the goal line when the opposition player skates the puck behind the net. With the emphasis on maintaining visual contact with the puck when it is in the defensive zone, play behind the net can present some distinct disadvantages for a goaltender. Because you have your back to the puck, your position is more vulnerable, and the challenge of maintaining visual contact becomes increasingly difficult. As the puck is moved from one point to another behind the net, that visual contact may be lost. Three potential attacks can develop from a behind-the-net puck position: a wraparound, a walkout, and a pass-out.

Because these attacks take place in close proximity to the net, if you lose visual contact at a critical moment, your ability to read the play will be diminished along with your ability to effectively respond to the situation. Reading and reacting to a particular play or set of circumstances is an essential part of a goaltender's skill set.

Tracking Down Low (Static)

Now let's move on to the actual tracking. Understand that this is a situation where the puck is already below the goal line or has been passed below the goal line, and the opposing player, in possession of the puck, is moving the puck behind the net. The term *static* reflects that the tracking technique is used when the puck carrier does not have speed. (A smooth follow is used when the puck carrier has speed coming around the net.) At this point, you should have already established a proper post position as described earlier. So with your head turned into the player and visual contact with the puck, you will maintain integration with the post until the puck is just inside or directly in line with the near-side post behind the net. Then you push off the near-side post, using the inside edge of your strong-side skate, to the center of the net, maintaining the same skate angle (30 degrees) as for your post position.

The result is that you are now positioned a little above the goal line at the center net (see figure 9.2a). Maintaining your skate angle allows you to keep excellent visual contact with the puck even beyond the center net. There are no adjustments from the post position stance or foot adjustments: just a simple, single shuffle in the direction opposite to the near-side post (see chapter 6 for an explanation of how to execute a shuffle). Therefore, there is no loss of balance or body control, which helps you keep track of the puck and move fluidly at the same time.

If the puck carrier continues to move the puck in the direction of the other post, simply turn your head to visually pick up the puck on the other side of your body. This head turn will automatically pivot your body at a 30-degree angle to the goal line. Should the attacker continue to move the puck in the same direction, simply wait until the puck is just inside that post, and then perform a simple shuffle movement to integrate with that post (see figure 9.2b). In the event the puck carrier moves the puck to the center net and has time to hold

Figure 9.2 Static puck tracking down low *(a-b)*.

that position, maintain your center net position with visual puck contact, reacting as we described earlier when the puck is moved to one side or the other.

As you can see, this is the least complicated method of puck tracking. It offers little in the way of opportunity for balance issues or panic situations because of lost visual contact with the puck in the early or late stages of its being moved behind the net. The only point where visual contact is lost is when the puck is directly behind the center net, and that point is equidistant from the nearest point of attack . . . the net post.

Hold-and-Release Puck Tracking Down Low (Static)

As is the case with much of goaltending, there is more than one strategy available when tracking a puck carrier behind the net. An alternative strategy to the one previously presented is the blocker hold and glove release. When the player moves from your glove side toward your blocker side in a static follow behind the net, you can maintain visual contact with the puck by releasing your post. After releasing the post, you shuffle toward your blocker-side post while continuously maintaining eye contact with the puck. Do not rotate your head until your last move to the blocker post. This allows you to keep the play over your glove side, which makes the puck easier to track, and you do not end up in the middle of your net with the potential of losing sight of the puck.

When the player moves behind the net from your blocker to glove side, you hold the post (see figure 9.3a). As the player moves toward the middle of the net, you watch him over your blocker shoulder through the window between your blocker shoulder, goal post, and crossbar. When you are about to lose sight of the puck, you rotate your head and find the puck over your glove-side shoulder (see figure 9.3b). Once you locate the puck, you have the puck carrier where you want him . . . over your glove side. You can then shuffle as required (see figure 9.3c). The goal of this technique is to put yourself in a position to trap the puck carrier over your glove-side shoulder. This method is ideal for the goaltender who thinks it is easier to track with the player over his glove side as opposed to his blocker side.

Figure 9.3 Hold-and-release puck tracking down low *(a-c)*.

Tracking Down Low (Smooth)

A smooth follow can be used to track the puck being passed behind the net, a teammate carrying the puck or an opponent carrying the puck with inside pressure. In this case we will track the opponent. When the puck carrier has approached the net with speed and continues to go around the net, perform a smooth follow. To execute a smooth follow, you may start at the post (see figure 9.4*a*) or, depending on the situation, you may establish greater depth generally with your toes on the top of the crease and next to the goal line. When the puck carrier begins to go around the net, you use backward C-cuts while keeping at a 30-degree angle. Stay a touch ahead of the player while matching his speed. When the attacker moves past the midline of the net, simply rotate (also known as a pivot) while in your stance; complete the rotation with the lead skate integrating with the post (see figure 9.4*b*). During the smooth follow, if you anticipate a wraparound, initiate a back diagonal slide into a paddle down.

Figure 9.4 Smooth tracking down low. *(a-b)*

JEAN-SEBASTIEN GIGUERE

One of the most difficult attacks a goaltender must defend against is from behind the net. Whether the play is a pass-out, walkout, wrap, or jam, when the puck is behind the net you are looking back, while the true scoring threat may be standing right out in front. Goalies employ different strategies and tactics while tracking a puck down low, and one of the best is Jean-Sebastien Giguere of the Anaheim Mighty Ducks. Giguere's ability to block the near side of the post does not allow the shooters a chance to find a hole when attacking from down low.

Jean-Sebastien Giguere was unbelievable as his Ducks fell short to Martin Brodeur and the New Jersey Devils in the 2003 NHL finals. A first-round draft choice of the Hartford Whalers in the 1995 entry draft, Giguere was awarded the Conn Smythe Trophy in the losing effort. In 2007 he was not to be denied as his Ducks captured the Stanley Cup. It took a while for Giguere to establish himself in the NHL, but he is now one of the league's dominant goalies.

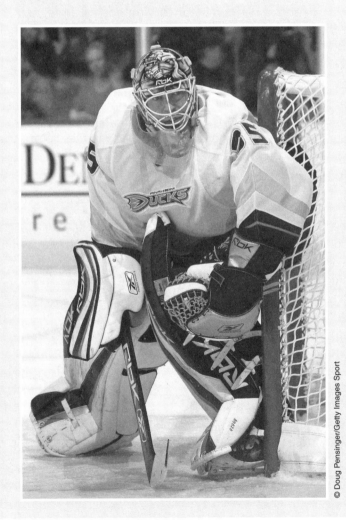

© Doug Pensinger/Getty Images Sport

DEFENDING WRAPAROUND ATTACKS

A wraparound with speed is a difficult play for a goaltender because the attacker is carrying the puck and has multiple options, adding to the danger of the situation. The attack can begin either above or below the goal line as the result of a dump, a broken play, or the attacker's accelerating wide around a defensive player. Depending on the proximity of defensive coverage, the attacker's options will diminish or increase. He may carry the puck behind the net and attempt a long wrap, entice you off the near post and stuff the puck there, make a pass to an uncovered teammate in the slot once the puck carrier has moved beyond the net, or attempt a walkout if defensive pressure to the far side does not materialize. As you can see, the speed of the attacker and lack of defensive support mean this impending threat demands your total focus and attention.

As is the case with plays beginning at or near the goal line, excellent post positioning is paramount in this scenario too. A strong post position will both encourage the puck carrier to bring the puck behind the net and also eliminate any attempt to penetrate your defenses at the near post. The delay caused by the necessity of carrying the puck around behind the net will hopefully give your team time to improve defensive coverage in the slot area and eliminate one of the key danger options.

Defending the Glove-Side Wraparound

The same process is followed for pucks that move across behind the net from your blocker side (see figure 9.5*a*). However, the paddle down stick position must be directly in front of the butterfly (see figure 9.5*b*). In this case, it is of little or no value in the event of a pass made to the slot or across the crease as the stick will not be able to block a passing lane. One variation of this technique is to go blade down with your stick as opposed to paddle down. This allows the blocker to stay raised and more options to use the stick. The one detriment of using this blade down techniques is that the paddle down puts you in better position to hold your ground if players are jamming at the puck.

On either side, if a situation develops where the attacker has time and space to bring the puck farther away from the post and gain a better shooting angle, you must adjust your position to a full butterfly to protect the upper portion of the net. Additionally, it may be necessary to adjust the gap between you and the puck by shuffling or pushing forward or in fact recovering to your feet if time permits. This enables you to fill more space and keep the puck from penetrating your position.

Figure 9.5 Defending the glove-side wraparound *(a-b)*.

One other dangerous situation that could develop is a pass from behind the goal line to the attacker's teammate in the slot. Because this is one of the more difficult situations to prevent, you need to be aware of the danger in front and anticipate or read the situation. If this occurs, you have the option of planting the back-leg skate and pushing into the path of the shot in the event of a close-in shot or even recovering to your feet and prioritizing center net coverage.

COACHES' TIP

The first instinct a goaltender must have is to beat the puck to the post using your skate, pad, and stick. If you get the ice covered first, you can build your coverage from the ice up using your body, arms, and gloves.

Defending the Blocker-Side Wraparound

With the near post sealed off with good post positioning, there remains only to track the puck carrier and puck as it is moved behind the net. Employing the same techniques as described earlier in this chapter, maintain visual contact with the puck. In most of these situations, goaltenders elect to make the save from a down position. Generally this method is employed because speed of movement is required, and that is more easily accomplished by moving into butterfly position. In most cases the attacker will attempt to beat you to the post and tuck the puck in along the ice, so therefore covering as much of the lower part of the net as possible is the goal. There is also the potential that the wrap will occur farther from the post because of the speed factor. That, in itself, implies that you will need to seal off a greater area of the net.

Let's follow the process where the puck is moved behind the net starting at your glove side. Since you should already be in good post position as the puck approaches, track its progress. Do not begin moving into the save position until the puck has passed the middle point of the net (see figure 9.6a). When it does, perform a short push, with the trailing skate driving the lead-leg pad down into the ice, and firmly make contact with the far post, sealing off that area completely. Pad and post contact should occur approximately in the middle to lower part of the shin. Although some goalies will lock their pads at the break above the toe area, pressing the pad at the middle to lower shin allows the upper torso to get closer to the post, allowing for less net exposure. The back-leg pad also is in contact with the ice, forming a butterfly although with far less width than usual.

At the same time as this is happening, drop your blocker hand, moving the stick into a paddle down position outside the post (see figure 9.6b). This brings the stick prominently into play. As a versatile part of your equipment, the stick's proximity and squareness to the attack not only serve as a primary defense but also, because of its mobility, to some degree can enable you to cut off passes to the front of the net or across the crease. If the puck carrier does not try to tuck the puck inside the post and elects to take an extra step to lift the puck over the lead pad, you can raise your glove-side pad in a traditional paddle down to gain more height with your upper body, or you can use a butterfly.

COACHES' TIP An aggressive play on a blocker-side wrap is a sweep check. When the attacker moves to the far post, instead of going paddle down, sweep your extended stick flush along the ice, knocking the puck away from the butterfly. You may want to try maintaining your hold on the shaft with just your fingertips to allow the stick to lay flat.

Figure 9.6 Defending the blocker-side wraparound *(a-b)*.

DEFENDING WALKOUTS

The walkout is perhaps the least dangerous of the near-net attacks we discuss in this chapter. It is not as dangerous because there are a couple of limitations to the shooter's position. First, we'll have to assume that the shooter chose this option because of defensive pressure or presence that otherwise prevents him from making a wrap with speed, attacking the net from the front, or passing to an open partner. Second, by making this choice, the attacker has limited his shooting angle and really given the advantage to the goaltender, provided the goaltender exercised caution and patience. Of course with the attack taking place near the net, good positioning on the part of the goaltender will automatically seal off all access to the net.

Let's look at the walkout that occurs off a potential wrap with speed. As stated before, the events leading up to the wrap are initial excellent post position, visual tracking of the attacker and puck behind the net, and a move to the down position to seal off the post. With this accomplished and the attacker's decision to forgo a wraparound attempt in favor of a walkout, you need to adjust your position relevant to the walkout.

1. The first element is to attain squareness to the puck in order to cover, or block, as much net as possible. You are not already square because your initial position at the post was based on the premise of a wraparound attempt. To square up to the puck, bring your back leg forward to rotate the body around the post while at the same time moving into a more upright butterfly position.

2. If time permits, attempt to close the gap by moving toward the puck.

Of course not all walkout situations occur from a wraparound with speed. Sometimes the walkout comes from below the goal line on the same side the goaltender occupies. In these situations and those where there is no urgency to get to the post, you will already be in a good post position on your feet. From that position, simply rotate out using a C-cut as the attacker brings the puck above the goal line. The attacker will not have the opportunity to take the puck to a better angle because of defensive pressure, so you can play him simply by assuming a compact position on your feet and moving a little closer to the puck. If the attacker is tight to the net, you may elect to load to the glove or blocker. If you choose to leave your feet on a walkout to the blocker side, opting to go directly into a paddle down blocks substantial net.

COACHES' TIP If a walkout is in tight, a goaltender may choose a blocking tactic. In this case you will load to the strong-side post, blocking any area of the net that the puck could enter. A popular strategy for the blocker-side walkout is the paddle down.

LOADING

One of the more recent tactics introduced to goaltending is the load. Loading seems to have taken hold to the point where a majority of goaltenders use this tactic whenever the puck enters the area near the goal line and close to the net. The load is a blocking technique that can be used when an attack develops along the goal line and the opposition has time and space with minimal pressure or when the attacker breaks around a defenseman. It involves sealing off the post completely with the near-side pad in a vertical position and sealing off the ice portion of the near side with the other pad in a horizontal position.

Essentially, the goaltender is on one knee with his torso upright and back-side pad at an angle that can range from 0 to 30 degrees to the goal line. Many times we see goaltenders with the back-side leg at a 45-degree angle or greater. This will severely hinder their ability to transition into a lateral slide to defend against a cross-crease or midcrease pass or shot. Alternatively, the back-side leg should not drop below the goal line. Again, this severely hinders the angle of the lateral slide process. The back-side pad position is determined by the back-side threat. If there is no backdoor play, the goalie can square more to the shooter. With the backdoor option, the goalie must keep his back-side pad close to the goal line to facilitate a push to the weak side.

The load is based on the premise that completely sealing off the bottom of the net during attacks is far easier from this position than any other method. This is especially true for near-post attacks. Loading can be an effective means of dealing with a cross-crease or backdoor pass because of the ease of transitioning into a lateral push across the crease from this position. It can also be used to defend against wraparound plays and low pass-outs.

Make no mistake, timing is a very critical element of this tactic. This is not something that is done as an offensive play is being executed. You must be in position before the play and set as it develops. Otherwise you run the risk of allowing stoppable goals. The load is an effective tool but should not be used as a crutch. Similar to when the paddle down was introduced, goalies have overused this technique, and we are now finding the correct usage. It is important that you maintain your feet when possible and not go into a load too quickly.

Loading the Glove-Side Post

In loading to the glove side, the outside of your glove-side pad should take away the short side in an upright position. Build coverage from the top of your glove-side pad to the crossbar by placing your glove on top of the pad. Your fingers should be facing 12:00 o'clock. Your blocker-side pad should be flush with the ice and cover low to the weak side in order to take away the weak-side low area of the net.

The near-side pad is vertically positioned and tight against the post, with the ankle touching the post. The glove arm is inside the post, with the palm of the glove facing forward and positioned above the pad. Your other pad rests on the ice, with the knee brought as close to the skate of the vertical leg as possible. The blocker arm is positioned out, away from the body so that the blade of the stick can be brought up to rest against the point where the top of the horizontal pad pushes against the vertical skate position, effectively sealing off any "holes" that may be present.

If the puck is extremely close and you are expecting the shooter to try to jam the puck through you, then you should have your paddle down to protect the ice and five hole (see figure 9.7*a*). If the puck is a little farther out than a jam situation, then your blocker should be up and the stick blade on the ice (see figure 9.7*b*). If the puck moves even farther out, you can drop the blocker elbow back in place at the bottom of your rib cage. By using the blade down as opposed to the paddle down in a load, you cover more area to the blocker side, and the blocker is ready for action.

Figure 9.7 Loading the glove-side post with *(a)* your paddle down and *(b)* your stick blade on the ice.

  ## Loading the Blocker-Side Post

On the blocker-side post, the near-side pad is vertically positioned and tight against the post, with the ankle touching the post. The glove arm is against the body, with the glove positioned above the top of the horizontal pad. The horizontally positioned pad rests on the ice, with the knee brought as close to the skate of the vertical leg as possible (see figure 9.8*a*). The stick arm is outside the post away from the body so that the blade of the stick can be positioned in front of the point where the top of the horizontal pad pushes against the vertical skate position, effectively sealing off any "holes" that may be present. The glove may be brought down to the ice, placed behind or at the end of the stick blade, if you are reading a jam (see figure 9.8*b*). This provides for an additional layer to protect the ice if the glove backs up the blade or additional width of coverage in the case of the glove extending from the blade.

If the puck is on the short side of the blocker and in tight, keep the blocker-side pad up and lay the glove-side pad flush along the ice, taking away the weak side. The stick blade should be covering the five hole. If the puck is very

Figure 9.8 Loading the blocker-side post *(a)* when you have space and *(b)* in a jam situation.

close to you, you can back up the stick blade with the glove if you expect the shooter is going to try to overpower you through the five hole. You may also lay the glove down in order to extend the blade of your stick. If you do not expect to be jammed, then the glove should build blocking coverage above the glove-side pad.

Puck Position: When to Load

Now that we have described the technique, let's describe the usual puck positioning for the tactic, as well as the primary purpose of the tactic and the situation where it is most effective. Essentially, a goaltender will move into this position when the puck is carried into the area below the goal line and within approximately 15 feet (4.5 meters) beyond either side of the net. It can also be used if the puck is in the area above the goal line but below the edge of the face-off circle and approximately 15 feet (4.5 meters) to the net. In these situations, the load is being used as a blocking tactic when the play is in tight. Although this is a more narrowly defined area of usage than we often see, it appears to defy logic to use this tactic when the puck is in other areas of the defensive zone when a strong stance will be adequate.

Loading is a progressive blocking technique that has proved to be very successful. Unfortunately, goalies who should be holding their feet an extra second are loading too early. The timing of the load is similar to the timing of going down in the butterfly—you don't want to leave your feet too early.

COACHES' TIP

DEFENDING PASS-OUTS

Pass-outs are the most dangerous of all attacks that take place at or near the net. This greater danger exists for a number of reasons, the most critical of which is the limited amount of time the goaltender has to reposition himself because the puck is being moved from one attacker to another as opposed to being carried by a single individual. Several elements add to the danger of the situation. There is a degree of uncertainty of the exact location of the pass recipient, since he may not be stationary but actually transitioning to a particular area of the ice. The recipient, who is positioned above the goal line and near the net, may have a more favorable angle. There is a potential for traffic that may directly hinder the goaltender as he tries to readjust his position. A screen situation as the shot is taken could be developing, and the goaltender must visually track the puck from below the goal line to its intended pass target and read the release and potential trajectory of the shot—all in a split second.

Understand that the situations we discuss pertain to passes made to an opposition player within a stick length or so of the blue crease area. These types of plays can be effectively defended with the traditional compact butterfly slide. The only exception might be where the pass is made to the far-side attacker and the goaltender thinks he will not have sufficient time to make the save using the traditional method. Here, because of the necessity to quickly seal off the bottom of the net, the goaltender may opt to begin the save process with a lateral slide; as he moves laterally, he extends his lead pad into the open net area, with his body falling toward the shooter in a low forward position. This move is referred to as a long body save and is discussed in the desperation saves segment in chapter 5. In this case it is mandatory that the goaltender use his glove or blocker to provide additional net coverage above the pad in the event the puck trajectory does clear the height of the lead pad.

In almost every case where there is a low pass-out, several elements favor the goaltender's chance of success: There is usually defensive pressure on the shooter; the shooter is normally tight to the net, so the amount of open net is severely reduced; the goaltender can be almost 100 percent certain that the shot will be made to the open side; and the shooter has a limited amount of time to release the shot.

When the pass-out is made to a player positioned outside the low pass-out area (i.e., more than a stick length from the crease), the situation is best handled with a step-out and reposition from the post if it is a near-side pass-out, or a strong T-glide or drop step and reposition in the case of a mid-ice or far-side pass-out (see figure 9.9 *a-c*). It is important that you arrive in position to make the save on your skates whenever possible, especially if it does not sacrifice

Figure 9.9 Defending pass-outs *(a-c)*.

angle, depth, or stance considerations. With the pass recipient farther from the net and the prime scoring area, it is more likely that the puck will be moved with a second pass or the puck recipient will carry the puck to another angle before shooting. Without the mobility of being on your skates, your ability to reposition if the puck is moved will be severely hampered.

If the puck isn't moved, then you simply play the shot from a strong stance position. Assuming you have followed the initial tactical sequence described for low-zone pass-out situations, then the only critical element left to ensure a high degree of success is that you "connect the dots"—following the puck from passer to pass recipient—and plan to arrive in a set position as the puck reaches the shooter's stick. From that point on, you play the situation as it develops.

Of course the easiest way to prevent a pass-out goal is to intercept the pass in the first place. With proper post positioning, you can shoot the stick blade off your toe to intercept the pass. In general, no puck should travel through the paint area of the crease; intercepting these passes is the goalie's responsibility. Do not break your knee flexion when trying to deflect a pass, as this may put you off balance and extended in the event you are not successful in making contact with the puck.

Same-Side Pass-Outs

In a same-side pass-out, the pass recipient is positioned on the same side of the net as the goaltender, in the low slot area, or is skating into that area to receive the pass. We can define the area into which the puck is being passed and where the shot will originate as a square starting at the post and extending along the goal line to a point approximately one stick length from the outer rim of the crease, then straight out to the edge of the face-off circle, back into the slot and parallel to the goal line, and then back to the near post.

The key component of making the save begins with proper post positioning while in balance and in control. The second component is to be alert as much as possible to the opposition's positioning or potential positioning in the danger area. Continuous use of peripheral vision and looking off the puck at opportune moments as the play develops before the pass is made will surely pay dividends here. The third component of making the save is coverage because of how close the actual shooter will be to the net when he receives the pass. Use a forward butterfly slide (see chapter 5) when the shot comes from close proximity, combining gap reduction and gaining angle simultaneously. If you read that the opponent will shoot immediately, you can effectively seal off the entire net opening with a compact blocking butterfly position because the shooter's location offers very little shooting angle and little net opening.

Low Slot Area Pass-Outs

A more dangerous pass-out scoring opportunity comes from the low center slot area, as reaction time to the actual shot will need to be extremely quick. The low slot area is from the top of the crease, about a stick length away, and extending out from both posts into the slot area. Again, proper post positioning comes into play as well as locating the potential pass target before the pass (see figure 9.10a). Angle becomes a more critical issue here, since the shooter is positioned in the primary scoring area, but generally, since this is the most highly defended area of the defensive zone, defensive pressure can potentially negate this factor. As was the case with the near-side pass-out, if you read that the opponent will shoot immediately, use a powerful compact lateral slide that can simultaneously achieve gap and angle on the shooter without negatively affecting either (see figure 9.10 b-c).

Figure 9.10 Covering low slot area pass-outs *(a-c)*.

Far-Side Low Slot Area Pass-Outs

The most dangerous pass-out without a doubt travels from below the goal line on one side of the net to the far-side low slot area . . . just the opposite of the same-side pass-out. It is the most dangerous for several reasons. The goaltender must travel a greater distance as well as turn her head a full 180 degrees to track the puck. Also, in most cases, the goaltender will not be able to locate the opposition attacker before the pass, so she may experience difficulty finding the exact point of release. If you are in this situation, take on a strong post position while the puck is located behind the goal line, and attempt to anticipate the positioning of opposition players based on the passing angle. Visually track the path of the puck from passer's to receiver's stick, and power into a lateral slide to gain angle position as the puck is passed; rotate square to the puck in the process of the slide. Let your momentum bring your body forward to improve the puck gap.

COACHES' TIP When properly post integrated for a pass-out, resist the temptation to lunge for the puck being passed. If you break your knee flexion and miss the puck, you will be in a very vulnerable position, leaving little chance to stop the shot.

chapter 10

BATTLING TRAFFIC AND MOVING THE PUCK

Tom Dempsey

One popular expression is "If it were easy, everyone could do it." Making saves is not easy, and to add an even greater degree of difficulty, sometimes goaltenders don't have a clear view of the puck because of traffic in front of the net. Also problematic is when a shot gets tipped or deflected while it's on its way to the net. This chapter teaches you how to handle a number of situations that will test your determination to find the puck and stop it.

The second part of the chapter is dedicated to puck retention. Puck retention is a goalie's ability to make sure he keeps the puck away from the opposition. This can come in the form of steering pucks, making pull-backs, and taking short pokes as well as playing the puck with clears and breakout passes. Puck retention focuses on the goalie's actions that will determine which team will end up with possession of the puck. If the goalie plays the puck by passing it to a defenseman, sweeping it away from an opposing forward, or steering it away from a potential rebounder, he has retained the puck for his team. Since puck retention includes puckhandling, the techniques of shooting a puck as well as how to control dump-ins are tackled as well.

TRAFFIC SAVES, TIPS, AND DEFLECTIONS

The term *traffic* in hockey simply refers to players on the opposing team driving to the front of the net or circulating around the vicinity of the net in an attempt to make it as difficult as possible for the goaltender to see the puck. Traffic increases the possibility that the puck will change direction on its way to the net and it will be harder to track. An old adage in hockey is that if the goalie can see the puck, then the goalie will stop the puck. Unfortunately, the opposite holds true as well so that when the goalie can no longer see the puck, his chances of stopping the puck are significantly reduced.

This strategy of creating traffic in front of and around the goalie is not new. However, with the increasing size and speed of hockey players today, it is indeed a more effective offensive strategy than in the past. Along with traffic comes a variety of complications for the goaltender. The most obvious is loss of vision. Not being able to see the puck is an extremely uncomfortable feeling. Another difficulty for the goalie facing a lot of traffic is the possibility of a deflection. Usually, when an opposing player goes to the front of the net, a defensive player will follow, adding to the visibility problem as well as the possibility of a puck hitting either player or either of their sticks.

Because of recent rule changes whereby defensemen are limited in their ability to "tie up" an opponent, teams are starting to put defensemen and forwards between the puck and the net in order to try to block as many shots as possible. This is a very effective strategy, resulting in very high numbers of shots blocked by defensive players. However, it also has several downfalls.

■ The strategy limits the goaltender's vision even more and increases the degree of difficulty for a goalie to make a save if the puck gets through to the net.

■ Traffic in front of the net can limit the goalie's ability to get out on top of the crease or to move from one side to the other.

- Finally, if the goalie does make a save on a screen shot or a deflection, it can take a fraction of a second to locate the puck, and this delay can inhibit the goalie's response to the rebound.

Other types of traffic that can cause problems are mobile traffic in the slot and traffic at the side of the net. These situations don't necessarily affect a goalie's ability to see the puck but can cause the goalie some anxiety in the case of a rebound. Side traffic can inhibit the goaltender's ability to play out at the top of the crease because of the threat of a backdoor pass and open rebounder, once again increasing the possibility of a rebound causing difficulty from the initial save. With opponents lurking to pounce on a rebound the goalie has to do a great job steering pucks to the corner and smothering. Let's take a look at the different types of traffic and see how a goalie can deal with them.

Defending Screen Shots

There are two different kinds of screen shots in hockey: One is a shot from the point along the blue line, with the front of the net crowded with both opposing players and defensive players; the other is when the player with the puck is in motion and uses a defensive player as a screen. This is usually associated with an opposing player cutting across the middle of the ice inside the blue line and shooting between the legs of the defenseman or shooting immediately after passing the defenseman. In this scenario, vision of the puck is temporarily lost.

The most important thing when combating the screen-shot threat is to attempt to maintain visual contact with the puck at all times. This can be done by looking over and around the screen (see figure 10.1) or getting down low and looking for the puck through the legs of the traffic. When standing, it is optimal to find the puck by staying big with a higher knee flexion. This allows you to move easier laterally in the case of a backdoor pass. High shots tend to discourage opposing players from going to the front of the net, so it makes sense that screen shots will be low most of the time. Establishing a strong position at

Figure 10.1 Defending the screen from a high stance.

the top of the crease and on the proper angle not only reduces the amount of net available to the puck but also keeps opposing players a little farther out in front.

Your main priority on the screen shot is to establish a position that takes away the low and center areas of the net. In other words, you should be at the top of the crease if possible and on the proper angle to butterfly on the shot.

A butterfly is often used on a screen shot because it takes away the most net, and since there is a good probability that the path of the puck will be altered on the way to the net, the butterfly establishes a strong blocking position. While in the butterfly, maintain a compact body position with arms tight to the body, thighs together, and pads and stick on the ice.

The butterfly should be as wide as possible, unless the shot is from an off-angle, and without compromising compactness. Finally, you should maintain a high chest and thigh position. This helps reduce access to the higher regions of the net and helps you respond to any rebounds to the side. Please check out butterfly techniques in chapter 5 and recovery techniques in chapter 7 for more technical resources.

Before going down in the butterfly, you must try to locate the puck within your stance. When doing so, it is very important that you keep your body square to the shot. You can move your head to the right and left, but you must not allow your body to move off target. Ideally, you would like to track the puck with your head on the strong side of the screen. Once again, you are trying to fill as much of the middle of the net as you can.

The body position as well as the stick position of opposing players can very often help you read where the oncoming shot is headed for. You can use your glove hand to control the position of opposing players tight to the net, allowing you to see "around" the screen. On screen shots, try to also "listen" for the release of the puck, and then go down and make as large a target as possible.

COACHES' TIP Goalies may want to create space between themselves and an attacker so they can move freely. Use your glove to push the hips of the opposing player. If you want him to move right, push his left hip and vice versa. Do not use your blocker hand as this will raise your stick off the ice. Also, using a straight-arm like a football player will give you extra leverage.

Handling Tips and Deflections

Deflections can occur in close to a goaltender or farther out in the high slot. The change in direction of the puck requires you to be perfectly positioned in both circumstances. Deflections are very difficult to stop even if there is no screen present. A key to making saves on deflections in tight is to get as close as possible to the point of the deflection in order to shut down the angle of the puck to the net. The butterfly will allow you to cover most of the net as there may not be enough time to react to the deflection. You must be careful not to be drawn out of the net too far, however. This makes a response to a rebound difficult.

When deflections occur farther out from the net, your reflexes will determine the outcome. As the point of deflection moves farther and farther away from

Figure 10.2 Gapping on a tip or deflection *(a-b)*.

the net, it is still crucial to establish a position that will intersect the path of the puck from the point of deflection to the middle of the net.

Deflections or redirects that occur at the side of the net (see figure 10.2a) are also complicated to handle. You must be aware of all traffic around the net in order to process the possibilities available to the puck carrier. Try to read where the opposing attackers are and the likelihood of each play happening in order to respond quickly. A butterfly slide can be used on a deflection from the side of the net (see figure 10.2b). This blocking technique will allow you to cover the ice and block much of the net.

Deflections that occur on a screen shot usually end up in the goal unless they hit the goaltender or miss the net. Your ability to "find" the puck after contact and your ability to move while down on the ice is critical when making saves on rebounds.

Handling Scrambles

Screens and deflections often result in rebounds that end up in the middle of both offensive and defensive players who are all fighting for possession of the puck. These situations are often referred to as "scrambles." Here is where technique frequently takes a backseat to a goalie's ability to battle, not only to regain vision of the puck but also to try to get into a position that will block the path of the puck to the net. Athleticism and a willingness to compete in a scramble situation will give you a chance to make the save. Dominik Hasek is a great example of a goaltender who has earned a reputation of being one of the best battlers in the NHL; he just never gives up on a puck.

Most of the time, scrambles occur right on your doorstep, so being down in the butterfly will cover the most net, and the number one priority is to block down low. You adjust to the angle of the shot with a butterfly push, knee shuffle, long body, or dive. The last two techniques are desperation saves. Ideally the goal is to stay in the butterfly, stay square to the puck, and cover any possible holes without going the desperation route.

PUCK RETENTION

Puck retention refers to a goaltender's ability to maintain possession of the puck after making a save or playing the puck with his stick. Preventing or minimizing rebounds is a step above controlling rebounds. Controlling rebounds usually means that the puck ends up in a "safe" location on the ice—usually the corners—where it is a relatively long way away from the net. However, in this case, the puck is still "alive" and could be acquired by the opposition, possibly resulting in another shot on net.

When you retain the puck after a save, the opposition has no possibility of regaining possession of the puck. Glove saves and body saves are the obvious examples of puck retention. Other examples are blocker saves or stick saves where the puck is deflected out of play, covering up loose pucks, or using the goal stick to pull pucks back toward you.

Puck retention includes stopping the puck behind the net and leaving it for a teammate, passing the puck up the ice, or leaving the puck for a teammate after a save. The key to playing the puck successfully is the ability of your team to maintain possession of the puck after you play it.

One of the most basic and, when used properly, most powerful weapons available for puck retention is the goal stick. The connotation attached to the word *weapon* should not be construed as an endorsement to wield your stick in an intimidating manner against opponents who get a little too close to you. Although a few goalies have become famous for protecting their domain with a penchant for "using the lumber," this segment is confined to the use of the stick as a defensive mechanism to repel or retain the puck.

The goal stick is first and foremost an integral part of a goaltender's stance. Its importance cannot be understated; improper stick placement can affect your balance and compromise all basic movements. Your stance must be comfortable and balanced on the balls of the feet—not leaning too far forward on the toes and not too far backward on the heels. Therefore, the stick should not be too far in front (causing you to be on your toes) or too tight to the skates (which can result in a lot of rebounds). In fact, the stick should be placed somewhere between these two extremes. This position will optimize your balance.

"Keep your stick on the ice." How many times is this phrase uttered by coaches at all levels of play? Goalie coaches agree—but not to the same degree as those who "run the bench." As a general rule, your stick should be on the ice at all times when there is the threat of a shot directed toward the net. However, there are many times during a game when a goalie should "relax," and if it means that the stick is off the ice, then there should not be any concern on the bench. Martin Brodeur may be the best example of a goaltender who knows when and how to relax during the heat of a game. Of course, a shot that goes along the ice and under a goalie's stick is unacceptable.

There are many ways in which a stick can be a "weapon" in a game. You can use your stick to defend against shots along the ice, to defend against shots from the middle of the ice, and to perform pull-backs and poke checks.

Defending Shots Along the Ice

Shots along the ice can be very nasty if they are not handled effectively. The biggest repercussion of a shot on the ice is the possibility of a rebound, and many goal scorers make a living feasting on juicy rebounds. In today's game, goalies universally respond to shots along the ice by using the butterfly technique. Extremely effective in taking away the lower part of the net, the butterfly is the save selection of choice. However, many goalies who use this technique have been instructed to keep their stick in the five hole, and the result can be a lot of rebounds off their pads. This is especially true in the case of shots from an angle to the far side of the net. Many teams actually employ a strategy of shooting to the far side, with a second player driving to the slot area where most rebounds will end up. The goalie has a low probability of making the save because of the distance he has to travel to get in the path of the shot from the rebound.

The way to combat this situation is to employ a very active and quick stick in order to direct these types of shots to the corner or up and over the glass for a stoppage in play. This technique requires a lot of hard work to get the stick on the puck. Typically, it is more difficult to get the stick on shots to the blocker side than to the glove side because it requires more strength. A goalie who is accomplished in this skill can reduce the number of scoring chances dramatically by keeping pucks out of the danger zone (slot). When practicing this technique, keep your stick far enough in front of the goal pad to allow clearance between the stick and the pad. Otherwise, a rebound can occur despite getting a lot of "wood" on the puck. If this happens, you must recognize why and make an adjustment for the next shot.

Another technical point to pay attention to is the angle of the stick blade. It should be tilted back slightly to form a "ramp" for the puck to climb up. In this way, you can really control the play by directing the puck out of the playing surface, putting the puck over the boards and out of play.

COACHES' TIP   One of the goals of a head coach is to limit the number of shots on net that his team allows. You can help the coach, your team, and yourself by effectively using your stick to control the puck. Being skillful at using your stick is as much about hard work as it is about talent.

Defending Shots From the Middle of the Ice

Shots from the middle of the ice require a different tactic to get the puck to go to the corners of the rink. In this case, the blade of the goal stick must be more perpendicular to the ice surface to form a larger, more resistant object to counteract the velocity of the puck. If the blade is tilted too much, pucks can deflect off the stick and go right into the net in between the arm and body.

To execute this stick save properly, push your blocker out more in front of your body, and turn the stick blade slightly to the corner of the rink so that the puck can be "guided" in the desired direction. The stick actually follows a semicircular path toward the puck in this case. Be careful not to "chase" the puck with the stick outside your leg pad. This can create an angle that could cause the puck to ride up the stick and enter the net (ramp effect). If the puck is shot along the ice and directly in the middle of the five hole, you can pull the blade of the stick back and absorb the puck and cover it. This technique cannot be used if there is power on the puck and should be employed only when the puck is controllable.

Using the stick to control and prevent rebounds is powerful, but it is not always possible to use the stick efficiently, such as when there is an opposing player in close proximity to the net who could deflect the puck. In this case, you should not attempt a stick save by following the puck with the stick outside the five hole. Instead, your stick should cover the five hole to counter the deflection possibility, and the save must be made with the leg pads on a low shot. This situation results in a rebound most of the time, but this is better than a goal on a deflection.

Pullbacks and Poke Checks

This is where a quick stick can be very effective. You can use your stick to "corral" the loose puck or poke it away from an opposing player. Do not extend past the length of the paddle to execute either technique, however. You do not want to compromise a balanced position so that if the pull or poke is not successful, you still have a chance to respond to the rebound while in a down position.

Pull-backs

If you have more time you can use a pull-back. A pull-back can be done from a standing position or the butterfly. In the butterfly simply reach out to the loose puck with the blocker on the paddle of the stick (see figure 10.3 *a-b*). Pull the puck towards you with the back of your stick blade and cover the puck with your glove while maintaining the butterfly (see figure 10.3*c*). After covering the puck protect your glove by placing your paddle in front of the glove. After this sequence you can then look up in case the opposition has backed off and there is a chance to move the puck to a teammate.

The decision to pull or poke is determined by many factors: Do you have enough time to pull the puck back and cover it up? Do your defensemen have the nearest opponent's stick tied up? You will be able to make the proper decision about executing these two techniques through practice and game experience.

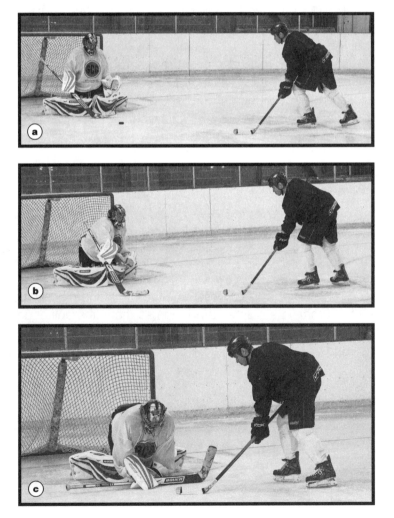

Figure 10. 3 Performing the pull-back *(a-c)*.

Poke Checks

Poking the puck can be done from a standing or butterfly position. The key is to poke the loose puck away from the opponent with the front of the stick blade and to an area where there is no imminent threat. In poking, thrust the stick blade at the puck directing it to where you want to go (see figure 10.4 *a-c*).

Pull-backs and short poke checks are most effective when done at paddle length and not at the end of the stick. End-of-the-stick poke checks are more appropriate when a puck carrier tries to cut to the front of the net while being pressured by a defensive player.

Figure 10.4 Performing a short poke check *(a-c)*.

PLAYING THE PUCK

The ability to handle the puck can mean the difference between playing in the games or watching from the bench. A strong stickhandling goaltender can aid his team in the breakout and can be looked at as a third defensemen at times. The significance of this has been made clear as the NHL has recently instituted new rules to try to limit the amount of puckhandling a goaltender can do. Playing the puck wisely and with confidence takes experience and a high level of skill. It cannot be stressed enough how important it is to practice playing the puck and not to be intimidated by the occasional miscue.

After stopping a dump-in, a goalie may be forced to attempt a pass, clear the puck, or cover it. You should make a pass only when there is a clear passing lane. Try to stay away from cross-ice passes, as they can be dangerous. If there is no passing option available, you can clear the puck by going diagonally off the glass and out of the zone. By going off the strong-side boards you make a safe play, clear the puck, and may even catch a forechecker in the zone. The safest play of course is to cover the puck, and this should be done when there is pressure and a risk of a turnover. Be aware that you cannot cover the puck below the goal line and outside the imaginary box that stretches from the goal line to the right face-off dot, across to the left face-off dot, and back down to the goal line.

Passing the Puck

Not everyone can handle the puck as well as Rick DiPietro. Being able to pass the puck well, however, may mean the difference between being a starter or second-stringer. Be sure to use the right stick—one that will not inhibit your shooting skills. The curve and rocker (discussed in chapter 1) on the blade can greatly affect your ability to play the puck.

MARTY TURCO

Having a goalie who can handle the puck is a huge benefit for teams. Finding the combination of having the strength and skill to handle the puck as well as the goalie sense to make the right decisions is a slam dunk. Marty Turco of the Dallas Stars is one of those goalies who have the ability to fire a puck up the ice and understand how important it is that their team retain possession of the puck after they play it. Turco was one of the first NHL goalies to turn his glove over to clear and pass the puck, and this technique has become very popular.

Marty Turco has been a star at every level of hockey he has played. In college he was the CCHA rookie of the year in 1995 and was named to the NCAA all-tournament team in 1996 and 1998 when Michigan captured the national championship. In the NHL he apprenticed under Eddie Belfour before taking over the starting duties for the Stars in the 2002-2003 season. Turco played in the NHL All-Star Game in 2003 and 2004 and tied the NHL record for most shutouts in one playoff series with three versus Vancouver in 2007.

© Dave Sandford/Getty Images Sport

Forehand Technique

You can choose from two forehand glove positions. The glove can be placed on the stick traditionally, with the fingers down (see figure 10.5a), or the glove can be turned over, with the fingers up (see figure 10.5b). To shoot the puck, grip the shaft of the stick comfortably with your glove, and grip the knob of your stick with the blocker. Start with the puck at the heel of your blade, off your hip and behind your body. Generate momentum by pulling the puck in while bending slightly at the knees and waist. As the puck crosses the center of the blade, roll your wrists and release the puck. Don't flick your shot by releasing it way ahead of your body. The power comes from leaning into the shot and being over the puck, therefore creating leverage. Because many goaltenders are overly concerned about the height of the puck, they neglect working on leverage and consistently shoot floaters that are easily picked off. Remember to look at your target.

Figure 10.5 Passing the puck from a *(a)* fingers down position and *(b)* fingers up position.

Backhand Technique

Slide your blocker up and grab the knob of your stick firmly. Find a comfortable place for your glove along the shaft, either in a traditional fingers down position or with the glove turned up. Apply the same principles to the backhand as you did to the forehand, remembering to start your movement with the puck behind your body and off to the side to get leverage on the puck. Keep the puck to the center of the blade. Even though goaltenders use a backhand shot much less than the forehand, it is an excellent skill to possess. How often do you see a goalie create chaos by trying to clear the puck out of danger with a bad backhand? Being able to ring a backhand around the glass is a great way to control a difficult situation. Remember to look at your target.

If you have a chance before or after practice, throw a bunch of pucks in the high slot. Practice shooting the pucks over the crossbar and against the glass, using both forehand and backhand techniques. Remember to stress technique over height.

COACHES' TIP

A great way to work on your ability to shoot the puck is to complete the 5,000-puck challenge. To complete the challenge, shoot 100 pucks per day, five days a week, for 10 weeks. This can be done at home with a shooting board. Younger goalies should start with player gloves and stick and as they get older graduate to the blocker, glove, and then goalie stick.

Stickhandling

Stickhandling is merely moving the puck from your forehand to your backhand. The key is to control the puck by cupping it with the blade of the stick. Goaltenders should join the other players in as many skating and stickhandling drills as possible. When stickhandling, your catching glove can be either turned up or down. The break of the glove pocket grips the shaft. Try to keep your glove from sliding too low. The closer the glove is to the blocker, the more skill you will develop. The blocker should be at the top of the shaft. It is important to control the stick at all times. Practice stickhandling with your head up so that in a game it will be easier to find the lane or potential outlet options. In game situations, try to limit the amount of stickhandling you do. Often a goalie will overstickhandle, only to realize he has run out of time.

STOPPING THE DUMP-IN

When the puck is shot directly at you along the ice, your first job is to control the dump-in before making a play. There are three ways to do this. If the puck is a threat to skip or bounce, you need to protect against a fluke goal. The easiest way is to drop your flared glove-hand knee to the ice and place your glove behind the stick blade, which stops the puck (see figure 10.6a). The glove acts as a buffer for the stick and provides security if the puck jumps. Do not use your glove to back up the paddle; although it adds to control of the stick, it does not back up and build coverage from your stick blade. If the puck is shot in flat and you are not overly concerned about it skipping, you can take a wide base in your stance and back up the stick blade with the glove without putting your knee to the ice (see figure 10.6b). If you are not afraid whatsoever of the puck's skipping, you can stop the dump-in while in a typical passing position.

If the puck is dumped in to your glove side, you can cover the extra distance by extending your stick out along the ice while dropping your blocker-side knee (see figure 10.6c). By tilting the paddle slightly forward, you can control the rebound off the paddle. If the puck is traveling away from the net on your blocker side, try to get there quickly in order to square with the puck, and use one of the three positions discussed. If you can't get there in time, you can slide your blocker up the shaft of the stick and hold it firmly for extra reach

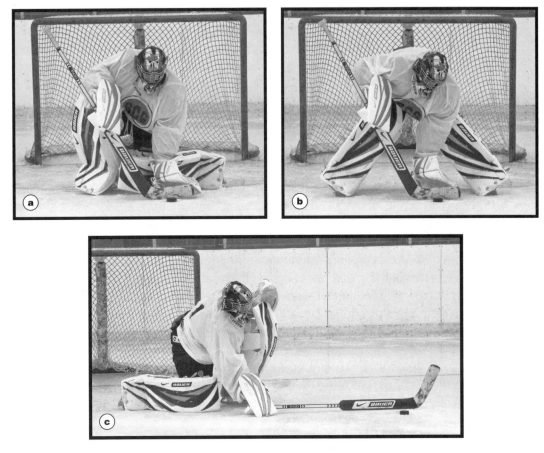

Figure 10.6 Stopping the dump-in with *(a)* a dropped glove-hand knee to protect against a skip or bounce, *(b)* a wide base if skipping isn't a threat, and *(c)* by extending your stick to cover extra distance.

while turning your stick over. Stop the puck using the back of the blade, or lay your stick flat, as for a dump-in on the glove side, for extra reach. If the puck is fired too hard for you to control, let it carom off the dasher (bottom of the boards), and stop it as it returns toward the goal line.

Looping Dump-Ins

When an opponent flicks a high dump-in in front of the net, you never know which way the puck will bounce. Play the puck; don't let it play you. The ideal response is to move out and catch the puck before it lands. If this is not possible, move as close to the landing spot as you can, placing yourself in a tight stance with your knees bent forward to control the rebound. If the puck is going to bounce well out in front of the net, stay put and react to the bounce—don't get caught out of your net in an unpredictable situation.

High Dump-Ins

If you have a chance to catch a dump-in with your glove, you should take advantage of this as opposed to trapping it with your body. After catching the puck, it is important to put it in a position where you can either clear it or set it up behind the net. When you drop the puck to the ice, do not drop it with the glove up high; rather, lower your glove close to the ice so you are in perfect control of placing the puck where you want it off your glove-side skate.

Setting Up the Dump-In

Properly setting up a dumped-in puck can be a big help to the defense. After stopping the puck, pull it to your glove side or push it to your blocker side, and then set it (see figure 10.7 *a* and *b*). You should always leave the puck flat and in an area that does not limit your defensemen's options. Do not leave a tail on the puck as it should be stopped, and make sure it is sitting when you return to your net. Leave the puck just below the goal line and 3 to 4 feet (0.9 to 1.2 meters) outside the edge of the crease. By leaving the puck away from the net, you limit the risk of your defenseman accidentally shooting the puck into your own net; this is also a position where, if something happens to the defenseman, you can smother the puck or shoot it yourself.

Avoid stopping the puck on one side of the net and placing it on another, because this can be confusing to your own players. Often when your teammates come back, they are tired. Or they may have bad habits and put their heads down as they skate back. In either case, they may not see that you've switched sides. Don't pass the puck to the location where you want to leave it. Rather, pull it or push it with your stick and set it—it requires a little extra work, but the defense will feel comfortable knowing that the puck will always be waiting for them at a specific spot.

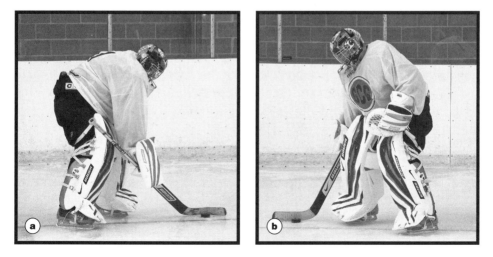

Figure 10.7 Setting the puck from *(a)* the glove side and *(b)* the blocker side.

While setting up a puck for your defenseman, place it far enough away from the net so he can pick it up on his forehand whether he is a right or left shot. By leaving it too close to the net, you may limit him to being able to turn only one way with the puck.

STOPPING THE RIM

You need timing and confidence, which come only with practice, to become skilled at stopping a puck dumped in behind your net. A team whose goaltender is weak in this skill will be forechecked harder, because the other team can sense a possible turnover, than one whose goaltender is consistently able to help take control in these situations.

When going back to stop the puck, your goal should be to stop it on the strong side of the net so as not to get caught in the middle. If your momentum takes you behind the net, you may keep going in your return, but ideally you would like to come back to the strong side. If anything was to go wrong, being directly behind the net would mean the greatest distance to getting back in position. From his stance, a goalkeeper must be able to explode toward the back of the net to the left or right of the posts. Some goalies use a T-glide, while others use one or two crossovers for that extra jump.

Glove-Side Rims

Arriving at the boards on your glove hand will leave you with two approaches. The most secure is to press against the boards with the outside of your skate and the tip of your stick (see figure 10.8 *a* and *b*). Your position should be similar to the basic stance, but with the glove closed and pressed against the glass. Angle your stick blade toward the boards so the puck doesn't ricochet out front. Placing the glove this way controls your approach into the boards and generates power as you push off with your arm, helping you return quickly to your crease. Once you control the puck, use the tip of the stick blade to pull it off the boards, where either the defenseman can easily play it or you can clear it. Return quickly to your crease on the same side you exited.

Be sure your defensemen understand that they should never cut between you and the net when going back to retrieve a puck. This can lead to accidental contact and chaos. It is essential that your defensemen leave you with the most direct path back to the net.

If you are playing on a quality ice surface where the puck should remain flat, you can stop the puck by setting up as if you were a forward receiving a pass. You will be able to move the puck quickly using this technique, but be careful because the puck may take an unpredictable carom off the boards, leaving you out of position. Try to be proficient in both techniques.

If forecheckers prevent you from leaving the puck for your defenseman, you should shoot using a forehand or backhand. By using the forehand, you shoot the puck in the direction you are facing—permitting you to follow its path and return to the net on the same side as the puck. If you use the backhand, you may need to return to the net on the side opposite the path of puck. Ideally your weak-side defenseman will release so you can make him a backhand pass. If you fire the puck for the clear, try to get it high off the glass. This will give you a few extra seconds to return to your net.

Sometimes you will be in position on your glove side when a puck comes off the boards about 6 inches (15 centimeters) away from the boards. Ideally you would like to control the puck and set it for the defenseman, but you're concerned that the spin on the puck will cause it to carom off your stick and back into play. In this situation, try angling your stick toward the boards to deflect the puck. With proper timing, you can make the puck come off the base of the dasher and stop in perfect position for your teammate to retrieve it, while you hustle back to your net.

Figure 10.8 Stopping a glove-side rim with *(a)* fingers down and *(b)* fingers up.

Blocker-Side Rims

In stopping the puck behind the net to your blocker side, before you reach the boards, you should be in your stance facing the direction the puck is coming from. Depending on the speed of the rim you can play it in a passing position or deep in your stance. Turn your stick over, and place the tip inward against the dasher board (see figure 10.9). After you control the puck, pull it away from the boards so your defenseman can easily gain control, and hustle back to the crease on the same side you exited. If you need to play the puck, use the same forehand or backhand technique as described previously. One of the cardinal rules of goaltending is to always face the play. When stopping the puck behind the net, do not turn your back to the rest of the playing surface.

Whether you stop the puck behind the net on your glove side or blocker side, do not venture directly behind the middle of the net. If a bad bounce occurs, you can be left stranded. Also, when the defenseman goes to pick up the puck with a forechecker tight on his heels, you may be caught in a traffic jam with limited room to return to the crease. In addition, never exit your crease on the side opposite to where the puck is dumped. You probably have seen enough blooper videos to know that the glass and boards are not always true and can send the puck in strange directions!

If you do go behind the net to play a puck, either the puck or your momentum may pull you toward the middle of the net. In this case you can allow yourself to go with the flow and come back to the net on the opposite side that you exited.

Figure 10.9 Stopping a blocker-side rim.

chapter 11

GOALIE SENSE

Jamie McGuire

It has been said many times by coaches, trainers, and scouts that a goal-tender either "has it" or he doesn't. We've all seen goaltenders make saves they had no real business making or anticipating plays before they happen and ending up in the right position in the crease so that the puck hits them. We've also seen really talented goalies let in horrible goals because they just didn't react in time.

Wayne Gretzky once said that he just knew where his teammates were on the ice and could sometimes pass without looking. Did someone teach him this "skill"? Becoming an elite goaltender is about more than just being skilled. There have been a lot of very talented goalies who could not succeed at the highest levels of play because mentally they were unable to adjust to the fast pace of the game.

Hockey Goaltending is about helping goalies around the world become more effective in the net and maximize their own individual potential, but how do you write about something that a goalie either "has" or doesn't? What does it mean for a goalie to "have it"? How can you help someone improve an area of his game that cannot be seen or videotaped and analyzed?

We are not convinced that "it" is something that can be taught. Martin Brodeur has "it"; Dominik Hasek has "it." These goaltenders are not the most fundamentally sound when compared with the majority of today's modern netminders. Yet, Brodeur and Hasek have arguably been the two best goaltenders in the world over the past 10 years. It's hard to believe that there's a goalie coach out there somewhere who taught these two goalies how to have "it."

So, if we can't all have "it," then where does that leave the rest of the goalies in the world, from mites to the professionals? This question is exactly what this chapter addresses. Although "it" cannot be taught, "goalie sense" can be. Goalie sense can't be defined in a single sentence or paragraph, but in a number of different parts that all come together. A goaltender with tremendous goalie sense needs to have the following 13 skills and characteristics:

1. Knowing where he is in the crease at all times
2. Being able to effectively read or see plays unfolding
3. Having himself in the right spot at the right time so that most of the pucks shot at the net hit his body
4. Correctly anticipating situations before they happen
5. Making effective decisions about playing or not playing the puck
6. Making effective decisions about save selection and rebound control
7. Communicating properly with teammates
8. Knowing his teammates' habits
9. Being able to learn from past mistakes
10. Being able to learn from past success
11. Always being aware of where the puck is
12. Being mentally strong
13. Being passionate about stopping the puck

SKILLS AND CHARACTERISTICS OF GOALIE SENSE

These 13 skills and characteristics are the basis of what we believe defines the term *goalie sense*. All of these things can be taught and, more important, can be learned. It will not be easy to master them all, but without even one or two of them, there will be glaring holes in your game. (And as goaltenders the last thing we need is bigger holes!)

Knowing Where You Are in the Crease at All Times

A goaltender who is always aware of where he is in the crease without looking down or behind him has simply developed effective methods of keeping track of his positioning through visual cues and physical habits. Find a marking in front of you that is easy to see that will remind you where the center of your net is.

Possible Visual Cues

- The painted logos on the ice (most rinks have them in each zone)
- The center-ice dot
- The net at the other end of the rink
- The hash marks in front of the crease (place yourself between them)
- The defensive face-off dots
- The blue-line stripe along the boards

If you are able to recognize where the center of your net is by using these visual cues, it will make it easier to know where you are standing. Another way to know where you are is to touch one post with the butt end of your stick and use your glove to touch the other post before you gap out of the crease or as you back in on an angle. This allows you to find the net behind you while still looking ahead.

Being square and positioned in the middle of the shooting lane is essential for being consistent. When playing in away rinks, spend time in the warm-up getting your bearing in net and not just stopping shots.

COACHES' TIP

Effectively Reading or Seeing Plays Unfold

Reading the play takes practice and experience. Goalies must pay attention to the habits of individual players and of players in general. You will notice many things, such as left-handed shooters usually shoot to the glove side (on a right-handed goalie), and right-handed shooters usually shoot to the blocker side (on a right-handed goalie).

Pay attention during practices when your coach is explaining offensive strategies to your own team, and watch as these unfold. Many of the same strategies are used by all teams so if you can pick up what is going to happen next your read and reaction time will be decreased.

RYAN MILLER

When you look for a great combination of athleticism, technique, and goalie sense, Ryan Miller has it all. He combines all the natural talent any goaltender would dream of but is also a student of the game and has mastered modern goaltending techniques. Many goaltenders who possess a natural instinct for stopping the puck do not make enough effort to improve their game technically, in contrast to less-talented goaltenders who depend heavily on technique. Miller plays an aggressive, smart, and calculated game. He has the ability to make the "big" saves when the team needs it as well as not give up the easy ones.

Ryan Miller is one of the top goalies in the NHL and currently ranks second on the Buffalo franchise's all-time list for playoff wins (20), goalie games (34), and goalie minutes (2,152). He set a new Sabres record with 40 wins in 2006-2007, was voted the Eastern Conference starter for the 2007 All-Star Game, and played in a career-high 76 games in 2007-2008. A U.S. college Hobey Baker Award winner, Miller won the Aldege "Baz" Bastien Memorial Award as the AHL's top goaltender and was named an AHL First Team All-Star. He also became the American Hockey League's first 40-game winner since Gerry Cheevers in 1964-1965.

© Icon SMI

Being in the Right Spot at the Right Time

Being in the right place at the right time is half the battle for goaltenders. This can be the difference between a solid performance and letting in six goals in a game. The best way to master this is to continually work on your skating. A goaltender who moves well will also move quickly. Getting up and pushing with the proper leg, keeping your stick on the ice, and pushing back to your post and not straight across are just a few examples of proper skating techniques. The right place is the combination of proper positioning, angle, and depth. But these factors continually change based on the location of the puck and opponents. Therefore, a goaltender is constantly using his goalie sense to decide on what the correct combination should be. The more that you work on understanding the game and reading the play the better you will be at being at the right spot at the right time.

Correctly Anticipating Situations Before They Happen

Anticipating the play is about knowing the game and studying opponents and their habits. It also may have a lot to do with the players on your own team. If you are facing a two-on-one situation and the defenseman on your team is weak, then he will most likely play the shooter, and the player with the puck will pass. If your defenseman is doing his job properly, he will take away the pass option, and you can expect a shot.

Making Effective Decisions About Playing or Not Playing the Puck

Goaltenders play the puck for only one reason . . . to help their teams. If you make a mistake, misplay the puck, make a poor decision, or miss the puck altogether, this does not help your team at all. It is therefore important that you be 100 percent certain before leaving the net to play the puck. Sometimes the best decision is to just stay in the net and leave the puck alone. The key to playing the puck is that your team maintains puck possession after you have played it.

Making Effective Decisions About Save Selection and Rebound Control

Save selection is a very important part of becoming a complete goaltender. The decision to stay up or to drop into a butterfly can make the difference between a rebound that lands 3 feet (1.0 meter) in front of you or one that is steered safely into the corner. There is no secret way for a goalie to master her save selection. It is all about practice, training, and repetition. The more shots you face, the better you will be able to determine what type of save is most effective for you.

Sometimes goalies can lose their focus in practice. A great way to train your ability to concentrate is to make sure you are controlling your rebounds and placing the puck where you want to so that in a game, it is second nature to dictate where your rebounds are heading.

Communicating Properly with Teammates

Hockey is a team game. In a team game, players must communicate with each other. As a goalie, you sometimes have the advantage of seeing things unfold that your teammates may miss. It is important to relay this information verbally.

- Let your teammates know that the linesman has waved off an icing call when they are coming back for the puck.
- Remind your defensemen on a two on one or three on two that you have the shooter.
- Let your teammates know if an opposing player is open in front of the net.
- Let your teammates know if they are being pressured or if they have time when they are coming back for a puck.
- Yell at your defense if an opposing player has snuck behind them.
- Let your team know that a penalty is about to expire.
- Give supportive and positive feedback between plays.

Knowing Your Teammates' Habits

By paying attention in games and practices, you will be able to notice certain habits of the other players on your team. You may have a teammate who is a great skater but always seems to make bad passes up the middle of the ice, resulting in turnovers. Certain players on your team may be slower than others, allowing opposing players to beat them in a one-on-one situation. If you are aware of these things, it will help you be better prepared during games.

Learning From Past Mistakes

When goaltenders make a mistake during a game, it can often lead to the opposition scoring a goal. Players, on the other hand, can make mistakes that may even go unnoticed. For this reason alone it is important that goalies learn from their past mistakes in order to try to prevent them from reoccurring.

For young goaltenders, mistakes are just part of the learning process. They are inevitable. What makes a good goalie great is the ability to recognize, accept, and then analyze those mistakes and try to understand how to keep them from happening in the future. If you can break down the play on a "weak" goal, you may be able to see something really small that you did wrong. Once you can recognize the problem, you can then work on fixing it.

Practice is the best place to work on these issues. This is where you can try new techniques or moves in order to complete your game. If you find you are getting beaten low stick side in games, then work on adjusting your angles in practice. If you are getting beaten over the shoulder in games because you are dropping too soon, then in practice you should concentrate on being more patient and staying up longer. We cannot emphasize how important it is for goalies to accept mistakes as part of hockey. Stay positive, and learn from your mistakes—they will end up being great learning tools.

Learning From Past Success

"Success is a choice." To be successful, we must choose to be. Part of that choice involves understanding what makes us successful so that we will be able to repeat the behavior. Just as we often make mistakes and we are not sure why, the same goes with our successes.

Being in a "zone" or bringing your "A" game can sometimes happen without your doing anything significantly different from usual. Or so you think. If you really look at your great performances in the past, you may be able to see things that you did really well on the ice, or a certain mood you were in before the game started.

Perhaps it was as simple as turning the wrist on your glove hand so the angle of your catcher was different, allowing you to cover more net and preventing any goals on the glove side. If you find something that works for you in a game, then make sure to try it in practice. The reverse is also important. If you are trying a new technique in practice and it is working, then do not be afraid to use it in your next game.

Being Aware of Where the Puck Is

As simple as it sounds, many goalies are not very good at finding and keeping their eye on the puck at all times. This comes down to focus and concentration. Goaltenders must always be focused and ready. They are not allowed the luxury of taking a shift off on the bench, as the other players do. Knowing where the puck is at all times will make the game significantly easier.

In scouting goaltenders at a game a few years ago, it was evident that when the play was in the other end, one of the goalies was more focused on moving the snow around in his crease than watching the puck. At the other end of the ice, the other goaltender never stopped moving his head, always watching the puck no matter where it was on the ice.

The second part of tracking the puck is being able to follow your own rebounds effectively. This is something you can easily work on in practice by asking your coach to slow down the shooting drills. This will give you a chance to feel the puck hit your body and then focus on moving to where the rebound went and squaring up. After you are set, then regroup and get ready for the next shot.

Another drill you can do is to have a teammate (one whom you trust!) take shots on you with your eyes closed. Make sure they hit your body. Without opening your eyes, try to square up to where you think the rebound went. Then open your eyes and see how close you were to getting it right. You will really have to focus on feeling the puck hit your body. Eventually you will begin to just automatically know where the rebounds are going to end up.

COACHES' TIP Having the chance to follow and line up on rebounds in practice is extremely important. This is what is going to give you the practice you need in order to stop a flurry of shots. Shooting drills that do not allow a goalie to follow the puck off his body do not help the goaltender.

Being Mentally Strong

Many hardworking goaltenders with all kinds of talent have not been able to reach their potential. One possible reason is their inability to be mentally strong. Goaltending requires a unique mind-set. Even the best goalies in the world still fail to stop the puck from going into the net two or three times per game. This fact alone is why the mental aspect of goaltending is so important. Failure is almost guaranteed every time you play. Goalies must learn to accept these failures and move on or start over each time a goal is scored.

Once you realize that getting scored on is just part of hockey, then it will become easier to accept it when it happens. Some goalies play an outstanding game for the first 15 minutes, and then they let in a goal . . . after that their entire performance suffers. On the other hand, successful goaltenders bounce right back and play even stronger after letting in a goal.

Allowing a goal during a game should be looked at as a wake-up call. After a goal you should take a moment to refocus and start over. Make sure you are ready to stop the next scoring attempt. If you are really bothered by the goal, you can try reaching into the net, picking up the puck with your glove, and handing it to the referee. This not only shows class but also allows you to calm down and keep focused.

Being Passionate About Stopping the Puck

Finally, you need to want to stop the puck. As obvious as this may sound, it is not always the case 100 percent of the time for most goaltenders. It is easy to say that you want to stop the puck and to even look good trying, but the ability to give everything in your heart and soul every time someone shoots a puck at you is rare. Never give up on a play. Force yourself to do everything in your power to make the save. Stay focused.

Make the extra effort to dive across the crease, even when you think you may not be able to get there in time. This passion is within all of us who have ever decided to put on a pair of goal pads and stand in front of a slapshot. The next time you are ready to give up or relax for even a second, remember how hard you have worked to get where you are, and then reach out and make that spectacular glove save.

Then you can honestly say you are one of those goalies who just "has it."

Great Goalies Are Forgetful

Adam H. Naylor, EdD, AASP-CC

Throughout hockey history, goaltenders have been called many different things . . . smart, focused, weird, tough, eccentric, and more. When thinking of a great game-day goalie, one should be sure to add "forgetful" to the list. It would be easy to argue that goalie is the most important position on the ice. The goalie is critical to a team's success, and furthermore the position can be tough on a player's ego. While it is an incredible rush to make a flashy glove save, cut off the angles on a breakaway, and cover up the puck when things are crazy in front of the net, it is equally (if not more) emotional to see the puck slip over the goal line.

The reality is that goals happen. Shutouts are rare, and even the best goalies often see the puck in their own net a time or two each game. Great goalies do not like to be scored on—they do however understand that it is part of the game. Most importantly, they know how to put it behind them and keep their head in the game. It is not easy to play the game with such forgetfulness. The good news is that any motivated goalie can learn to be game tough. With practice and commitment, every goalie can learn to focus as if they are working on a shutout at all times.

The first step to becoming a resilient goalie is to embrace a few basic principles of tough goaltending:

1. Make your opponents earn their goals. Before each game determine two keys to your goaltending success (some examples are control rebounds, stay out of the net, keep your stick down). Next, focus on executing these two things throughout the game. If a goal is scored on you and you were successful with your keys to success, no problem. You made your opponents "earn it."

2. Remember the crease is sacred. If you are not focused on watching the puck and cutting off angles, get out of the crease! If your mind is focused on the last shot or your emotions are out of control, get out of the crease! Goalies have the great luxury that it is rare that an official will drop the puck if the goalie is not in the net. When frustrated or unfocused, skate to a corner to calm down and refocus. When in the crease, your game and team need a goalie that is clearly seeing the puck and focused on his/her keys to good goaltending.

3. There is a time to think about the goals you let in; game-time is not that time. A good goalie does think about goals that slipped past him/her. If mistakes were made, it is important to learn from them. The time to do this learning is after the game is over. During the game, things are too emotional and too exciting for great learning to take place. All good players focus on one or two keys to success and leave big thoughts to after the game is over.

Understanding and committing to these principles will allow a goalie to play focused consistently during the game. Sometimes these ideas might be tough to remember or difficult to believe during the emotions of a game. Therefore it is important for a goalie to create a few mental anchors to keep him/her on track throughout each game. Anchors can be actions that help calm the body, symbolic activities that ready a goalie, and/or simple thoughts that help a goalie focus on the right thing at the right time. Here are a few examples:

- Calm the body. A lot of mental mistakes are made because a goalie gets too excited, causing the mind to race and muscles to tense. A good goalie needs to be calm in the net so that the body remains flexible and the mind is able to focus on the puck. An easy way to help yourself find this state is to breathe deeply. Exhale for a count of four, and follow this up with a full breath in for a count of four. Getting oxygen to the body and mind will calm, energize, and focus a goaltender.

- Trigger focus. Great goaltenders often have simple actions or rituals that remind them to get their mind into the game. Perhaps one of the most famous rituals was Ron Hextall's (Philadelphia Flyers former goalie) hitting the posts and the crossbar at the beginning of every period and during the intermissions. These actions do not have to be so dramatic; having a sip of water, adjusting one's pads, tapping the stick, or skating out of the crease for a moment or two can all be great ways to refocus. Choose an action that allows you to refocus and say, "I'm ready."

- Think on target. Oftentimes a few focused and/or positive words can keep a goalie in the game. What is a brief phrase (two or three words) that sums up what you need to do to play well? "Heads up." "Stick down." "Get out." When your mind is wandering to a goal let in or a tough series, say your phrase to put you back on target.

Take a few moments to develop these anchors for yourself. Try them out in practice in order for them to be game ready. Remind yourself of them before the puck drops on game day. Commit to them throughout the season. These actions combined with the three principles of mentally tough goaltending will allow you to develop the "forgetfulness" of a great goaltender.

Practice hard. Play smart. Have fun.

About Dr. Adam Naylor

Dr. Adam Naylor is the director and sport psychology coach at the Boston University Athletic Enhancement Center (www.bu.edu/aec). He wrote the previous article exclusively for the Goaltending Consultant Group. Adam has authorized the use of his article for *Hockey Goaltending,* as it provides goalies with perspective and tools to help them be stronger mentally.

Dr. Naylor also leads Telos Sport Psychology Coaching (www.telos-spc.com). For more educational articles and sport psychology information, visit the Telos SPC Web site. Dr. Naylor can be reached for consultation or coaching at adam@telos-spc.com or 617-821-7133.

chapter 12

DEVELOPING A SHUTOUT MIND-SET

Brian Daccord

Many elements go into becoming a successful goaltender. You must be technically schooled, in great condition, and able to read the play. Equally as important as skill, strength, and goalie sense is the mental aspect of goaltending. In this chapter you will read about how the four Cs (confidence, character, competitiveness, and composure) can help bring your game to a whole new level.

Being mentally tough is an important quality for a goalie to possess, as well as working well with his coach and goaltending partner. A goalie must be a leader on her team and act as the quarterback on the ice. This chapter helps you prepare yourself for goalie-specific situations. The ability to overcome adversity and setbacks is essential for succeeding between the pipes, and these topics are covered in the sections on overcoming nervousness and dealing with a slump. Finally, preparing mentally to be successful through goal setting is all part of the equation. Although this is the last chapter in the book, it may just be the most important for those goalies looking for that extra edge.

THE FOUR CS: CONFIDENCE, CHARACTER, COMPETITIVENESS, AND COMPOSURE

The technical side of the game means little if a goalie does not have confidence. Having the inner confidence that you will stop the puck is a huge determinant of whether you will be successful between the pipes. Therefore, the big question is where does confidence come from, and how do you build and maintain it? Confidence is derived from various factors. Character, competitiveness, and composure play significant roles in determining confidence.

Confidence

Inner confidence says a lot about your character. Very rarely do you find an athlete with true inner confidence who does not have strong character traits. Words to describe these character traits are *competitiveness, passion,* and *sportsmanship.* These traits don't happen overnight—they are developed over time. Please don't mistake the hot dog for somebody with confidence, as the athlete who tries to put on a big show is usually battling a lack of inner confidence.

Feeling good about yourself, your skill set, and your performance ability is key. To feel good about yourself, conduct your actions in a manner you can be proud of. Work hard on the ice at all times to make yourself better, and take that same work ethic into the classroom and your home.

Character

Having character involves being a quality teammate and person. Surrounding yourself with positive people who also have strong character and make the right decisions is very important. If you are selfish and lazy, it is hard to feel good about yourself and therefore difficult to have that inner confidence. You will find that confidence is something that will grow like falling dominos and continue to pick up momentum. Take part in activities and associate yourself with people that will help build your self-confidence.

Competitiveness

One thing you can say about all successful athletes is they are extremely competitive. Passion for the game and a desire to win are absolutely necessary to become the best you can be. You must be able to channel this competitiveness in a positive way and when you compete leave nothing on the ice. With this type of competitive spirit, even if a game is lost you can still take pride in the fact you gave it everything you had. Use defeat to drive you to train harder, focus better, and perform at a higher level to ensure success.

Composure

Composure is all about controlling your emotions when things start to get out of control. Out of control can mean both good and bad things happening. You must not allow yourself to get caught up in the emotions that will take you out of your game. Try to keep an even keel and stay away from the dreaded peaks and valleys. Keep your head in the game at all times, and don't let situations or the actions of others get you sidetracked. Having composure is so important when it comes to goaltending, and it is a quality that can be worked on and developed over time.

Exuding confidence is very important when trying out for a team. Coaches will be looking for the goalie who doesn't get rattled and will provide them with the most consistent goaltending.

COACHES' TIP

DEVELOPING GREAT PRACTICE HABITS ON AND OFF THE ICE

We all know that games are fun, but it is what we get out of practice and training that gives us the ability to have fun in games. Therefore it is essential that you maximize your time and effort to gain the most rewards for your commitment. Don't practice or train just to get it done. Practice and train to get better. You do this by pushing yourself and never being complacent.

On the ice, do not be satisfied with a mediocre performance in practice. Challenge yourself to contest every shot. If you push yourself in this manner, the games will become mentally and physically easier.

One of the hardest working goaltenders over the last 20 years is by no surprise one of the worlds most successful. Whether it was a regular practice, a morning game-day skate, or a pregame warm-up, Dominik Hasek never gave up on a shot and contested every puck. It was easy to see why he was one of the best goalies of his era.

If you think your coach doesn't push you enough in practice, then take it upon yourself to work harder. There are several things you can do on your own within practice.

- Line up on every rebound as if a player is going to be there to shoot the puck, even if there isn't.
- Work on communicating with your teammates throughout practice.
- Do small crease skating drills on your own. Get on the ice early or stay later if you can.
- Communicate with your coaches about how to make practice more beneficial for the goalies. The goaltender is in the easiest position to cruise though practices. Don't let it happen to you.

Off-ice training as you get older becomes extremely important. Set goals for yourself with respect to your training. Push yourself to attain those goals. Think about how what you are doing off the ice is going to affect your success on the ice. If you are not sure what you should be doing off the ice, seek assistance and make sure you are maximizing your time. If you are not putting time and effort into the off-ice training component of development, you can rest assured that there are other goalies working hard at bettering themselves.

COACHES' TIP   Working hard and working smart go hand in hand. When putting together your on- and off-ice training program, be sure it is a well-choreographed plan that addresses all the areas of development necessary for you to reach your potential.

MENTAL TOUGHNESS

Not all coaches have the same strategy in preparing a team, and not all goaltenders have the same mental approach to the game. Some goalies like to be all fired up and mad at the world when they compete; others prefer to play in a calm and conservative manner. Other people can't tell you what your approach should be, but they can help you see some of the factors that can contribute to your success.

A self-evaluation is part of the goal-setting form at the end of this chapter. Be sure to note on your self-evaluation what state of mind you had at the beginning of the game in question as well as throughout the game. By analyzing these forms, you will likely find that you consistently play at a higher level when you compete in a specific state of mind. Prepare a list of emotions you have when you are in this particular state. Go over this list before the game, and see if you can place yourself at this emotional level.

MARTIN BRODEUR

The importance of a goalie's confidence level cannot be underestimated. An inner confidence can mean the difference between greatness and mediocrity. One of the greatest goaltenders playing in the NHL is Martin Brodeur. The interesting thing about him is his ability to perform at the highest level, stay focused, and compete courageously while at the same time being relaxed and enjoying the game. One reason for his character on and off the ice is his confidence in his own ability to stop the puck. This confidence is due in part to his commitment to practice and to his motto as a younger goalie to "never get beat twice" in practice. Working hard to not give up two consecutive goals in practice allowed him to maximize his training time and to focus on the next shot as opposed to worrying about the puck that just went in.

Martin Brodeur has had a legendary career, winning the Stanley Cup three times with the New Jersey Devils. He won the Calder Trophy in 1994 and has appeared in nine All-Star games. Brodeur has also won the William M. Jennings Trophy four times as well as the Vezina Trophy on three occasions. As if all the NHL hardware wasn't enough, he also won an Olympic gold medal in 2002 as the starting goaltender for team Canada in Salt Lake City.

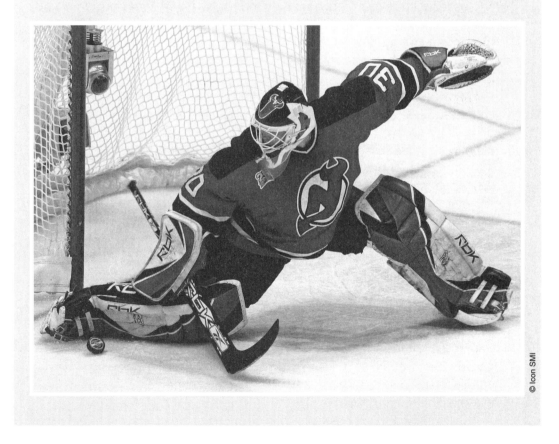

© Icon SMI

Athletes are often notorious for their rituals and superstitions. Players may need to eat the same meal before every game or park their cars at specific spots. For players who have such superstitions, following through on them can help induce the right frame of mind for playing the game. Goalie legend Patrick Roy, for example, would not skate over the blue lines while skating to and from his net—he actually hopped over them. This little ritual, performed at game time, helped him stay concentrated and in the zone.

COACH–GOALTENDER RELATIONS

A goaltender's needs are very specific, and they differ from those of the rest of the team. Open communication between coach and goalie is extremely important. Players often are too intimidated to discuss situations with their coaches. To be successful in this competitive position, however, you must do everything possible to improve your performance—and that may require communicating with the coach.

Most coaches were not goaltenders themselves, and sometimes they have trouble grasping the concepts and mentality of goaltending. It is up to you to become knowledgeable about the fundamentals by watching videos and reading manuals such as this one. Then, if there is a point the coach is missing, it is up to you to explain it.

There are appropriate and inappropriate times to approach your coach with suggestions. To be successful, the coach must have the players' respect and discipline—so if you believe a practice drill is counterproductive for you, don't express your feelings there on the ice. Wait until after practice, and sit down with the coach in private when he'll have an open mind and time to analyze your suggestions.

Never question his skill or judgment in front of the other players. The last thing you want is to back him into a corner. Even in your private conversations, always leave him a dignified way out of a controversial situation. After you've talked with him, don't keep bugging him. Give him time to set the drill up differently for the next training session. After that practice, if you can tell he still doesn't grasp the concept, bring him the video or manual with the explanation, and present it to him in a respectful manner.

There must be mutual respect between you and your coach. Show him you want to learn and improve your game by working 100 percent in practices and games. Demonstrate your desire to do everything possible, including analyzing practices and games with him and discussing what can be changed to make things better for you.

Always show a willingness to play in all circumstances. Never project a lack of self-confidence to your coach, even if you are in a state of low self-esteem.

This will reduce the confidence level the coach has in you and make his decision to go with the other goaltender easier. Never look to the bench after a goal. Get ready to keep playing, and shake it off. If the coach yanks you, skate to the bench with your head high, and get motivated for your next chance to play. Don't lumber to the bench hanging your head like a defeated warrior, as this will negatively affect the morale of your entire team. If you don't agree with a move, don't pout on the bench; rather, encourage the other players and goaltender. After the next practice, where you've worked 100 percent, respectfully discuss with the coach why you were pulled and what you need to work on to improve your standing in his eyes.

Perhaps the most discouraging thing for a coach and his players to see is a beaten goaltender. After a goal, avoid lying on the ice or shaking your head. Let the referee pull the puck from the net, and either go for a brief skate or get back immediately to your set position. Keep your chest and head held high, and show that you're ready to compete. Reacting this way puts you back into the correct mental state and makes your teammates feel secure.

BECOMING A GREAT REGULAR-SEASON GOALTENDING COACH

Many goaltenders get caught up worrying about the game, and it drains them physically. A coach can settle down the starter by telling him two or three specifics on which to concentrate during that game. Instead of worrying about 100 different scenarios, he is able to focus better and stay calm. Another coaching strategy is to break the game into three parts and have players think about the score after each period. This breaks the contest into three short games, each with a distinct beginning and ending. Goalies get a break after each period and are ready to start the "next game" with a fresh outlook.

It is important that coaches understand what motivates their goaltenders. Some goaltenders are motivated to achieve success, while others are motivated by fear of failure. A player motivated to achieve success will be up for the best competition but may have trouble getting enthusiastic about playing a weak team. A player motivated by a fear of failure will look either for the easy win or for a game so tough the odds are overwhelmingly in the other team's favor. The coach's responsibility is to identify trends in a goaltender's mental approach and improve on them. For example, if you're going into a game against a weak team and your goaltender is motivated by success, give him specific goals and challenges to inspire his play. If your goaltender is motivated by fear of failure, work on building his confidence and creating an outlook for him that transfers responsibility to the team rather than just him.

Most head coaches are very open about the fact that they are not up to date on the most recent goaltending techniques and strategies. But this does not mean they can't be great regular-season goaltending coaches. It is a goaltender's responsibility to seek goalie-specific training on top of what is provided by the team. It is therefore the coach's responsibility to do his part during the season to assist in goaltending development. The following are suggestions for head coaches who want to be great goalie coaches.

1. Plan practices so that goalies have 5 to 10 minutes at the beginning of the ice session to do their goalie-specific skating drills. Goaltender skating drills are different from player skating drills, so allow goalies time to get their work in.

2. Assign an assistant coach to be responsible for the goalies. This coach does not have to be a former goalie or goalie educated. He simply will make sure that the goalies are working hard and maximizing the practice time. This coach should watch to see if the goalies are competing, are controlling rebounds, and are vocal during situational drills. You don't need to be a goalie coach to track these things. This coach should also add positive reinforcement when the goalies are practicing hard and create accountability if they are dogging it.

3. Add the five-second rule to your practice drills. After a shot is taken in drills, the players often go directly to the next line, and neither the shooter nor the goaltender follows the rebound. To create a gamelike situation, tell the players that after each shot is taken to imagine five seconds left in the third period of a tie game. This will prompt the goaltender and attackers to play the rebound, allowing for scrambles, walkouts, pass-outs, wraparounds, and so on. These drills will make not only the goalies better but the shooters as well. It will also add tremendously to the goaltenders' conditioning and not affect the tempo of practice.

4. Play to the whistle in practice drills. Once again trying to create more gamelike situations, coaches can use their whistles not only to start drills but to end them as well. In this situation, the players and goalies are trained that, after the initial shot is taken, they should continue to play until the whistle. The next group starts only after the whistle is blown. This creates a number of situations for the goalies to handle, and it helps in their training of following the puck and battling until the whistle.

5. If there is going to be downtime for goalies in practice, prepare accordingly. If a head coach is going to work just one end of the ice and leave the other goalie standing around at the far end, the coach responsible for the goalies should be prepared. Have an assistant ready to either have the goalie work on skating drills or dump pucks in to work on his stick skills.

6. Let the goalies know they are part of practice. So many times a head coach is so consumed in practice that he does not take a second to recognize the goalies. Head coaches should make it a point to include the goalies and communicate with them in practice. This will create more accountability and add to goalie and coach relations.

7. Don't treat your goalies differently from any other player. The old cliche of "just leave the goalies alone" has long passed. A goalie is a member of the team just like anybody else. He should be encouraged, instructed, and accountable just like any other player on the team.

8. Communicate with your goalies. The number one problem in any relationship is communication. The more you communicate with your goalies, the better they will be able to play. By keeping them guessing or playing head games, a lot of negative energy can be created. Try to create an environment where there is open communication, and if that isn't your style, have the assistant coach responsible for goalies act as the liaison.

When utilizing the five-second rule in practice, have one coach at each end responsible for making sure the effort at both ends is 100 percent. To make it fun, the coach can yell a countdown of 5, 4, 3, 2, 1 to create a sense of urgency.

COACHES' TIP

GOALTENDER COMPETITION

Through tryouts, the regular season, and the playoffs you will be competing for playing time with other goalies. There is often jealousy and conflict, with players even lobbying for one goaltender or the other.

Competition is essential for you to reach your maximum potential. Welcome the challenge, and realize you will improve more by being pushed than if you had no pressure. Don't take the challenge on a personal level; your competition wants to play hockey and be successful just as you do. The starting job should be won on the ice—not by backstabbing and politics, which disrupt the chemistry of the team and lead to bickering and disharmony. You have a responsibility to yourself, your coach, and your teammates to do everything you can to help the team win, whether by starting or being prepared to come off the bench.

Because goaltenders play a unique position, there is usually a bonding among a team's goalies. If you are on a team with two or three goaltenders, you will hopefully experience relationships of mutual respect. Even if there is tension among you, try to maintain the highest level of sportsmanship. By watching another goaltender practice and play throughout the season, you pick up habits from him. Analyze his game completely, and borrow from his repertoire aspects that will improve your style. You can mutually raise the level of your play by acting as each other's goalie coaches and pointing out positive and negative points in each other's game. By doing this, you raise the quality of the entire team. An adverse relationship among competing goaltenders will only distract and detract from your potential improvement.

OVERCOMING NERVOUSNESS

Nervousness is a sensation that all goaltenders experience. It can slow your reflexes and lead to bad decisions. If you are scared to make a mistake, you will hesitate—and that hesitation can translate into a goal. You must learn to translate your nervous energy into power. There are three keys to beating a case of nerves, each of which are covered here:

1. Practice
2. Focus
3. Attitude

Practice

Remember the nervous feeling you had when you went into an exam for which you studied only the previous night? Was the feeling different when you had prepared adequately? An honest player who works 100 percent at practice is a player with integrity. Integrity translates into respect for yourself, and that respect translates into confidence. Self-confidence and pride will defeat a bout of the nerves.

In practice, you have the chance to prepare your response to many different situations. By thinking about how you will play certain situations and knowing what to do before they even happen, you will develop much quicker reaction times when they do happen. Practice is not just physical: Think the position!

Focus

You cannot perform to the best of your ability without concentration. Your state of concentration must remain constant throughout the game, without lapses. Often a bad goal can open the floodgates, or a bad game can cause a slump. A successful approach to dealing with events that can break concentration is to focus on future results. If you know the results you are looking for down the road, you'll find it easier to deal with minor setbacks.

If your desired result is to not give up any goals, you are being unrealistic, and a bad goal may throw off your game. But if your goal is to give your maximum effort for 60 minutes so your team has its best chance to win, a bad goal may easily be forgotten. If your desired result by the end of the season is to have improved your ability as much as possible in order to play at a higher level next year, you can consider a bad game as a learning tool that provides motivation to work harder.

Attitude

Successful athletes maintain an attitude that allows them to have the self-confidence to perform at a high level. That attitude gives them the ability to react without hesitation. Making split-second decisions is a big part of goaltending. If you are afraid to make a mistake, you will not play to the best of your ability. Fear promotes hesitation. Hesitation creates internal second-guessing that can only lead to trouble. If you have worked hard at learning and understanding your position, this knowledge is inside of you. Your solid fundamentals will show without your having to consciously think about them. When the puck drops, let your instincts take over, and have fun!

The key is to focus on the positive. Everyone has a positive attitude somewhere inside of him; it is up to you to bring it forward. When you step on the ice before your next game, ask yourself this question: "How would I feel if I were not afraid?" The answer would probably be "Great!" The chance to compete in a sport you love, playing with friends, with people cheering you on—these are the reasons you chose to play hockey in the first place. Once you've put your fears away, you can perform to the best of your abilities.

DEALING WITH A SLUMP

No one is immune to the dreaded slump, but a smart goaltender will come out of a slump faster than one who does not think about his position. Try to do the following to help you get out of a slump:

- Take advantage of your evaluations to note what kind of goals you are allowing and what you can do about them. Be determined to stop that type of shot.

- Take a new outlook or philosophy into a game, and see if this new approach can give you a jump-start.

- Put on a show. Go out for your next game determined to make it your best of the season.

- Exaggerate your saves a little, or try a little "trash talking"—anything to provide a spark.

- Be someone else! Remember as a kid when you used to pretend you were a great NHL superstar? Why not try it again? How about being Marc-Andre Fleury for a game? It will take the pressure off of you and place it on him!

MENTAL PREPARATION THROUGH SETTING GOALS

There comes a point in an athlete's career when he has to look at himself for motivation. When you were a child, your coaches and parents were always there to pick you up and give you a push when you needed it. Moving ahead often requires leaving security behind—even a screaming coach will motivate you for only so long.

A big part of remaining constantly motivated during practices and games is focus. You must be clear about why you are putting in all this work and what you want to achieve. If you are unclear inside, you will not be able to perform at your highest level and will not carry the respect for yourself and for the game necessary to be a winner.

Once you initially have a clear focus, your next task is to maintain that focus, and you do that by setting goals. No one can tell you what your specific goals should be, but the following five principles will help you set goals.

1. Set both long- and short-term goals. It's not enough to say, "I want to play in the NHL one day." Rather, set short-term goals such as playing on a travel team, midget AAA or varsity at high school, then college or major junior, and then the minors.

2. Make your goals realistic but tough to achieve. Set a goal such as finishing in the top three goaltenders in your league or winning 70 percent of your starts. The idea is to challenge yourself with a goal for which you really need to work hard.

3. Set goals that can be measured. A goal to become a better goalie is good, but you need a way to quantify your progress. Use statistics such as save percentage, number of starts, and goals-against average to make it easier for you to see the results.

4. Make a written plan describing how you will achieve your goals. Set specific criteria for improving as a goaltender. Your plan may entail more off-ice work, form and film analysis, or extra time at camps and clinics.

5. Evaluate, evaluate, evaluate! Good goal setting requires that you continually evaluate your progress toward achieving your goals. Make a photocopy of the goal-setting form provided on pages 256 and 257 and fill it out; constantly read over your goals to track your results. This will provide motivation, praise, and encouragement in bringing your game to the next level.

A major component of goal setting is writing down your goals. It is not good enough just to think about them. After they are written down, put them in a place where you can see them frequently. Seeing your goals written down on a consistent basis will keep them in the forefront.

GOAL EVALUATION FORMS

One final useful tool is the goal evaluation form on pages 258 and 259. Make several photocopies of this form, and give them to a coach, a parent on the bench, or your team's other goalie to fill out for you during a game. Specific notes on each goal scored against you will help provide valuable feedback, and you will be able to find areas for improvement. By studying these, you will know how to stop the puck in similar situations in the future.

PLAN FOR SUCCESS

Goaltending is not easy. If you are mentally weak, you will have a tough time meeting the challenges and dealing with the pressure. But if you have a plan and a sound philosophy on how you will deal with the peaks and valleys inherent in the life of a goaltender, your chances of success will improve dramatically. Go out and play with passion, and enjoy every minute you spend on the ice. Playing goal is tough. Going between the pipes and putting yourself on the line shows how strong a person you are. Just facing this challenge alone shows that you are a success!

GOAL-SETTING FORM

Long-Term Goals

_____

_____

_____

_____

_____

_____

_____

_____

Short-Term Goals

_____

_____

_____

_____

_____

_____

_____

_____

Plan to Achieve Goals

_____

_____

_____

_____

_____

_____

_____

Evaluation of Goals

_____

_____

_____

_____

_____

_____

_____

_____

GOAL EVALUATION FORM

Team: **Date:**

SHOT

Time of goal: [   ]   **Period:** [   ]   **Score:** [   ]

Type of shot (circle one):

- Slap shot
- Wrist shot
- Backhand
- Snapshot
- Deke

Where did the puck beat me?

[   ]

SHOOTER

Shooter (circle one):

- Left
- Right

Attack (circle one):

- 3-on-2
- 3-on-1
- 3-on-0
- 2-on-1
- 2-on-0
- 1-on-1
- Breakaway
- In-zone

Situation (circle one):

- Power play
- Shorthanded
- Even strength

Zone in which puck was shot?

[   ]

Position (circle one):

Standing

Down

In between

Type of save attempted (circle one):

Butterfly

Butterfly slide

Butterfly push

Glove save

Blocker save

Two-pad stack

Long body

Dive save

Stick save

Poke check

Half poke

Comments:

_____

_____

_____

Where was I positioned?

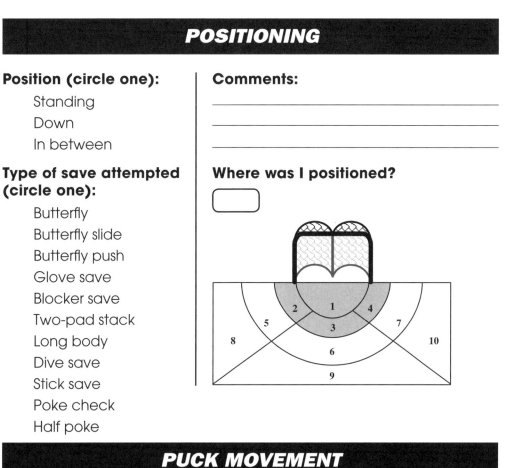

PUCK MOVEMENT

Scored by (circle one):

Forward

Defenseman

Type (circle one):

Screen

Deflection

Clear look

Pass near crease

Goalie error

Wraparound

Fluke

Rebound

Note: if goal was scored after a rebound, mark an R where rebound was left.

Comments:

_____

_____

_____

What was the movement of the puck?

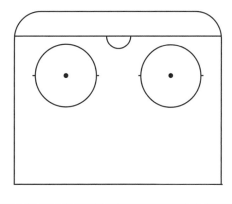

INDEX

Note: The italicized *f* and *t* following page numbers refer to figures and tables, respectively.

ABOUT THE EDITOR

Brian Daccord is a former goaltending consultant of the Boston Bruins. His "Ask the Coach" column appears in each issue of *Goalies' World* magazine, and he can be heard across North America on his weekly radio segment "Between the Pipes With Brian Daccord" on the Fast Hockey Show on XM radio. Coach Daccord was featured in *Hockey News* as one of the NHL's top goalie coaches with "crease clout." He has worked with more than 30 professional goaltenders since 1999, including 2003-04 NHL Rookie of the Year Andrew Raycroft, NHL record holder for consecutive shutout minutes Brian Boucher, and Scott Clemmensen, NCAA national champion from Boston College. Daccord has also helped develop 23 NHL draft picks. His current clients include top NHL, AHL, ECHL, college, and junior goaltenders.

Currently, Daccord trains many of the top goaltenders in the country at Stop It Goaltending. He is also the director of the Goaltending Consultant Group, which features many of the top goalie coaches in North America. He is a former coach and player at Merrimack College (NCAA Division I) and played seven seasons of professional hockey in Switzerland. He has coached at every level of youth hockey as well as the U.S. prep school, junior, college, and professional levels. Daccord holds a master-level coaching certification with USA Hockey and also has earned a master's degree in sport science. He was born and raised in Beaconsfield, Quebec and currently lives in North Andover, Massachusetts, with his wife, Daniela, and two sons, Joey and Alex.

ABOUT THE CONTRIBUTORS

David Alexander

David Alexander (author of chapter 5) is currently a goaltender coach at the University of Maine and is a Head Director at Alexander Goaltending. He played three years in Ontario in the OPJAHL and won a provincial championship at the Midget AAA level. He has worked as a goaltending consultant to the NB Program of Excellence and, along with the Tommies, coaches the Fredericton Canadians Midget AAA team. He has worked as an instructor with Alexander Goaltending for 7 years and has a reputation of being one of the brightest young minds in the world of goaltending. David has worked with several Pro, Major Junior, and NCAA Division I goaltenders and has a tremendous passion for the position.

John Alexander

John Alexander (author of chapter 9) is the former goaltending coach for University of Moncton Blue Eagles and is currently in his sixth season as a goaltending consultant to the Amherst Junior A Ramblers and head scout of the MJAHL and is goaltending consultant to the HNB High Performance Programs and the Team Atlantic Female Program. He has coached at all Youth Hockey AAA levels winning both Atlantic and Provincial Championships. John holds an Intermediate Coaching Level with the Canadian National Coaches Certification Program, and lectures regularly at hockey Coaching Certification clinics. He has coached goaltenders for over 15 years and is the owner of Alexander Goaltending, which has operated camps and clinics in the area for the past 11 years. Among his current and past clients are some of the top names in youth and Junior hockey.

Terry Barbeau

Terry Barbeau (author of chapter 6) is entering his sixth season as the Sault Ste. Marie Greyhounds' goaltender coach in the Ontario Hockey League. Terry's ability to develop young goaltenders is well documented, having worked closely with Buffalo Sabres standout Ryan Miller, as well as former Greyhound Adam Munro. Prior to working with the Greyhounds, Terry was the goaltending coach for the men's hockey team at Lake Superior State University. Locally, Terry is renowned for his work at summer goaltending camps.

John Carratu

John Carratu (author of chapter 1) is currently a goaltending director at Northeastern University as well as a goaltending director at Stop It Goaltending where he trains NHL, Minor Pro, and NCAA Division I goalies as well as goalies of all abilities at the youth level. In college, he led his NCAA Division II Plymouth State team to the ECAC playoffs while graduating with a degree in education. While entering the teaching profession in the Seattle area, John began his career as a goaltending consultant. While in Seattle, he was a member of the USA Hockey Pacific District selection process and coached goaltenders that played in the NAHL, BCJHL, and NCAA as well. A strength of John's is his knowledge of equipment and advising clients in the proper selection and purchasing options. He owned and operated his own hockey shop in the Seattle area, which catered primarily to goaltenders. Upon his return to New England John became an assistant coach with the Salem Ice Dogs in the IJHL and helped lead them to two playoff berths. He coached at numerous goaltending camps and clinics before bringing his knowledge and enthusiasm to Superskills Hockey. John has also served as a goaltending consultant to US Prep School power Cushing Academy and this season will serve as a consultant with Nobles and Greenough in the ISL.

Tom Dempsey

Tom Dempsey (author of chapter 10) is in his sixth season as the goaltender coach of the Ottawa 67's in the Ontario Hockey League. He has trained several professional goaltenders including Robert Esche, Marc-Andre Fleury, and Dominik Hasek. Tom has coached goalies on a full-time basis at the Junior A and Major Junior levels for the past 16 years. Tom also runs elite level camps and clinics for goaltenders as well as conducts private sessions in the Ottawa area.

Dave Flint

Dave Flint (author of chapters 2-4) is the assistant coach of the US National Women's Team and is responsible for the development of the country's Olympic team, U-22 team and U-18 team goaltenders. Dave is currently the head coach of Northeastern University's women's program. Until 2008, Dave was head coach of St. Anselm College women's program, where during the 2006-2007 season, his team posted its third-straight 20-win season, finished with a 24-3-0 overall record and claimed its first-ever ECAC East Regular-Season title with an 18-1-0 league mark. Flint was named as the ECAC East Coach of the Year for the third straight season. Over the last four seasons, Flint's teams have compiled a record of 88-15-2, giving him the best winning percentage in Division II/III in that period at .823. A certified athletic trainer (ATC) and strength & conditioning specialist (CSCS) Dave has been training professional and amateur goalies on and off the ice for the past ten years.

Jamie McGuire

Jamie McGuire (author of chapter 11) has been a professional goaltender instructor for the past 15 years. Jamie has trained goalies from youth hockey to the pros and owns McGuire Goaltending and Hockey Development (www. mcguirehockey.com) in Ontario, Canada. His client list includes several NCAA goalies, Major Junior Goalies as well as a number of top ranked youth goaltenders. He currently serves as the goalie coach of the York University Lions (CIS), the 2008 Canadian University All-Star team, and is the assistant coach/ goaltending coach for the Mississauga Chiefs. A former draft pick of the London Knights (OHL), Jamie played four years of varsity hockey for the St. Mary's Huskies. Jamie won a world championship as head coach of Canadian National Amputee Hockey Team in 2004, 2006 and 2008 and is a Sport Specific Personal Trainer and Nutrition and Wellness Specialist.